PUBLIC SPEAKING

Second Edition

WAYNE C. MINNICK
The Florida State University

HOUGHTON MIFFLIN COMPANY   BOSTON

Dallas   Geneva, Illinois   Hopewell, New Jersey   Palo Alto   London

FOR LENORE

Cover photograph by James Scherer.

Printed in the U.S.A.
Library of Congress Catalog Card Number: 82-83203
ISBN: 0-395-32627-3

CONTENTS

PREFACE

The second edition of *Public Speaking,* like the first, is designed to teach the basic skills students will need in all kinds of speaking situations. Most of the book deals with formal situations, but it also gives instruction in small group and interpersonal communication. In this edition I have added a chapter that extends this instruction to speaking on radio and television.

Like the first edition, this new edition presents a concise but full theoretical base and then emphasizes the skills for preparing and delivering speeches.

The first chapter acquaints students with the history of public speaking dating from Aristotle. Although my basic approach is traditional, I have modified and supplemented that tradition with concepts and evidence from modern rhetorical theorists and scholars. In this revision I have expanded and tightened the connections between theory and practice. In the chapter on informative speaking, I show how principles of learning should be applied in the construction and delivery of such speeches. In the chapter on persuasion, I indicate how theories of attitude change, such as balance and cognitive dissonance, help in composing and in listening critically to persuasive speeches. There are fuller discussions of credibility and emotional proofs, as well as the use of persuasion to intensify attitudes and to make people resistant to change. This theoretical material helps students not only to make better speeches but also to become more careful and critical listeners. Another important emphasis of this book is making students conscious of their role as consumers of speeches.

Units and chapters are developed in a logical pedagogical progression, moving from simple to more complex communication tasks. Students are first taught about the complex nature of a communication transaction; people are both speaker and listener as they influence or are influenced by others. This two-way process reveals why speakers must perceive and clearly formulate a purpose when speaking. In early chapters, I explain general and specific purposes so that students can focus their first speech correctly. Early units give instruction in the wording of this purpose, in basic outlining, in suitable organizational patterns, and in the use of specific forms of supporting materials, including the use of visual aids (a section that has been completely revised and updated). These principles are then applied in the students' first major speech, a one-point speech in which they are asked to use a variety of materials to support a single idea.

From a first one-point speech, students are led into more complex informative and persuasive speeches. The chapters on informative and persuasive speaking have been completely rewritten to include new principles and specific types of informative and persuasive speeches that were not discussed in the first edition, i.e., a descriptive speech, a process speech, a speech to convince, and a speech to activate.

After informative and persuasive speeches, I offer a greatly expanded chapter on speaking in special circumstances. Instead of simply discussing the structure of such speeches, as I did in the first edition, I have now used full speech models as examples—a full text of a speech of introduction, a humorous speech, a eulogy, and a commencement address. I cover all common types of occasional speeches, but in addition I have a section on job-related speeches—job interviews, oral reports, convention presentations—and an entirely new unit on parliamentary speaking in which students are introduced to the purposes and procedures of parliamentary rule.

An entirely new chapter on radio and TV speaking follows. I have tried to show students how to adapt to the studio demands of the electronic media and how to prepare a manuscript speech for the radio-TV audience by including devices for holding attention and by casting speech material into structurally simple and attractive formats. I also call attention to the fact that, when students take part in debate or interview formats, they must present a logically adequate case and be able to respond to questions and objections.

I have added pedagogical aids to this new edition and increased the use of concrete examples. All chapters have an overview of materials to be covered, a chapter summary, and a selection of classroom exercises designed to help teach the principles set forth in the chapter. This edition has many more student outlines, representing all key types of public speeches, which are placed near the explanation for preparing that particular type of speech. Whole speech models, by students and by known figures, are also placed close to the sections dealing with their preparation. In this way, students can immediately see, through outline and model, how the theoretical discussion and the instructions have been transformed into an actual speech. Whether outline, excerpt, or whole speech, I have selected historical and contemporary examples that show excellence of practice.

Daniel J. O'Neill of Youngstown State University has prepared an entirely new Instructor's Manual for this edition. I am much indebted to O'Neill for this contribution.

I wish to thank publishers who have permitted the use of copyrighted material, especially the publishers of *Vital Speeches of the Day,* from which numerous examples in the text have been taken. I wish to thank again those who read and criticized the original manuscript: David Jabusch, University of Utah; Allan Kennedy, Morgan State University; Steve McDevitt, Victor Valley Community College; Ted Smith, Eastern Kentucky University; Voncile Smith, Florida Atlantic University; Al R. Weitzel, San Diego State University; Frazier White, University of Miami; and Darlyn Wolvin, Prince George's Community College. These reviewers offered many discerning suggestions that helped immeasurably in the preparation of the first edition. I hope their insights have been preserved.

Thanks are also due to reviewers of the manuscript of the second edition: Anthony D'Angelo, Peirce Junior College; Fred Dowling, University of Wisconsin, Stevens Point; Ileen Kaufman-Everett, formerly of the University of New Hampshire; Thomas R. King, Florida State University; John R. Lyne, University of Iowa; Joyce Nader, Petersburg Junior College; Curt Siemers, Winona State University; and Al Weitzel, San Diego State University. Their comments and suggestions have been very helpful in expanding and refining this edition.

Also, I want to thank Tom King of Florida State University for help in preparing test items. And I want to thank the editors and staff of Houghton Mifflin Company who made positive contributions to the improvement of this edition.

Finally, I want to thank my wife, Lenore, for her help in the preparation of this revision and for her patience and encouragement.

W. M.

Chapter One
INTRODUCTION

OVERVIEW

A short history of public speaking
Why the study of public speaking is important
Public speaking as a transaction between speaker and audience
Important responsibilities in preparing to speak
The significance of freedom and responsibility in speech

A HISTORY OF PUBLIC SPEAKING

All living creatures communicate with one another in some way. The form of communication may be as simple as a female moth giving off an odor to attract a mate or a rabbit thumping on the ground to warn other rabbits of danger. Or the form of communication may be more complex. For example, the voice may be used, as when monkeys vary their screeching to signal different messages. No matter how complex communication is, however, its purpose is always the same: one member of a species wishes to let others know of his or her presence, to establish a relationship with them, and to share ideas with them.

Human beings have the most elaborate communication system of all creatures. Like animals, they speak with signs and bodily gestures and with elementary noises such as sighs, groans, and chuckles. But they also use highly organized and complicated systems of symbols, the most common of which is language. Although much of the linguistic communication of human beings is written, the greatest part of it is oral—reflecting, perhaps, that people learn to speak long before they learn to write.

Because speaking is humanity's most common form of communication, it is not surprising that people have spent considerable time and effort studying the process. Beginning with the first civilized, literate societies and continuing to the present, public speaking has been the object of formal and informal instruction. Archaeologists have found the remains of a speech textbook written in 2675 B.C. by Ptah-Hotep among the relics of ancient Egypt. Many scholars of ancient Greece, such as Corax, Tisias, Protagoras, Socrates, and Plato, wrote on the topic of rhetoric, a term that was then used primarily to mean oral argument. The best known of the Greek writers, however, was Aristotle; his book the *Rhetoric* was written around 330 B.C. and has had a great influence on later writers. Aristotle said that the content of a speech (its arguments, proofs, and demonstrations) had to be molded and adjusted to the attitudes and beliefs of the audience. Thus, his notion of an effective speaker was a person who uses both logic and psychology.

Of the Roman writers who elaborated on Aristotle's basic premises, Cicero and Quintillian were the most significant. By the end of the period in which they wrote, rhetoric was seen as consisting of what became known as the five canons, or principles:

1. *Invention,* or the discovery of the ideas and arguments that form the content of a speech
2. *Arrangement,* or the organization of the parts of the speech
3. *Style,* or the use of language in composing the speech
4. *Delivery,* or the manner in which the speech is projected to the audience
5. *Memory,* or the means by which the speaker keeps the ideas of the speech in mind during delivery

The Middle Ages and the Renaissance added little to rhetorical theory. Most writers, like Augustine, Ramus, and Wilson, repeated the classical canons. They paid more attention to some canons than others, though, and they emphasized how to apply the canons to different subjects, such as politics and religion.

In the nineteenth and twentieth centuries, writers on rhetoric, while still owing much to the classical tradition of Aristotle, began to relate their subject more closely to the field of psychology. James A. Winans, a teacher at Cornell University, wrote a book in 1917 in which he identified attention as central to speaking. In fact, he defined speaking as "the process of inducing others to give fair, favorable or individual attention to propositions."[1] Some time later, Alan Monroe popularized the "motivated sequence," in which a speaker gains attention, arouses the audience's basic motives, demonstrates how the aroused motives can be satisfied, and provides specific steps for attaining satisfaction.[2]

As they adapted their writings to the field of psychology, the majority of rhetoricians gave up the classical method of looking at personal experience and the experience of successful speakers for proof of the general rules of effective communication. Instead, they turned to an experimental-quantitative approach. They designed experiments to test the effectiveness of various message elements, such as fear appeals, and they supported their

---

[1] James A. Winans, *Public Speaking* (New York: Century Company, 1917), p. 194.
[2] Alan Monroe, *Principles and Types of Speech,* (New York: Scott, Foresman and Company, 1935), *passim.*

conclusions with the results of these experiments. Many of the hypotheses about communication that are tested today come not from writers in the field of rhetoric itself but from scholars in the fields of psychology, sociology, and allied areas. Their reliance on experimentation has produced fresh theories that offer provocative ways of viewing the communication process.

The usual approach to studying communication, even among modern behaviorists, has centered on formal speech making, and especially on public speaking. This emphasis reflects the importance of public speaking in society. In Aristotle's time and in the time of Cicero and Quintillian, legal and political decisions were usually made by a large public forum of citizens. A person's ability to present views persuasively to such a forum and to counter the arguments of opposing speakers thus became an important skill.

Offsetting the scholarly emphasis on formal speaking, some present-day rhetoricians place heavy stress on interpersonal communication: the kind of speaking in which one person speaks face to face with another person or with persons in a small group. In the study of interpersonal communication, scholars emphasize the importance of interaction and give-and-take dialogue among participants. Although it cannot be denied that the interpersonal speaking situation is common and that much of society's business is transacted through interpersonal communication, the importance of the formal public speech should not be underestimated.

It is commonly believed that few people ever make a formal public speech. The fact is that the demand for formal speeches is frequent. A study done by Kendall in 1973 showed that ordinary people are often called upon for formal talks. Kendall asked a sample of 202 blue-collar workers in Albany, New York, "In the last two years, how many times have you spoken to a group of ten or more people at once?" About half (46.5 percent) said that they had spoken to a group of ten or more at least once in the previous two years. Kendall also found that the higher the subjects' level of education, the more frequently they were called on to speak. It stands to reason, therefore, that college-educated people would be likely to make even more formal speeches than blue-collar workers. Occasions for speeches mentioned by those interviewed in this study were church gatherings, driver-safety lectures, talks with day-care parents, and union meetings.[3]

---

[3] Kathleen Kendall, "Do Real People Ever Give Speeches?" *Central States Speech Journal,* 25 (1974), 233–235.

Many other occasions require public speaking. For example, the city commission of a large American city recently considered rezoning a portion of a single-family residential area to permit the construction of apartments. Residents of the area feared that a change from single-family zoning would cause congestion and reduce property values. Accordingly, they appeared at the commission hearing to protest. Plumbers, business-people, homemakers, and teen-age high school students found themselves standing up before an audience of 150 persons to speak in public defense of their interests.

Dozens of other occasions that demand formal speaking come to mind: hearings for utility rate increases, legislative hearings on proposed laws, political rallies on behalf of candidates, meetings of civic and religious organizations, testimonial dinners, and so on. In the business world, executive and middle-level managers are required to address seminars, convention gatherings, and employee groups of all kinds. So important is skill in speaking that firms like Coca Cola and Sears Roebuck currently pay public-speaking experts $100 per hour to coach company executives, and they pay $500 each to send executives to a three-day public-speaking seminar. Effectiveness in public speaking is clearly a useful commodity and in great demand.

WHY STUDY PUBLIC SPEAKING?

Aristotle wrote his book to explain an art much used in his day. Today, too, pragmatism is still the chief motive for the study of public speaking. People study public speaking because it contributes to their personal growth, development, and achievement and because the ability to speak publicly enables them to perform useful and necessary functions for society. Of course, speaking can be studied as an art form just as literature and painting are studied as art forms. But public speaking is primarily a useful art and only secondarily an aesthetic one. In other words, public speaking is more functional than artistic. Thus, most persons study public speaking as a skill that can be applied. They do not enjoy it for itself but for what it can do. Public speaking, therefore, is an instrumental art.

The study of public speaking, as we have noted, benefits the student. The first and most obvious benefit is the development of personal confidence that promotes self-esteem. The Dale Carnegie Institute has used this benefit as a major selling point in soliciting thousands of students, and no doubt the Carnegie instructors have nurtured confidence and self-esteem in many. College teachers of public speaking are likely to regard gains in confidence and self-esteem as by-products of instruction and not as goals to be aimed at directly. They see the study of public speaking not as personal therapy but as training in a basic human skill—a skill necessary to the welfare of both the individual and society. In their eyes, training in public speaking develops two very important intellectual abilities. First, it teaches students the ability to investigate a topic and gather reliable information about it. Second, it teaches them to think: to draw sound conclusions from evidence, to weigh and evaluate ideas.

Likewise, college teachers are not likely to stress public speaking as a tool for gaining personal power and influence. Its usefulness in helping a person attain power and influence cannot be denied, however. Most influential people, such as politicians, managers, lawyers, ministers, and professors, have substantial public-speaking skills and credit much of their success to their speaking ability. Opinion surveys have repeatedly shown that business and professional people rate public speaking and communication as among their most valuable college courses. Nevertheless, although college courses in public speaking may contribute to personal success, that is not why they are included in the curriculum.

Most college instructors prefer to justify the study of public speaking for what it does for society as a whole, although they may recognize that it will also benefit the individual. They believe that a society organized on democratic principles, as ours is, needs to promote the general welfare. This welfare requires that ideas and information be communicated rapidly to vast portions of the population. The social welfare depends on political and policy decisions that affect the fortunes of all. And the success of any democratic system relies on maintaining the commitment to the shared political and social values of society and its subgroups. How public speaking contributes to the satisfaction of these needs will soon be apparent.

The rapid spread of ideas and information is necessary to create informed, productive, and progressive citizens. Underdeveloped countries in the Middle East and elsewhere have used lectures and demonstrations on radio and television to spread agricultural innovations and to convince people to use socially desirable practices like birth control. In developed societies, such as that of the United States, news broadcasts give all sorts of information on such diverse topics as the stock market, the energy crisis, and the causes and effects of inflation. Public speaking obviously plays an important role in this process.

In America, we make collective political and policy decisions in a variety of ways. One possible way of influencing public policy is through persuasive speech addressed to whatever audiences can be attracted. An evangelist illustrates well this type of influence. People like Billy Graham promote themselves and then address the audiences they have attracted through advertising and word-of-mouth publicity. Political candidates running for elective office do the same thing. By influencing the attitudes of the general public, such advocates hope to gain support for themselves and for social changes that they deem desirable. But most public decision making is channeled through agencies designed for that purpose, such as legislatures, courts, arbitration boards, and collective bargaining panels. These agencies are designed to permit committed advocates to express opposing views. For instance, a legislative committee contemplating the drafting of abortion legislation will hold public hearings to give right-to-life advocates and abortion-on-demand advocates free opportunity to be heard. Likewise, in our courts contending parties are represented by hired, highly skilled advocates who present the best possible case for each party. Finally, having heard all interested parties, the agency involved makes up its mind and renders a decision.

Underlying this process is the assumption that if information and ideas are widely communicated in a society, its people will be able to influence the legislatures, the courts, and other agencies to make decisions that are reasonable and beneficial for everyone. This assumption might be valid if everyone trying to influence decisions was honest, well informed, and well intentioned. We know in fact, however, that almost everyone acts selfishly in political and business dealings. We also know that a lot of people are uninformed and misguided. Perhaps worst of all, we know that many people are downright manipulators who aspire to use other people unfairly for their own gain. Given these facts, how can we expect the corporate decisions of social agencies to be reasonable and fair to all?

It has often happened that rich and powerful individuals have been able to influence political and economic policy to their own benefit and to the disservice of others. American government is shaped in many ways by people from great industrial, military, and political organizations; these people have influenced the adoption of policies that may be good for them and their constituents but that are not always good for the majority.

To combat this tendency, Americans have placed a great deal of reliance on freedom of thought and expression. They believe that a free press can keep people informed on public issues, expose the strategies of selfish interest groups, and shed corrective light on the activities of dishonorable politicians. And the press has often done this job well. We as individuals, however, cannot depend on someone else to protect us from exploitation. Instead we must depend on our own ability to investigate issues, to formulate our own conclusions, and to communicate those conclusions forcefully to others. Freedom of speech does not merely free the press to investigate and publish without restraint; it also frees individuals to criticize, examine, and discuss all public policy and conduct. It frees us to denounce, if necessary, and to cry alarm, as did early American patriots like Patrick Henry. If we each are to play the role of individual social critic responsibly and effectively and to guard our own interests, skill in public speaking, discussion, and debate is essential.

Finally, a society sustains itself by maintaining a common core of shared values and beliefs. This does not mean that differences cannot exist; to the contrary, a number of subcultures coexist in America. Unifying our subcultures, however, there needs to be a common commitment to certain basic premises, such as the rights to work, to a life of dignity and respect, and to equal access to the advantages of the system. Public speakers foster the preservation of this common commitment to basic ideals, especially on ceremonial occasions. Recall the speeches during the Bicentennial of the American Revolution or at a national political convention selecting a candidate for the presidency. In such instances, public speakers seek out and reinforce the identifications that unite a diversity of people. With their words, speakers strive to build other unifying identifications. This ceremonial, stirring renewal of common cause is an important cement in holding a nation together.

So public speaking is worth studying. It will benefit you by showing you how to investigate issues, assemble and organize material, and present that material effectively to an audience. Your confidence in yourself, your methods of thinking about and investigating issues, and your ability to influence others should improve. Your awareness of the workings of a democratic and individualistic society will gain focus, and your appropriate participation in the nation's affairs will increase. Surely these are valuable outcomes and deserve your eager effort.

THE COMMUNICATION PROCESS

Engineers have studied human communication using as a model the process involved in sending a message electronically. According to this analogy, the speaker puts a message into a transmitter, like the telephone, and the message passes through a channel to another person. Figure 1.1 diagrams this process. The diagram calls attention to details of the speech

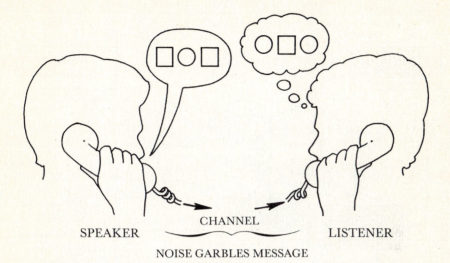

Figure 1.1 SIMPLE COMMUNICATION MODEL OF A ONE-WAY
RELATIONSHIP BETWEEN SPEAKER AND LISTENER.

situation that are often taken for granted, but it also focuses on perceptions that are often neglected. For instance, it demonstrates that one
cannot transfer a message (ideas) directly from the speaker's head to the
listener's mind. Instead, the message must pass into a transmitter, across a
channel, into a receiving mechanism, and then into the mind of the
listener. During this journey, the message is subject to distortion, or *noise*;
noise may garble the message so badly that the listener may not receive it
at all or may seriously misunderstand it.

One shortcoming of Figure 1.1 is that it portrays communication as a
simple, linear process in which the message moves from sender to receiver, with the receiver playing a relatively passive role. Refinement of
the diagram corrects these impressions and presents a truer picture of
what happens during communication. Look at the model of the process
shown in Figure 1.2. This diagram, like the first one, calls attention to the
existence of noise or distortion that interferes with communication. It also
indicates, however, that distortion may occur not only during transmission, but in the responses of the audience as well. In addition, the second
diagram spells out more clearly the actions of the speaker and of the
audience. In particular, it indicates that audience feedback is a communication variable during all stages of receiving and responding to the
speaker's message. Members of an audience do not passively receive a
message; they must consciously attend to the channel, receive and understand the message flowing through the channel, evaluate and interpret the

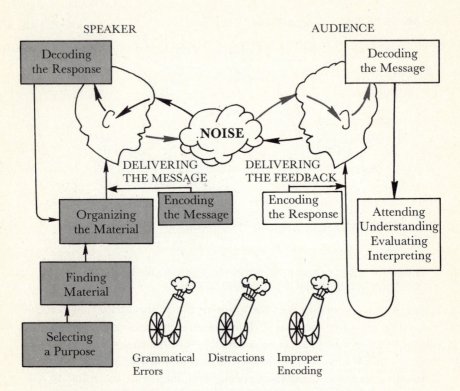

SPEAKER   AUDIENCE

Decoding the Response

Decoding the Message

NOISE

DELIVERING   DELIVERING
THE MESSAGE   THE FEEDBACK

Organizing the Material

Encoding the Message

Encoding the Response

Attending
Understanding
Evaluating
Interpreting

Finding Material

Selecting a Purpose

Grammatical   Distractions   Improper
Errors   Encoding

Figure 1.2 COMPLEX COMMUNICATION MODEL OF A TWO-WAY
RELATIONSHIP BETWEEN SPEAKER AND LISTENER.
This figure illustrates the circular nature of communication by emphasizing
feedback between audience and speaker. It also indicates the prevalence of
noise or interference.

message, and then respond accordingly. If speakers are to elicit the
response they seek, they must be sure that an audience is actively playing
its role in the communication transaction. As shown, they monitor this
variable through feedback channels. They need to make corrections when
they note that an audience is failing in its responsibility or is distorting
meaning because of interfering noise.

Public speaking may be defined as a circular process by which one
person tries to influence the knowledge, attitudes, and conduct of another.
At one end of the circuit, the speaker transmits over an available channel a
verbal message that is accompanied by gestures or by audio-visual or
other nonverbal cues. To complete the circuit, the audience receives the
message and returns verbal or nonverbal feedback to the speaker. Based

on such feedback, the speaker is able to adapt the message to the mutual needs of both speaker and audience. A public speaker is thus both a sender and a receiver of messages, and a good public speaker is adept at this process of give-and-take.

THE SPEAKER'S TASKS IN PREPARING A SPEECH

Certain requirements of a public-speaking transaction stand out from the above discussion—requirements that speakers must consider in order to successfully discharge their responsibilities. Now that the communication process has been described, let's look at the specific things a speaker must do in preparing a speech.

ADAPTING TO THE AUDIENCE AND THE OCCASION

A speaker delivers a speech to influence other people. These people, a few individuals or a multitude, make up an audience. During the preparation and during the actual presentation of the speech, the speaker must adapt to the characteristics of the audience—their knowledge of the subject, their attitude toward the speaker and the topic, their age, sex, income level, and so forth. A public-speaking situation is usually a one-to-many circumstance with limited opportunity for the audience to respond orally to the speaker. But successful speaking involves activity on the part of both speaker and audience. Hence, speakers often seek to ensure audience participation by soliciting questions during their presentations or afterward. At all times good speakers are alert for nonverbal messages from the audience, like facial expressions, inattention, and bodily movements. Such messages give the speaker clues as to how the audience is reacting to and taking in what is being said. Good speakers adjust their remarks to verbal and nonverbal signs from the audience, so that their speeches, without being broken up into dialogue, are somewhat like enlarged conversations with the audience.

Next, speakers must consider the occasion: whether it will be formal or informal and whether they will address the audience directly or through some electronic medium like television. They must think about what the audience will expect them to do under the prevailing circumstances. They must, in effect, realize that the occasion imposes certain required behavior on them. At the same time, there will be restraints—things that they may not do. A speaker will behave differently when addressing a congressional investigating committee than when addressing an informal gathering of war veterans. The differences in behavior will come, at least in part, from perceptions, imposed by the occasion, of acceptable and unacceptable behavior.

DETERMINING A PURPOSE

People engage in public speaking because they need to do so, because by influencing others through speech they can secure some satisfaction or reward for themselves and for the audience. Nobody makes a speech just to be making a speech. A speaker always has a purpose. The basic purpose is to influence, that is, to get some kind of response from the audience. A speaker usually sets out to get one of two responses: (1) an increase in the audience's knowledge and understanding, or (2) a change in the audience's attitudes toward events, and corresponding changes in conduct. Some speakers, such as teachers, may be wholly concerned with the knowledge-explanation-understanding function. These speakers will measure their success by the accuracy and amount of what the audience recalls and by the audience's ability to grasp and use what they have learned. Politicians, on the other hand, will measure their success by how well they are able to sway the attitudes and the votes of their audiences or, perhaps, by how well they intensify existing favorable attitudes. They may incidentally provide the audience with much information and explanation, but the transmission of knowledge is not their purpose.

As we mentioned earlier, at times speaking has a ceremonial purpose. On the occasion of awarding a gift, commemorating an anniversary, or the like, speakers will devote themselves to discharging the purposes of the occasion, not to trying to instruct or to influence attitudes on public questions.

GATHERING INFORMATION AND IDEAS

At some point (perhaps in a continuing or ongoing process), a speaker must collect the information, the evidence, and the arguments that will form the content of the speech. This process has both a confirming and a learning function. The evidence found may serve to confirm the speaker's views, reinforcing the position to be advocated. It may also, however, cause the speaker to modify and restructure a presentation so that it better reflects reality as he or she perceives it. Effective and responsible speakers seek to base their presentations on the best evidence and the soundest reasoning. They try to meet this standard because of ethical consider-ations and because discourse that reflects the realities of life makes for the most enduring and effective kind of instruction and persuasion.

ORGANIZING CONTENT

Once they have gathered the information and ideas that will make up the substance of a speech, speakers must turn to organizing the message. All speakers do not structure or organize speeches the same way. Some speakers begin with a statement of purpose and then offer evidence in somewhat random fashion, to support that purpose. Some speakers care-fully structure their speeches and attempt in each part of the speech to draw a particular response from the audience. Such structured speeches usually have an introduction that includes a statement of purpose, a body that includes a series of reasons supporting or illustrating the purpose, and a conclusion. In every speech, however, there are two parts: a disclosure of purpose, expressed or implied, and an array of information and ideas supporting the purpose.

EXPRESSING CONTENT

The way in which a speaker puts a speech into words is called *style*. A speaker's use of language tends to be highly individualistic; hence, style may be said to be the way an individual uses language. This definition emphasizes that what is in a speaker's mind has no independent existence, but can only be discovered in the speaker's words. Only through the speech can we know the speaker's ideas and general outlook on the world, habitual view of the things in life that are important, and customary ways of thinking about these things. Thus, a speaker's use of language is bound to be unique, and its uniqueness reveals the kind of person that speaker is. Because of the utilitarian nature of public speaking, clarity and forceful-ness are characteristic of good speech style. Speakers aim to influence their audiences. Clear language that hits the audience hard is most likely to have the desired effect. Embellishment, imagery, and impressiveness may well be important in public disclosure, but a speaker's chief aims are to avoid misunderstanding and to make an impact.

DELIVERING THE MESSAGE

Finally, the speaker is ready to transmit a message to the audience. *Delivery*, as it is called, is a bodily function; the larynx, mouth, tongue, and lips are used to form sounds. How a speaker uses these organs will determine whether the tone of the words strikes the audience as agreeable or irritating, whether the sentences drone on or sound meaningful, and whether the total presentation has pace, variation, and emotional appeal. The way in which the voice is used says something to the audience about the speaker's attitude, sincerity, and conviction, and about the relative importance he or she gives to various ideas.

Likewise, an audience receives information from a speaker's body. Posture, muscular tensions, gestures, and movements may all convey impressions of confidence, trustworthiness, expertise, and self-command. In a sense, speakers encode and transmit a message not only in words, but also with vocal inflections and bodily movement. In reality, they transmit on two channels: an auditory channel and a visual channel.

This way of describing its nature shows that the act of public speaking consists of the following series of steps:

1. *Determining a purpose* that relates to the needs of the speaker and the audience
2. *Gathering information and ideas* that will become the content of the speech
3. *Organizing the content*
4. *Encoding or putting into words the material*
5. *Delivering the message*

This brief description omits many details, all of which will be discussed in later chapters. It also tends to focus on the speaker as the central figure in public speaking and to show little of the give-and-take between speaker and audience.

We can now quickly spell out the obligations of a person who wants to practice the art of speaking:

1. A good speaker must perceive the limitations and problems imposed by the occasion and the audience.
2. A good speaker must work within the constraints and possibilities of the subject and purpose.
3. A good speaker must know where to gather information and how to select and use material that will seem valid and relevant to the audience.
4. A good speaker must be able to organize and arrange content materials to insure understanding by the audience.

5. A good speaker must be able to word ideas for understanding and impact while avoiding practices that foster interference.
6. A good speaker must be able to use body and voice to effectively transmit a message through whatever channel is available.
7. A good speaker must be able to evaluate the probable effectiveness of a speech and make appropriate adaptations.
8. A good speaker must listen intelligently and critically to others.

The rest of this book takes an in-depth look at each of these principles. Each principle will be the subject of a chapter. Some principles will be discussed in more than one chapter. If you master the content of this text and are able to apply it, you can train yourself within a reasonable span of time to become an effective public speaker.

THE SPEAKER'S ETHICAL RESPONSIBILITIES

Earlier in this chapter, we noted that communication plays an important role in spreading information and in forming public policy. A free society operates on the premise that individuals have the right to know, that there are no forbidden topics or hidden areas. Other premises of a free society are that individuals have both the right to decide for themselves what they will believe and the right to urge others to accept their views on any controversial topic. Thus, freedom to communicate, whether through public speech or by any other means, is a respected article of faith in our society and is protected by the Constitution as interpreted by the courts. Students of public speaking should be aware of the national commitment to freedom of speech and its attendant responsibilities. Freedom of speech means not only your right to express yourself, but also the right of others to express their views to you, no matter how misguided those views seem or how unpopular they may be. The Speech Communication Association of America has adopted a *Credo for Free and Responsible Communication in a Democratic Society.* This credo, or statement of belief, expresses principles that all public-speaking students should know:

Recognizing the essential place of free and responsible communication in a democratic society, and recognizing the distinction between the freedoms our legal system should respect and the responsibilities our educational system should cultivate, we members of the Speech Communication Association endorse the following statement of principles:

We believe that freedom of speech and assembly must hold a central position among American constitutional principles, and we express our determined support for the right of peaceful expression by any communicative means available to man.

We support the proposition that a free society can absorb with equanimity speech which exceeds the boundaries of generally accepted beliefs and mores; that much good and little harm can ensue if we err on the side of freedom, whereas much harm and little good may follow if we err on the side of suppression.

We criticize as misguided those who believe that the justice of their cause confers license to interfere physically and coercively with the speech of others, and we condemn intimidation, whether by powerful majorities or strident minorities, which attempts to restrict free expression.

We accept the responsibility of cultivating ... a respect for precision and accuracy in communication, and for reasoning based upon evidence and a judicious discrimination among values.

We encourage our students to accept the role of well informed and articulate citizens, to defend the communication rights of those with whom they may disagree, and to expose abuses of the communication process.

You should study this credo and understand its principles. In the minds of many people the proper functioning of a free and orderly society depends on the willingness of its citizens to honor the concept of free expression and to practice it with responsibility.

SUMMARY

Public speaking is as old as civilization. The ancient Greeks and Romans transformed a public-speaking forum into a kind of legislature by which they governed their countries. Since it has played such an important role in society, scholars have studied speech making intensively and stress that speech is an interchange between a speaker and an audience, not merely a one-way flow of ideas from the speaker.

To effectively interact with an audience, a speaker must (1) analyze the audience and the occasion, (2) determine his or her purpose, (3) gather information and ideas, (4) organize the content, (5) express the content in words, and (6) deliver the material effectively.

Because public speaking serves society as a means of exchanging ideas and determining matters of public policy, freedom of expression is essential. Free speech guarantees you the right to express your ideas and opinions; likewise it guarantees that right to others.

Exercises

1. Divide into discussion groups of six or eight persons. Choose and discuss one of the following topics, describing what communication about it should be like and the ethical responsibilities of speakers in each case.
   a. The role of public speaking in a social movement, such as the anti-nuclear weapons campaign.
   b. The role of public speaking in the affairs of a public figure, such as a United States senator, a corporation president, the president of a great university, or a religious leader like the Pope.
   c. The role of public speaking in spreading new ideas, such as those associated with space technology and space exploration.
2. Watch a ''60 Minutes'' broadcast and respond to the following questions:
   a. Were the segments of this program informative or persuasive?
   b. Are such segments composed of objective representations of fact?
   c. The program has been criticized for sometimes offering unfair and slanted views. Do you agree? Why or why not?
3. Consider a movie such as *The China Syndrome* or *Network,* or some current ''message'' film. In what sense are these films similar in purpose to some kinds of public speaking? How do they differ in content? Do you think these films are educational? Are they effective?

Chapter Two
AUDIENCE AND OCCASION

OVERVIEW

Basic needs and values of an audience and how to relate speech
    materials to them
How to gain and hold attention
Adjusting to how the audience feels about your topic
Various kinds of speech occasions
A check list for analyzing audience and occasion

The audience and the occasion that has prompted them to assemble are key factors in shaping a speech—its contents, the language that characterizes it, and the style in which it is delivered. It is not difficult to see why audience and occasion are central in shaping a speaker's effort. Assume that you wish to speak on the subject of decriminalizing marijuana use. Assume further that you will on one occasion address an audience of police officers who are attending a meeting of a statewide sheriffs' association, and that on another occasion you will address convention delegates at a meeting of a national association of college student/government officers. Different arguments, different language, and different styles of delivery are clearly called for. A speaker selects the specific variations to use as the result of an analysis of the audience and the occasion.

ADAPTING TO THE AUDIENCE

Every audience has unique characteristics that are not shared by other audiences. But each audience is also, in a way, like every other audience in that the people who compose it share motivations, knowledge, and needs that are common to their culture and their time. Their basic likenesses may be expressed in individual ways, but their actions spring from common necessities. Thus, audience analysis is an art that consists of predicting the probable attitudes, behavior, and specific responses of a group of people by estimating how they will express their general needs and goals. For the public speaker, it is important to analyze the audience in this way. A speech, a discussion, or a debate must be tailored to fit its intended audience. For instance, what do the members of an audience need to know of a particular topic to understand it? What will the audience gain from the knowledge offered in an informative speech or from the proposals recommended in a persuasive one? A speech that does not take these things into account ignores the fact that communication is a give-and-take transaction between speaker and audience.

In the following pages, we will discuss some of the general needs and values that are the concern of practically all people. Then we will discuss some particulars that speakers must keep in mind as they try to apply a list of general tendencies to a particular audience.

BASIC NEEDS AND VALUES

While the differences among people are great, their similarities are even more remarkable. Regardless of their nationality, ethnic background, and economic status, they eat and sleep, look for and hold jobs, buy and own property of various kinds, make love and marry, raise children, wear clothing, quarrel with others, create governments, and build things such as houses, bridges, locomotives, airplanes, and armies. Imagine that a living creature from another planet were to hover above New York City at 100,000 feet observing the behavior of its people through glasses that allowed it to see inside homes and buildings. Such a creature would probably conclude that human beings could not be distinguished from one another successfully any more than we could distinguish a separate bee in a teeming hive.

Scientists try to look at human beings as would the imaginary space traveler just described. They adopt this approach because they are interested in consistent, repetitive events from which they may infer laws or principles that will make predictions possible. Social scientists who study human behavior are impressed by the variety in that behavior. Some of them doubt they will ever be able to predict it with any degree of accuracy. Their problem springs from the wish to predict the behavior of individuals, rather than that of groups.

When we speak of a catalogue of human needs and values, we mean a set of general tendencies to which all individuals respond in roughly similar but not identical fashion most of the time. One such catalogue of values has been put together by Abraham Maslow. His list of common human needs is paraphrased and adapted here:[1]

---

[1] A. H. Maslow, "A Dynamic Theory of Human Motivation," *Psychological Review,* 50 (1943), 370–396.

  I. *Physiological needs*:
     A. Hunger
     B. Thirst
     C. Maintenance of health
     D. Sexual gratification
 II. *Security needs*:
     A. Freedom from physical danger
     B. Avoidance of emotional disturbance
     C. Protection from hostile environmental influences, such as cold, excessive heat, aridity
III. *Love and belonging needs*:
     A. Sense of family or group cohesiveness
     B. Love of mate
     C. Acceptance by others
 IV. *Esteem needs*:
     A. Having the respect and admiration of others
     B. Exercising power and influence
     C. Acquiring self-respect by achievement and effort
  V. *Self-actualizing needs*:
     A. Full development of capabilities and ambitions
     B. Freedom of opportunity for growth

Maslow thought of these needs as being arranged in a hierarchy, with the strongest ones at the base and the weaker ones at the top. Physiological needs obviously are the strongest. We must have food and water to live. Hence, we work to satisfy our physiological needs before tending to other needs. In fact, when necessary we may sacrifice higher needs to satisfy our more basic ones. For instance, a man who is starving may beg for food at the cost of his self-esteem. Or a big-city dweller may remain at home, rather than going to a concert or play—barricading herself behind locked doors because the need for security overcomes the need for self-actualization.

Maslow's hierarchy of motives may be thought of as a pyramid like that shown in Figure 2.1. Given that the base of the pyramid represents the number of people involved, we can see that *all* people are motivated by physiological needs, somewhat fewer by security needs; the number involved in other motivations steadily declines to the top, where considerably fewer respond to self-actualization needs. That relatively few people

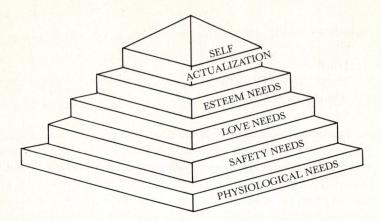

Figure 2.1 A. H. MASLOW'S HIERARCHY OF NEEDS.
Extracts and data for diagram based on Hierarchy of Needs in "A Theory of Human Motivation" in Motivation and Personality, *2nd Edition, by Abraham H. Maslow. Copyright © 1970 by Abraham H. Maslow. Reprinted by permission of Harper & Row, Publishers, Inc.*

respond to higher needs reflects the fact that most people, on a worldwide scale, must spend most of their time and energy in satisfying their physiological and security needs. Thus they have little time left for higher needs.

Self-actualization is the highest need in Maslow's hierarchy, and the least concrete. You can get some idea of the meaning of self-actualization by looking at the personality characteristics of persons who have strong self-actualizing tendencies. Such persons show the following traits:

1. More efficient perception of reality and more comfortable relations with it.
2. Increased acceptance of self, of others, and of nature.
3. Spontaneity, simplicity, naturalness.
4. Problem-centered rather than ego-centered.
5. Increased detachment and desire for privacy.
6. Ability to be independent of their physical and social environment.
7. Freshness of appreciation and richness of emotional reactions.
8. Higher frequency of "peak," mystic or transcendent experiences.
9. Increased identification with and feeling for mankind.

10. Deeper, more profound interpersonal relationships.
11. A more democratic character structure.
12. Strongly ethical, clearly distinguish between means and ends.
13. A philosophical, unhostile sense of humor.
14. A natural spontaneous creativity.
15. Ability to be detached and resist his culture.[2]

This list suggests that the self-actualization motive is the desire to have a fully rounded, healthy, developed personality; it also indicates that self-actualization is a motivation that does not appear in all people, and perhaps exists only in a minority. In fact, Maslow himself acknowledged that self-actualization might be impossible for many young people in American society today.[3]

In using such a hierarchy to analyze an audience, a speaker needs to do two things: (1) determine the needs of the audience that are not fulfilled or whose continued fulfillment is threatened; and (2) find the information or specific actions that, when presented to the audience, will show them how to cope successfully with the problem. To illustrate the application of this type of analysis, we will look at a couple of actual speaking situations. The first is from a speech by John H. Perkins, president of Continental Illinois Corporation. The speech was delivered at the University of Chicago, November 18, 1976. Perkins appeals immediately to one of the audience's strongest physiological needs, the need for adequate health care. He declares that the continued satisfaction of this need is threatened by the ever-increasing cost of medical care.

By any measure you wish to use, health care costs have gone up at an alarming rate and are continuing to go up—for government, for business and industry, and for institutions of every kind. Health-care costs per employee and per taxpayer are increasing—and doing so much faster than other costs and income. They are growing, in short, as a major financial burden to the nation and its people.

At Continental Bank, from 1971 through 1976, the cost of health insurance benefits will have increased more than 91 percent and has

---

[2] A. H. Maslow, *Motivation and Personality* (New York: Harper and Row, 1954), pp. 153–174.
[3] Ibid., p. 150.

gone up faster than the costs of salaries and other benefits. We believe this is a fairly accurate reflection of what is happening to employers generally, and the growing public debate on the subject bears out that conclusion.

You may be familiar with the dramatic statistic that in 1975 General Motors paid $375 million for hospital, medical, and dental expense coverage for its U.S. employees—an average of $1,500 per employee.

You also probably are acquainted with the findings of the latest HEW study, issued last month, which projects that, even without national health insurance legislation, but assuming a 5.2 percent annual inflation rate, the national health-care costs will increase by about 40 percent to $224 billion a year by 1980. That amount of spending will consume 9.7 percent of the Gross National Product, compared with 8.3 percent in 1975.

. . . there is little doubt that we have a problem of epic proportions on our hands. Health has always been regarded as a priceless quality, not only by the individual but more broadly by society because of its inestimable value to the survival of the group. This is even truer today, as the expectations of society have escalated in all areas, and particularly in health care. Health does not have a conventional market value, and it is, of course, priceless. But this does not mean that we are not and will not continue to be concerned with health costs and their proper control. The cost of health, like health itself, has a high national priority in the determination of our directions and goals. Fortunately, there are, indeed, things that can be done.[4]

In the second example, a history professor, Michael D'Innocenzo, makes a strong appeal to the need for love and belonging. Again the speaker uses a threat that the fulfillment of an important need is slowly being eroded and that finally we will all experience a state that the speaker calls "intimacy deprivation":

---

[4] John H. Perkins, "Business Looks at Health Care Costs," *Vital Speeches of the Day,* 43 (1976-1977), 211-212. Reprinted by permission.

Families are under fire—the evidence seems increasingly persuasive.
One reads and hears with disturbing frequency that

    families don't dine together—food is not only consumed sepa-
rately, but often quickly, and on the run.

    families don't talk together—it's hard to communicate when
you are not in the same place at the same time. It is hard to
communicate when a pattern of not talking has persisted. It
is hard to communicate when mutual respect, love and
individual dignity have not been established.

    families don't play together—he has his tennis game; she has
hers. Occasionally they get together for a few mixed sets,
which he does not really enjoy. But who plays with children
or with their own parents? How many families take a
spontaneous walk along a beach, go on a picnic, a museum
visit, to a concert or a sporting event? Are the chasms of
interests really so great that only one generation at a time
can be involved in separate activities?

    families don't read together or interact on shared intellectual
and cultural levels. The point is simply that in many families
there are precious few points of contact.

    increasingly, families don't even watch TV together. Most
households have 2 or 3 TV sets—sometimes even more.
American children grow accustomed to their own rooms,
watch their own TV's, listen to their own music, and, before
long, they are even riding alone in their own cars. Can
anyone really be surprised that the sociologist Philip Slater
characterizes our generation of Americans by a "pursuit of
loneliness."

    one hears disturbing reports that families do not have physical
closeness. Mother and father do not embrace, kiss or touch
children. In strikingly large numbers of instances, it seems
that husband and wife don't even embrace, kiss or touch
each other. Women complain that the only time their husbands caress them is as a direct prelude to intercourse. It is
not surprising that sex-therapists (a rapidly growing profession!) view American men as being more concerned with
product than process. Clinicians refuse to use the word

''foreplay'' because they want to encourage the affirmative idea of ongoing sexual pleasuring and physical closeness rather than a preoccupation with orgasm and a release of one's own tension.
what much of this points to is intimacy deprivation—for individuals, within generations and between generations. . . .

There may come a time—and not in the too distant future—when intimacy deprivation will be regarded as a problem near the magnitude of food deprivation.[5]

Whenever speakers fail to show how their messages affect the needs of the audience, they are open to the charge that their ideas are irrelevant. Audiences do not respond to irrelevant ideas. Speakers must be sure that audiences see how their proposals will be of use to them.

THE APPEAL TO REASON

Most people think of themselves as rational beings. Our society values intelligence and the ability to solve problems. We have a scientific orientation, and science prizes thinking, judgment, and objectivity. Thus, speakers who provide the audience with good evidence (statistics, scientific surveys, experimental studies, and the testimony of experts) and use this evidence to draw justified conclusions will receive favorable audience attention. A detailed discussion of logical processes appears in Chapter 5. At this point, a brief description of the rational approach will do.

People do not begin to think until confronted with a problem. *Problem,* in this sense, means any obstacle that gets in the way of satisfying a person's needs. Thinking is the process of inventing ways to overcome such obstacles. A person needs several things to reason: first, data or information about the problem; second, an awareness of how this information is to be interpreted; and third, a way of confirming a solution and, possibly, changing it.

Evidence, or data, consists of facts, as reported in reliable sources, and of the opinions of experts. Evidence is interpreted by inductive or deductive reasoning. Inductive reasoning is the process of drawing a conclusion about a class of things after observing a sample composed of examples drawn from the class. This conclusion is a generalization. For instance,

---

[5] Michael D'Innocenzo, ''The Family Under Fire,'' *Vital Speeches of the Day,* 43 (1976–1977), 431–432. Reprinted by permission.

the statement "Nuclear power plants are so poorly built that dangerous accidents are frequent" is a generalization. Deductive reasoning is the process of applying a generalization to a specific situation. If we believe in the validity of the generalization about nuclear power plants, we can then make a deductive prediction: the proposed nuclear power plant to be built at Crystal Lake will have a high risk of experiencing a dangerous accident. A simple example of reasoning as used in public speaking shows how to appeal to the rational side of an audience.

You might make a speech in which you argue that college and university grades no longer show the difference between good and poor students. You denounce this condition as "grade inflation." You compare the number of A and B grades given in the past at several typical universities and colleges with the number given today. You show that there have been percentage increases in the number of A and B grades ranging from 50 percent in some schools to as much as 150 percent in others. You also provide examples to illustrate the point: In one university, a theater course enrolling 2,450 students during an academic year recorded 2,225 A's; in another university, a beginning course in criminology recorded 225 A's among a total student enrollment of 310. You then cite figures to show that scores on the Scholastic Aptitude Test (and scores on other college aptitude tests) have dropped by several percentage points during the same period. You reason that the increase in higher letter grades could not, therefore, have come from better-trained or more intelligent students. You suggest that this failure to record different levels of student achievement is undesirable because it lessens the motivation of all students to learn; it especially affects the brighter students, because it makes it exceedingly difficult to pick out the abler students who should be admitted to professional and graduate schools. On this basis, you propose that university and college professors return to curve grading, in which only a fixed percentage of A's and B's are awarded.

The rational method, as illustrated by the preceding example, commands respect but does not necessarily convince an audience. One listener might be a medical school admissions officer who resents the fact that students with high grade averages sometimes do not perform well in medical schools. This person would probably find your logic irresistible. Another listener, a student who wants to be admitted to a graduate school after getting a bachelor's degree, rejects the reasoning. To this student, it is not sensible to support a proposal that may reduce the chances of being accepted by the graduate program that he or she wants to join.

The instruction in the example is clear: The most effective speaking presents listeners with the hope of satisfying their needs and values by adopting a logical and reasonable course of action.

THE PROBLEM OF HOLDING ATTENTION

Some topics are naturally interesting to certain audiences. If speakers discuss a subject that affects a need or goal important to the welfare of an audience, they will have little trouble in getting and holding interest. Therefore, the first principle of holding attention may be stated as follows: Offer your listeners something they want and need. The difficulty here, of course, lies in convincing the audience that you are offering them something that they really need—something that will actually bring them a satisfying reward, not merely a huckster's promise. Nevertheless, a person whose house has just been flooded will listen to talk of flood insurance; a person who is unemployed will lend an ear to descriptions of a training program that will guarantee a job; and a person with cancer will not ignore a discussion of new remedies that promise a cure for the disease. When a speaker's message offers a reasonable chance to satisfy a listener's felt need, the listener will pay attention to it. Thus, speakers who want attention must always try to connect their speech with the goals of their audiences.

The second principle for getting and holding attention is to fill the speech and the occasion with strong and varied stimuli. Such stimuli arise from several sources. The speaker's surroundings are a part of the message. Displayed posters, blown-up photographs, flags, statuary, stained-glass windows—all can add mood and perhaps specific ideas to the speaker's presentation. Likewise, the speaker conveys nonverbal messages by dress, posture, and physical behavior. Finally, the ideas and thoughts that the speaker expresses may be vivid and forceful in themselves or because of the way they are worded. If the speaker's surroundings, nonverbal cues, and verbally expressed ideas show the following characteristics, they will probably get and hold attention:

> intensity
> activity
> variety
> order

Intensity. A loud sound will be more noticed than a soft one, bright colors more than muted ones. Thus, if the speaker makes the delivery forceful and intense, he or she improves the likelihood of getting attention. Likewise, if intense rather than drab stimuli decorate the podium and the room or hall in which the speech is delivered, the effect will be to help the speaker focus and maintain interest on the subject. Care should be taken, however, not to surround the speaker with distracting or overpowering stimuli.

Language may also have intensity. Intense words are generally words that make the strongest sensory impression, that are unusual or varied, or that are accusatory or even taboo. The facts and ideas presented may also deal with intense human feelings and beliefs. Note how the following passage holds attention because of the strong wording and the conviction of the speaker as he expresses basic human emotions. The passage is from a speech by Malcolm X, a Black Muslim minister and civil rights leader who was assassinated in 1965:

The political philosophy of black nationalism means that the black man should control the politics and the politicians in his own community; no more. The black man in the black community has to be reeducated into the science of politics so he will know what politics is supposed to bring him in return. Don't be throwing out any ballots. A ballot is like a bullet. You don't throw your ballots until you see a target, and if that target is not within your reach, keep your ballot in your pocket. The political philosophy of black nationalism is being taught in the Christian church. It's being taught in the NAACP. It's being taught in CORE meetings. It's being taught in SNCC [Student Nonviolent Coordinating Committee] meetings. It's being taught in Muslim meetings. It's being taught where nothing but atheists and agnostics come together. It's being taught everywhere. Black people are fed up with the dillydallying, pussyfooting, compromising approach that we've been using toward getting our freedom. We want freedom now, but we're not going to get it saying "We Shall Overcome." We've got to fight until we overcome.[6]

[6] "The Ballot or the Bullet," in *Malcolm X Speaks*, ed. George Breitman (New York: Grove Press, 1965), p. 38.

Activity.   Activity attracts attention, whereas stationary objects tend to be overlooked. Speakers who effectively hold attention usually display a great deal of movement; they may pace about on the platform, display facial expressions, gesture with their hands and arms and use movements of the head and trunk. Such movements are not random, however, but are in tune with the speaker's verbal communication in much the same way that an orchestra conductor's movements are coordinated with the music. A speaker's movements should be like those of an actor, supplementing dialogue and enriching it with additional meaning.

Action, however, is not confined to actual movement by a speaker; it may also be blended into the content of a speech. Demands for action, as well as fast-paced narrative forms or quick movement from one grammatical structure to another, may give a passage a sense of rapid pace. What follows is an example from a speech by Robert W. Bunke, president of Cencom, an industrial corporation:

We forget also that in business today many large companies are afflicted with committeeitis. You know what I mean: Every decision must first be submitted to a faceless committee. Then after some months of leisurely luncheon meetings the committee submits its report written in gobbledygook. The report is impersonal because nobody dares to take any responsibility for it. And the report usually pussyfoots around the problem instead of wrestling that problem down to the mat and making it say uncle.

Let's listen to General Patton again—and the more I ponder his words the more I miss that abrasive but wonderful American. General Patton said:

"A good plan violently executed now is better than a perfect plan next week."

Or as Jesus told Peter:

"Launch out into the deep. ..."

Amen. I do not of course recommend rash behavior but I do recommend taking a calculated risk whenever necessary.

Action. Action. Action. The small company does that best. And as Emerson warned:

"In skating over thin ice our safety is in our speed."[7]

---

[7] Robert W. Bunke, "Learning a Lesson from David," *Vital Speeches of the Day,* 43 (1976–1977), 378. Reprinted by permission.

Variety.   Variety modifies intensity and action. Any stimulus that is repeated over and over tends to become monotonous. Speakers use variation to break the stimulus pattern and to renew interest. A speaker who has been talking intensely and loudly for some time may profit from lowering his or her voice and slackening the pace. If the speaker has been moving about and gesturing a lot, he or she may relieve the audience by standing still and moving only the face and the head and shoulders. The opposite is also true. If the speaker has been talking quietly with subdued gestures and movements, an increase in volume, intensity, and activity will help the audience stay with the message.

Variety in speech content is achieved by avoiding clichés, trite forms of expression. The speaker must have a fresh approach, some element of novelty, or distinctiveness in substance or style. Note how Herbert Richey, chairman of the board of the U.S. Chamber of Commerce, used a novel approach in his speech to members of the Ohio Chamber of Commerce. His subject, economics, was old stuff to his audience, and Richey needed to give it a fresh look if he wished to capture their attention. Here is how he did it:

I'd like to talk about modern economics today. I'm sure many of us are already familiar with that. But for those who are not, I can illustrate the theory with a story:

Jed is a part-time farm worker with a flair for applied economics. One day he "borrowed" a country ham from the farmer who employs him ... without bothering to tell the farmer.

He went downtown and sold the ham to the grocer for $27. Then he used $20 of that money to buy $80 worth of food stamps.

With the food stamps he bought $48 worth of groceries. He used the remaining $32 worth of food stamps to buy back the ham.

Then he returned the ham to the farmer's smokehouse.

So the grocer made a profit, the farmer got his ham back, and Jed has $48 worth of groceries plus $7 in cash.

If you see no flaw in that process, then you are already familiar with modern economics.

On the other hand, if you suspect that someone, somewhere, has been "taken" for $80, then the rest of this speech is dedicated to you.[8]

---

[8] Herbert Richey, "The Real Causes of Inflation," *Vital Speeches of the Day,* 43 (1976–1977), 386. Reprinted by permission.

Order. When people look at a set of stimuli that are jumbled and incomplete, they show two tendencies. One is called *closure.* Closure is the tendency to complete a fragmented impression by closing up the gaps in it so that it becomes a whole, unified stimulus, instead of several incomplete impressions. The constellations that people see in the stars are a good example of closure. The Big Dipper, for instance, is simply a closing up within the human mind of a pattern of stars that are really a random arrangement. The other tendency people show when they encounter a random set of stimuli is *organization.* It is similar to but not the same as closure. The tendencies toward closure and organization show that the human mind prefers orderly rather than disorderly input and tends to impose order when order does not really exist. We prefer music to noise, for instance, because of the pattern or organization in music.

In listening to a public speaker, an audience prefers an organized, patterned speech. They find such a presentation easier to listen to, and they can interpret it more accurately. Speakers stir greater interest and attention if they work from an outline that gives their speech a visible structure than they do if they speak spontaneously and randomly. In Chapter 4, we will take a close look at the principles of speech organization and how they benefit a speaker's effort.

Keeping attention is vital to successful speaking. In fact, as we noted earlier, one writer has said that success in speaking consists almost entirely of the speaker attracting fair and favorable attention to his or her proposals. This view has some merit. We obviously respond to things that attract our attention in a favorable way, but it is dangerous for speakers to assume that they can be successful merely by gaining the attention of the audience. Speakers cannot be successful without getting attention, but it is also true that they can get attention and still fail.

In analyzing an audience, speakers should try to predict what will help them get and hold attention. What are the needs and values that are uppermost in the minds of the listeners? Why are the listeners concerned? How can the speech be phrased so as to reveal its relevance to those needs and values? How can a speaker vary stimulus, incorporating movement, change, intensity, and variety into his or her behavior? How can these elements be included in the speech content? Will the audience's attitude place limits on the speaker's behavior? Will the audience react negatively to high intensity, to too much movement, to novelties in presentation that are too surprising? By answering such questions, the speaker hopes to create effects intelligently and to maintain the audience's constructive interest.

ANALYZING AN AUDIENCE

Several considerations about an audience can help a speaker make intelligent choices concerning the content and delivery of a speech. These considerations are age, sex, knowledge of subject, attitude toward the speaker's subject, and general audience orientation. Each of these factors deserves a brief discussion.

Age.   The individuals in an audience may range from very young to very old, but often those in an audience are of similar age. This is so because a human being's needs and values change with maturity and because a person tends to get together with others who have like needs. Age, therefore, affects audience formation and is a useful clue to the group's goals and motivations. Young adults will be interested in problems of family (acquiring a home, raising children, career expectations, and so on), whereas older adults in their fifties and sixties will be less concerned with these factors and more absorbed in security, esteem, and self-actualizing needs. Very young audiences (teenagers, for instance) will be concerned with their self-image, with their relations to the other sex, and with their education and career choices.

Of course, economic status modifies all of these age factors. The description just given assumes a middle- or upper-middle-class group. Lower-middle-class or lower-class people will have goals and wants that are affected by their economic needs, which should thus be taken into account when analyzing an audience. Age may also be a useful clue to the audience's education and to their probable knowledge of and interest in the speaker's subject. Some evidence also suggests that young people tend to respond to a speaker's prestige, while older youths and adults respond more to the content of a message. Conclusions drawn from the age of an audience, however, are clearly risky. Other evidence supporting them is usually needed to increase their reliability.

Sex.   The interests of males and females are currently coming closer together. Many women, in attempts to break out of sexual stereotypes, are competing in sports, entering professions like science and engineering, and working at a variety of jobs outside the home. But the majority of women still seem to be more oriented toward children and the home than men. They also tend, even though working, to cluster more than men in professions such as those of secretary, teacher, nurse, social worker, librarian, and so on. Useful judgments of the needs of both men and women may be drawn from such differences. But such judgments should be made with care. According to communication research, women, for reasons that are not clear, also tend to be generally more persuadable than men. Again, as is the case with age, there is risk in trusting the reliability of judgments based on sex factors.

Knowledge of subject.   An audience's familiarity with a subject is important to the speaker because it gives clues about where to start the discussion, how many and what terms need defining, and how complex and detailed explanations need to be. The audience's knowledge of the subject will suggest organizational choices: whether one can proceed inductively, whether it would be better to go from simple to complex, or perhaps whether there should be a psychological or logical plan of development. For a persuasive speech, valuable clues about the audience's probable attitude toward the speaker's position may come from knowing the extent and nature of the information to which they have already been exposed.

Attitude toward subject.   When speakers aim to inform or instruct, they can ease their work if they find out whether the audience is interested or disinterested in what the speech will be about, or even resentful of instruction. If the audience is disinterested, speakers know that a primary task is to stimulate and maintain interest. If the audience is already interested, speakers can gauge the interest elements on which they can build to encourage the reception of the message. If members of the audience are resentful of instruction, speakers know that they may have to start with material that is possibly irrelevant but is designed to reduce resentment and create a receptive or at least neutral frame of mind.

When speaking persuasively, the communicator needs to know whether the audience is favorable, neutral, or hostile toward the proposal. Attitude evaluation should be as precise as possible. Usually it can be plotted on a continuum like the following:

Strongly Agree	Agree	Undecided	Disagree	Strongly Disagree

Attitudes will usually not be the same throughout an audience. Maybe 85 percent will agree and 15 percent will disagree. The speaker must then decide what the persuasive task should be. Should it be to intensify the attitude of the 85 percent, forgetting the others, or should it be to convert the 15 percent on the assumption that the others are safety in the fold? If much of an audience strongly disagrees with the speaker's position, the persuasive task is exceedingly difficult. Evidence from survey and experimental studies show that highly committed persons are difficult to influence, especially if the speaker's position is markedly different from their own. Sometimes, to move the audience a step closer to the ideal position, the speaker may choose to support a position less radical than what he or she would really like. For instance, a speaker might try to get a hostile audience to endorse abortion in the first few weeks of pregnancy when abortion on demand is the speaker's true position.

Whatever the speaker's plan, whether to compromise somewhat or to remain with an ideal, he or she must be prepared to link proposals to the needs and wants of the audience and to provide listeners with good reasons for following advice.

General audience orientation. Often it is useful for a speaker to judge the probable orientation of the audience toward his topic. The audience's knowledge of the subject and their attitude toward it will determine their orientation. Four kinds of orientation are possible and awareness of them helps the speaker choose the content and strategies that will be most effective in accomplishing the purpose of the speech.

1. *The reward orientation* Audience members with a reward orientation want to know how something will be useful to them—how they can profit from it. If, for example, you were to speak to older Americans on funding problems of the social security system, you would know that their chief concern would be how any change in the program would affect their pocketbooks. Not only will the speaker's judgment of acceptable changes in the program be affected by this knowledge, but he or she will know the kind of arguments to be used and the objections to be overcome in securing acceptance of any proposed change.

   Subjects that deal with the buying and selling of merchandise, upgrading someone's abilities in the marketplace, finding a job, increasing earning power, coping with taxes, and the like, tend to attract the reward orientation.

2. *The ego-defensive orientation* Sometimes a subject will challenge an audience's sense of esteem, pride, or devotion to a chosen philosophy or way of life. Such a challenge will make an audience feel

threatened. As a result, they can become remarkably resistant to change or, on the other hand, they might begin to favor unwise hasty action that appears to avert the threat. When President Carter spoke to the American people about his handling of the Iranian hostage crisis, he had always to confront American pride. He was constantly obliged to adjust to demands for military intervention or other precipitous action.

Subjects that usually attract ego-defensive orientations are ones that question deeply held convictions. Such convictions most often relate to religion, politics, patriotism, or ethnic origin.

3. *The value-supported orientation*   People tend to support programs that advance their political, social, economic, religious, and aesthetic values. They will join political action committees to advance conservative economic legislation; they will engage in campaigns to further a right-to-life amendment; or they will join parades and protest marches to prevent projects they think will threaten the environment. Others will spend countless hours and no small fortune to create a symphony orchestra or a community art center. Whenever a speech's subject runs counter to cherished values held by an audience, the speaker must be aware of that fact. Such knowledge will allow the speaker to choose appropriate appeals and avoid others that are value threatening.

4. *The knowledge orientation*   Audiences will be relatively ignorant about some topics. They will, therefore, be motivated by curiosity and a need for information. If the speech can relate instruction to some reward and to ego- and value-supportive needs so much the better. Often, however, knowledge will be valued for its own sake, as with topics relating to space travel, new inventions, medical breakthroughs, new social trends, and the like.

ADAPTING TO THE OCCASION

A speech must not only be designed to fit a particular audience, as has been described; it must also be adapted to the occasion of its delivery. Occasions for speeches are of many kinds, and each occasion places different obligations on the speaker. Occasions may be classified in several ways, but probably the best way is to view them in light of the kind of speech expected.

CEREMONIAL OCCASIONS

During the Bicentennial of the American Revolution in 1976, many organizations, such as civic clubs, veterans' groups, and patriotic societies, held one or more meetings where public speakers played a prominent role. On these occasions, speakers were expected to dwell on the nature of the American Republic, the principles set forth by its founders, and the relevance of those principles to today's American society. Speakers, of course, were given great flexibility in their treatment of this basic theme. Most of them tried to handle it in an innovative manner, but all pretty much had to hold to it; certainly, none would have been unwise enough to give a lecture on the economics of shrimp farming at such a gathering.

There are many ceremonial occasions where appropriate speeches are expected: the inauguration of the president of a university; the retirement of a long-term employee of a business firm; the death of a respected colleague; the induction of new members into a club, society, or other organization; the launching of a new merchandising program; and so on. In each of these circumstances, the speech is expected to fit the requirements of the occasion; usually, this means the delivery of an inspirational address that praises persons and/or ideals and calls for rededication to common purposes and values.

LEARNING OCCASIONS

The typical learning group will focus on some particular kind of information. A learning group may be a literary guild dedicated to the study of novels (or drama or poetry), it may be an Audubon society or a Sierra Club specializing in nature study, or it may even be as formal as a college class focusing on a specific subject, like political science or economics. An invitation to speak before such a group usually requires an essentially informative speech and assumes some expertise on the speaker's part. The speaker will be aware that the audience is already knowledgeable on the topic and should try to build on their background with appropriate new information. Persuasive speeches based mainly on information may also be appropriate on such occasions; for example, a speech to a nature club may call for an environmental protection lobby in Congress, or a speech to an economics class may demand that we abandon Keynesian economics.

DELIBERATIVE OCCASIONS

A deliberative occasion calls for study about decision making or problem solving. A typical example is a congressional committee gathering information and opinions prior to introducing proposed legislation. On such an occasion, a speaker is expected to supply information having to do with the issue and to express a view. Other occasions that require deliberative speaking are city and county commission meetings, meetings of school boards, meetings of corporation boards, political rallies, meetings of political-action groups such as Common Cause, meetings of lobbying groups, and so on. Deliberative speaking is essentially persuasive speaking; this type of speaking is so common that Chapter 10 will be devoted to it.

AMBIGUOUS OCCASIONS

Not every occasion clearly specifies the purpose of a speech. Often someone is invited to speak before a civic club or other organization at a luncheon or banquet meeting. The speaker may be asked to talk on whatever he or she wishes. Thus the speaker has a lot of flexibility. He or she may seek to entertain or amuse the audience, to offer them inspirational material reflecting the ideals of the club or organization, to inform them on a topic about which the speaker is enthusiastic and knowledgeable, or to speak persuasively on an issue of concern to the audience. The choice is pretty much up to the speaker, who is restricted only by what he or she knows of the audience and how it will probably respond.

ADAPTING TO TIME, PLACE, AND FORMAT

Just as the occasion strongly suggests the purpose of the speech, it also suggests opportunities and limitations that affect speech performance. The location, for instance, may be a help or a hindrance. An indoor hall may have poor acoustics that will not be evident until the speech has begun. It may be so large that it requires a sound system that will inhibit the speaker's activity. It may be poorly arranged, so that part of the audience will have a poor view of the speaker. On the other hand, the location may provide the speaker with an excellent central platform and a background that allows the display of such mood-enhancing items as flags, posters, and slogans.

The occasion may provide for music, which may create an emotional climate that enhances or detracts from the speaker's purpose. If possible, a speaker should influence the choice of musical selection to his or her advantage.

Outdoor meetings offer a difficult challenge. Usually, audiences are much less confined than when indoors, and individuals are likely to drift in and out. The audience may find it difficult to hear. Distractions are more frequent than in a hall. The speaker must be prepared to counter all these negative influences.

The occasion may call for other speakers as part of the program. If so, what these speakers say and the amount of time they take will influence what a speaker does. The order in which speeches occur is important. In a series of speeches, a speaker may prefer to be last so that the impact of the message is not reduced by later speeches. But the last speaker in a series may have to contend with boredom and inattention resulting from the audience's having been exposed for too long to verbal assault. Other speakers may say things that set the audience against a subsequent speaker. When Henry Grady addressed the New England Club of New York City in 1886 for the purpose of drawing out sympathy for the New South (as he called it), the efforts of two previous speakers made his task difficult. First, T. Dewitt Talmage spoke glowingly of the striking achievements of the Grand Army of the Republic in defeating the rebellious Southern Army, and then General Sherman described his famous march from Atlanta to the sea in terms that belittled the South. Following Sherman's address, the audience rose and sang "Marching Through Georgia." Then Grady was introduced. Grady's success in overcoming the negative atmosphere created by the previous speakers paid tribute to his skill as an orator.

The occasion will usually restrict a speaker's time. The limits may be very strict, as in a debate against other speakers, in which the participants must observe a signal such as a buzzer or a bell. Time cards may be used to measure the speaker's progress minute by minute. In many cases, although the time frame is not so precise, it will be clearly understood that twenty-five or thirty minutes of discourse is expected. Talking much longer than expected may seriously diminish a speaker's credibility.

Finally, the occasion may call for confrontation with opposing speakers or for questions and answers from the audience. A debate format means adjusting to attack from an opponent or opponents who will share the platform. In most cases, a thoroughly set speech won't work in a debate. A structure of important points and supporting evidence should be prepared, but the pattern of presentation should be left open to deal with

opposing arguments. This may mean sacrificing some neatness of organization. If the speech is to be followed by questions and answers from the
audience, its content may be pretty well structured in advance. However,
the speaker must be prepared to defend its major points with additional
evidence and arguments when challenged by the audience.

INVESTIGATING AUDIENCE AND OCCASION

The foregoing discussion clearly indicates that a speaker needs to
investigate the audience and the occasion prior to delivering a speech.
Often the investigation is limited to what the speaker can learn indirectly.
If, for instance, a women is to address the county school board, she will
have to depend on what she can read in the newspaper or learn from
friends about the attitudes of board members. She may want to attend a
board meeting prior to the date of her appearance so as to be familiar with
procedures and aware of the board's reactions.

When speakers are invited to make a speech, they can ask questions.
They will learn the approximate size of the audience; its makeup in terms
of age, sex, economic status, and education; and so on. They will be
informed of the meeting place and of who and what will apear in the rest
of the program. They may, by request, be able to control a number of
factors, such as seating arrangements, order of speeches, and particularly
the content of the speech that will introduce them to the audience.
Although it may be time consuming, an extensive investigation of the
audience and the occasion is well worth the effort. In fact, speakers ought
to use a simple check list of items based on the factors discussed in this
chapter.

A check list for analyzing the audience and the occasion follows. If
speakers get the information called for on this list, they can be sure they
will be armed with the knowledge necessary to adapt intelligently to the
circumstances of the speech.

I. *The speaking occasion.*
  A. What is the date and hour?
    1. Is the date a work day, a holiday, an anniversary, or
       another special day?
    2. Is the time a lunch hour, late evening, or another hour that
       deserves special consideration?
  B. What will be the size of the audience?

C. Where is the meeting place?
  1. Is the meeting place an auditorium or large room?
     a. Is there a speaker's lecturn or platform?
     b. Is a microphone present or is one needed?
     c. Is there a blackboard or a place to exhibit charts, graphs, or slides?
     d. Where are the electrical connections? Where are the light switches? Can window shades be drawn?
     e. Can heating and air conditioning be controlled?
     f. Is the lighting on the speaker's platform and in the auditorium satisfactory?
  2. Is the meeting place a small room with a small audience? What are the seating arrangements? Lighting, heating, and so on?
  3. Is the meeting place outdoors? What problems will this cause?
D. What type of meeting is it?
  1. Is it a regular meeting of a club, a class, or a special gathering?
  2. Who is sponsoring the meeting, and for what purpose?
  3. What will be the mood or atmosphere?
  4. Is there a planned program of announcements, reports, other speakers, or music?
  5. Will there be an open-forum question period?
II. *The audience itself.*
A. What are the audience's characteristics and common interests?
  1. Age: Uniform age group or mixed?
  2. Sex: All men, all women, or mixed?
  3. Race: All white? Racial minorities? Wholly a minority group?
  4. Educational status: High school graduates? College graduates? Other?
  5. Economic and occupational status: Wealthy, middle income, or poor? Kinds of jobs? Students, homemakers, retired persons?
B. What are the audience's attitudes toward your subject?
  1. Indifferent, uninformed?
  2. Undecided, uninterested, or interested?
  3. Opposed? Strongly or moderately so?
  4. Favorable? Strongly or moderately so?

C. What general orientation will the audience have?
  1. Reward orientation?
  2. Ego-defensive orientation?
  3. Value-supportive orientation?
  4. Knowledge orientation?
D. What are the audience's attitudes toward you as a person?
  1. Are you like your audience in age, sex, race, religion, economic status? Will any differences make your audience less responsive to you?
  2. Does the audience know of your background and your purpose in speaking to them? Will your education, occupation, titles, and so on, command their respect?
  3. Do you have special qualifications to speak on the topic?
  4. Will the audience initially greet you with favor or prejudice?

PROCESS ANALYSIS

Up to this point, we have discussed prior analysis of the audience and the occasion, stressing the things a speaker needs to know before the address is given. During the presentation of the speech, the speaker needs to be observant of the audience to detect how well the message is being received. If the speaker fails to observe the audience's response, he or she neglects the principle of feedback. (See Figures 1.1 and 1.2 in Chapter 1.) Feedback is essential to effective communication. Without it, the speaker is unable to gauge the responses of the audience that convey misunderstanding, objections, perplexity, or simple indifference to the speech. Without this information, the speaker cannot adjust the speech to the communication needs of the audience. What kind of feedback, then, should the speaker look for from the audience? The following list indicates the things that a speaker should look for:

I. The speaker should estimate the degree of attention and interest.
  A. Implicit indicators: Is the audience restless? Experimental study has confirmed that gross bodily movement provides a measure of broad levels of audience interest. Much movement means lack of interest. Whispered conversations, evidence of sleepiness, yawning, and the like imply boredom. The frequency and amplitude of laughter and applause may be indicative as well.

B. Explicit indicators: Shouts of encouragement, booing, hissing, and the like, are obvious signs of audience reaction.

II. The speaker should estimate the probable accuracy of the audience's understanding of his message. This factor is exceedingly difficult to evaluate. Information may be derived from the following sources.

   A. Interest level: If attention is poor, understanding is likely to be fragmentary. Misconceptions of the speaker's meaning are almost bound to occur.

   B. Gross physical activity: Nodding or shaking of heads, whispering together, and certain gestures may be taken as indicating lack of understanding.

   C. Facial expression: Recent studies have shown that practiced observers of facial expression are usually able to infer correctly the emotion expressed when they know the situation which produced the expession. Experienced speakers are able to infer bewilderment by keenly observing facial changes in their audience.

III. The speaker should estimate the degree of emotional involvement and suggestibility in his audience.

   A. Again, an estimate of attention level will help gauge emotionality and suggestibility. A highly emotional and suggestible audience is not easily distracted by extraneous stimuli. Furthermore, their reactions tend to be more expansive. Hence, the fewer the observed responses to distractions and the greater the amplitude of reactions such as laughter and applause, the higher the probable emotionality and suggestibility.

   B. Facial expression, bodily tonus, and gesture are also ready indicators of emotion. The kind and degree of emotion can be roughly calculated by an experienced speaker.

   C. Response to direct suggestions may be observed. If cries of "No! No!" or "Yes! Yes!", or applause, or other overt responses greet direct suggestions, then suggestibility can be roughly gauged by observing the number of persons so responding and the expansiveness of their response. If direct suggestions are greeted with silence, the audience may be suggestible, but probably only to a slight degree.

   D. Observation of emotional response provides a speaker with a rough way of estimating the probable effectiveness with which he has adjusted his message to the needs and wants of the audience.

IV. The speaker should estimate the degree of credibility the audience attaches to his statements.

    A. He should look for evidences of belief or disbelief in facial expression, gesture, and movement. Since things not understood are not believed, correct understanding necessarily precedes belief.

    B. The speaker should estimate the probable degree of his personal prestige. Do the members of the audience appear hostile or friendly, or are their attitudes mixed? Do they respond readily to friendly overtures, or are they cold and reserved? Are they paying attention? Dullness has an adverse effect on a speaker's prestige.

    C. Does this audience appear to respect the sources of the speaker's information, as well as the speaker personally?

    D. Is there any apparent reaction to his train of reasoning? Does the audience lose interest during logical exposition? Loss of interest is a sure sign that argument is ineffective.

V. The speaker should estimate the degree of effectiveness with which he or she has adjusted the message to the needs and values of the audience. This is accomplished in III above when the speaker estimates the degree of emotionality and suggestibility.[9]

POSTANALYSIS

After a speech has been delivered, a speaker should try to measure the outcome in terms of audience response. This step is especially important if the speaker has additional opportunities to address the same audience, because it will reveal what needs to be done to make future messages more effective. Even if the speaker cannot address the same audience again, however, it will help to know generally what elements of the presentation were effective or ineffective and why. Only by evaluating each speech experience can a speaker hope to improve on later occasions.

How effective a speech has been can be learned from the following:

---

[9] Wayne C. Minnick, *The Art of Persuasion* (Boston: Houghton Mifflin Company, 1967), pp. 271–272.

1. Opinion ballots or agreement-disagreement scales the audience is asked to fill out
2. The kinds of questions and comments from the audience in an open-forum period
3. Personal testimony from members of the audience after the speech is over (This kind of face-to-face interaction must be qualified because the speaker will be able to reach only a few members of the audience and because they may be unwilling to state their opinion honestly in the speaker's presence.)
4. Any editorials, opinions, or news stories about the speech that may appear in the press
5. The behavior of the audience

If the audience acts as the speaker recommends, the speech methods used may have been effective. One cannot be sure, however; audience members may have been favorable to the action before the speech, and the speech may have had little effect on them. But if the audience's attitudes were known to be initially unfavorable or indifferent, then the speech can reasonably be assumed to have had some effect on audience behavior.

SUMMARY

All audiences share certain basic needs such as physiological needs, security needs, and needs for love, esteem, and self-actualization. Appealing to these needs by showing how your material satisfies one or more of them is a good way to get and hold attention. However, your speech should have other attention-getting characteristics, such as intensity, action, variety, and order, if you expect to hold interest at a high level. In analyzing an audience you need to consider things like age, sex, knowledge of the subject, attitude toward it, and general orientation toward the topic. Adapting to the occasion means you must know the requirements of various ceremonial, learning, and deliberative circumstances in which speeches are called for. Audience analysis can be made prior to the speech, during its delivery, or following its presentation.

Exercises

1. The class should be divided into groups of five or six. Each group should use the check list given in this chapter for analyzing the same audience and occasion. Compare the results among groups and discuss differences.
2. Analyze the class itself as an audience to be addressed by student speakers. For example: What kinds of subjects will it be interested in? What needs and goals will appeal to it? Choose a one-point speech topic suitable for the class and prepare and present a short informative speech.
3. Select an audience composed of university people, such as fraternity or sorority, the student senate, a general meeting of the faculty, an alumni group, a student honorary society, the staff of the student newspaper, and so on. Prepare and submit an analysis of this audience based on the check list given in this chapter.
4. Bring to class and discuss examples of attention-getting materials in magazines and newspaper advertisements. Select the two best advertisements. Why are these the best?
5. Listen to a live speaker whose audience can be observed. This can be a teacher lecturing, a prominent figure speaking on the campus, a local minister preaching, a member speaking to the student senate, and so on. Write a process analysis of the audience using the check list given in this chapter.
6. Prepare a three-minute speech on ''How to Register for Classes,'' or some other student problem. In this speech emphasize one or more of the attention-getting factors discussed in this chapter.

Chapter Three
FINDING SPEECH MATERIALS

OVERVIEW

Guiding principles for selecting a subject and a purpose
A description of general speech purposes
How to find content material for your speeches
How to prepare for your first speech
How to deal with stage fright

SELECTING SUBJECT AND PURPOSE

In Chapter 2 we saw that a speaker should choose a subject that the audience is interested in. Audience expectations, created by the particular speaking occasion, should not be ignored. Neither should the speaker ignore the age, previous experience, sex, or economic status of the audience. When the speaker can choose a subject and purpose that seem appealing to the audience, this may be a wise thing to do. However, a speaker should be careful not to sacrifice other important considerations to find a topic that will appeal to the audience. What are these other considerations?

The speaker's own experience, knowledge, and interests are perhaps more important to selecting a subject and purpose than the audience's preference is. The ideal, of course, is a sensible mixture of both speaker and audience considerations. Let us look first at the speaker's experience and knowledge. When people speak about what they have experienced or what they have learned through extensive study, they usually speak with confidence, animation, and zeal, all of which are characteristic of effective communication. If you are a camera enthusiast or a serious stamp collector, you have not only a set of valuable experiences, but also a wealth of knowledge picked up from the reading you have done on your hobby. If your audience is not expecting a speech on a specified subject, you may elect to choose photography or stamp collecting as the subject of an informative address. Although your audience may at first have no interest in these subjects, your enthusiasm and expertise should be able to kindle attention quickly and sustain it.

Interest in the topic may sometimes cause a speaker to elect a subject in which he or she has little experience and only indirect knowledge. Usually such choices involve questions of personal conduct and public policy. How do you feel, for instance, about abortion, about the use of drugs such as alcohol and marijuana, about the use of illegal means by the FBI and the CIA to collect information on radical groups? Are you satisfied with the grading system in your college, with the way student government is organized, with the balance between teaching and research demanded of your professors, with the student or administration method of handling student offenses? You may find that you have strong feelings on one or more of these topics (and possibly on several others). Perhaps you have not had direct experience with the problem area, or you may not know much about it. This should not stop you. Your interest and concern will keep you going through a research program that will make you knowledgeable enough to express informed views.

The selection of speech topics should also be guided by *an awareness of the social utility of communication.* In Chapter 1, we noted that speech making plays an important role by exposing people to a variety of attitudes and opinions that will provide a basis for informed choice. Speech making also plays an important role by informing about new techniques and processes and about culturally valuable ideas. Thus speech topics should be considered for their value to both audience and speaker as an aid in decision making on public issues and as part of the ongoing learning process expected of all citizens in a free and enlightened society. Speech topics, properly chosen, can expand the horizons of both the speaker and the audience. Both should gain new insights into current issues and an increased awareness of humanity's exploding knowledge about itself and the universe.

In choosing a speech topic, consider *the availability of material and its quality.* Suppose you choose to speak on the possibility of visitors from outer space to this world or on new theories about the death of John F. Kennedy. You should be aware that much of the alleged new evidence on these questions is based on unreliable human observations. These observations, in turn, are often based on unproved, sensational assumptions. If you choose to tell an audience about the speculations on such topics, you should do so with a grain of salt. It is extremely difficult to establish as fact the guesses and alleged revelations that surround such topics, but you might wish to try.

Other topics offer plentiful evidence that is factual, statistical, or scientific and is easily found in your school's library. For instance, you might want to speak on the changes in your school's student population caused by fee increases in the past six or seven years. You would be likely to find in your library hard evidence about the following: the annual percentage increases for both in-state and out-of-state students; differences in fees and rates of increase between undergraduate and graduate students; and changes in the nature of the income of students' parents (that is, how many students are from lower- versus middle- and upper-income groups). From these facts, you can paint a picture of what has happened to the student body and what future trends are likely to be. You may choose to stop here, content simply to inform the audience of the facts, but you may also choose to move into policy questions, recommending changes in fee structure in line with your perceptions of what is good for the nation as a whole and for its citizens.

Value-laden topics, such as the right-to-die controversy, require as much factual support as do matters of fact and policy. In discussing the right-to-die topic, you need to establish factually the nature of the predicament of terminal patients—how long they can be kept alive and by what means, how much it costs to prolong their lives, and so on. But the question really turns on moral, religious, and ethical issues. You must be factually informed on the issues but also prepared to handle them emotionally as well as logically. You should investigate how other advocates have injected their arguments with moral, religious, and ethical appeals. Then you should develop emotional proposals of your own to counteract them. Before you attempt to prepare a speech on a given topic, however, it is comforting to know that the needed information is available.

Finally, in selecting a topic and a purpose, you should consider the *available time*. Classroom speeches may be as short as three or four minutes. In nonclass situations you may have from thirty minutes to an hour. The complexity of the subject may prevent you from choosing it if you have only a few minutes. Likewise, if your purpose is to persuade, four minutes may not be enough time to accomplish your purpose. You may therefore be required to select a topic that is sufficiently narrow or simple to fit the time frame; or you may choose to deal only with part of a more complex topic. If you are preparing a persuasive speech, you may try to convince your audience, because of the time limit, of only one aspect of a larger issue.

DISTINGUISHING GENERAL AND SPECIFIC PURPOSES

In this chapter and the previous one, the general purposes of a speech have been mentioned. To reiterate, these purposes are:

1. *To stimulate* The term *to stimulate* refers to the kind of speaking that has elsewhere been called ceremonial. *To stimulate* may not be

a universal term (some authors have called this type of speaking *evocative,* and Aristotle called it *epedictic*), but the term is intended to cover speeches of introduction and presentation, entertaining speeches, and speeches that seek to stir and sustain interest. It even covers such things as funeral orations. In all these cases, the speaker does not aim primarily at increasing the audience's knowledge or affecting their attitudes. The speaker seeks to perform a ceremonial function: stimulate the audience's feelings and heighten their awareness of their reason for assembling.

2. *To inform*   The speaker's purpose is to give information. For example, a speaker may attempt to explain processes, such as how to build things or how to understand the operation of human-made or natural objects. A speaker may try to clarify areas of knowledge, such as economics and physics, and the theories underlying them. In general, the purpose is to enhance the listener's knowledge and understanding of the world.

3. *To persuade*   Here the speaker proposes to work a change in the attitudes and behavior of the audience. The topics are perplexing issues or problems that confront the individual and society. In persuading, the speaker must communicate knowledge, but any facts and evidence that he or she uses are designed to support the arguments set forth to influence attitudes. A persuasive speech that seeks to influence the attitudes of the audience primarily by reasoning is called a speech to *convince.* A speech that seeks to get the audience to take some action by appealing to their motives is called a speech to *actuate.*

When speakers select a topic, they decide on their general purpose by weighing the nature of their own interest in the topic against the needs of the audience. If a speaker knows a lot about the subject and the audience is largely ignorant of it, he or she may feel that an informative speech is clearly called for. If the subject is a controversial one about which the speaker has strong feelings, and if the speaker judges the audience to be uncertain about it, he or she may want to give a persuasive speech. If the occasion so indicates, the speaker may be clearly required to give a ceremonial speech of presentation, introduction, or whatever.

When the general purpose is clear, the speaker must translate that general purpose into a specific one. That is, the speech must state clearly what the speaker wants to inform the audience of or persuade them to do, or what frame of mind the speaker wishes to stimulate in them. A few simple illustrations will clarify the process of selecting a specific purpose. The first example states the purposes of an informative speech:

General purpose: To inform the audience of some of the problems involved in taking good nature photographs
Specific purpose: To demonstrate how composition and lighting are key factors in successfully photographing animal subjects

Note that the general intention is to inform the audience about the art of nature photography. This general purpose already limits the broader field of photography as a whole. The speaker will ignore portraits, sports and documentary photographs, and other topics to focus on nature photography. The specific purpose represents an even tighter restriction of the subject matter. The speaker will not be concerned with the whole field of nature photography (scenics, flowers, and so on), but just with animals. Neither will the speaker be concerned with all of the considerations that go into taking a successful animal photograph (film, exposure, and so on). Just two essential elements, composition and lighting, will occupy the speech.

Sample specific-purpose statements that might be used for informative classroom speeches are:

1. The surgery-for-fee system used in America medicine results in unnecessary operations.
2. The operation of the space shuttle is a miracle of ingenuity.
3. The theory of evolution has undergone a number of modifications since Darwin's time.
4. Modern techniques of treasure hunting are fascinating.
5. Discrimination against women can be demonstrated through salary figures and job-placement records in business and the professions.

For persuasive speaking, the statement of a specific purpose has the same selective and focusing function just described:

General purpose: To persuade the audience that the cost of health care in the United States is a serious social problem

Specific purpose: To persuade the audience that the widespread use of prepaid health-care clinics can lessen the serious deprivations caused by the high cost of medical care

Again, the selection of a general purpose has limited the subject to some degree. The speech will deal with the cost of medical care, not its quality or regional availability (except as these are related to costs). The specific purpose further narrows the subject to a single alternative among a number that might be available for easing the problem.

Here is a list of specific-purpose statements that might be used for persuasive classroom speeches:

1. The grading system now in use at this school—A, B, C, D, and F—should be replaced by a system that uses ratings of satisfactory or unsatisfactory achievement.
2. There should be a student representative on the board of regents (governors) of this university or this system.
3. The legislature should adopt a state lottery for the support of education.
4. Our country should abolish the system of selecting the President of the United States by vote of an electoral college.
5. Congress should create a federal cabinet office for consumer protection.
6. This state legislature should adopt a law legalizing the possession of small amounts of marijuana for personal use. (This goes beyond the present action of some states, where possession of small amounts of the drug is a misdemeanor).

Defining a specific purpose for a stimulating speech often depends on the occasion. If it is a speech of introduction, the speaker's thinking might run like this:

General purpose: To introduce Mr. Joe Walters to the Pilot Club in an appropriate and effective way
Specific purpose: To acquaint the audience with the educational qualifications and the professional experience that have made Mr. Walters a recognized literary critic, while at the same time portraying him as a warm and friendly person

One would use a similar approach if the occasion is the retirement of an employee of some organization, the award of a prize to an individual for valuable work, or a eulogy on the death of some respected person.

If the speaker wanted to entertain an audience, as is appropriate on many luncheon or banquet occasions, he or she might approach the task as follows:

General purpose: To entertain the evening banquet of the convention of cleaners and dyers and to present a tribute to this hard-working group of professionals
Specific purpose: To provoke mirth and laughter by telling amusing stories of the odd habits of customers and the kinds of things they leave in the pockets of garments—end by stressing the usefulness and worth of the cleaning profession

Examples of general-purpose statements suitable for entertaining classroom speeches follows:

1. Dating games played by men and women
2. The idiosyncrasies of professors
3. How to find a parking place without going mad
4. Dining-hall food and other nutritional atrocities
5. The TV commercial
6. The world as reflected in song lyrics

FINDING MATERIALS

For every hour that professors teach in the classroom, they are expected to spend four hours in preparation. To suggest the same ratio for the preparation of speeches would not be unrealistic. In fact, many speakers devote an even greater amount of time to gathering evidence for their talks. Robert LaFollette, a Progressive Party senator from Wisconsin in the early part of this century, provided what is perhaps a model of careful preparation. When he was faced with an important address, he would first sit down and write out all his present ideas on the topic. Next he would talk with persons knowing a lot about the subject. Often these were persons working in government and industry on tasks related to his topic; frequently, they were college professors at the University of Wisconsin.

After this talking stage, he would personally search the resources of the library at the University of Wisconsin or, when pressed for time as he frequently was, he would hire graduate students to make the necessary search for him. LaFollette would thus compile a large batch of material, which he then read over carefully. If he detected gaps or insufficiency, he would use appropriate means to locate the needed material. If we make a careful inspection of LaFollette's methods, we will have a useful model for discovering the information needed for a responsible and effective speech.

YOUR OWN EXPERIENCE AND READING

What can you draw on from your own experience and reading? Many students have summer or part-time work experience. Such experience might illustrate ideas about the economic problems of the country or the personal problems that young people confront in fitting into and understanding their society. A greater fund of useful experience comes from your memory of things like formal classroom instruction, television news and dramatic broadcasts, motion pictures, and the reading of articles, essays, and both fiction and nonfiction books.

From formal classroom instruction, you may draw ideas and sources of great value. Have you had courses in such areas as death and dying, marriage and family life, race relations, mass communications, social problems in literature, business or educational psychology, philosophy of religion, environmental economics, interest groups in democratic politics, collective behavior, or the social psychology of groups? If you haven't had such courses, you will have had a dozen like them. Draw on them for speech topics and for basic information on which to build the speech.

When you look to your television, motion picture, and reading experience, you have a wealth of ideas and information. What does the success of Archie Bunker suggest about American ideals? Does the violence that appears nightly on prime-time television shows like "Hill Street Blues" and "Magnum P.I." have any relation to the occurrence of and attitude toward crime in America? What do movies and books you've read have to say about current issues? Not only do such programs, movies, and books offer ideas for speeches; they also supply a ready source of examples and illustrations to support your speech proposals.

You should not, however, try to rely solely on material drawn from experience, observation, and general reading when you prepare a talk. Such material does not give a well-rounded sample of information on the topic; in fact, it tends to be highly selective and needs to be supported from other sources. Conclusions drawn from the behavior of Archie Bur\`er, for instance, need to be confirmed (or refuted) by the testimony of experts or by the results of carefully conducted surveys.

INTERVIEWS

Much useful information can be found by talking with persons who know a lot about a subject. If you plan to speak on coin collecting, talk to a local coin dealer to find out what coins are rare and why, what controls the cost of collectable coins, and how coins are collected, preserved, and protected. Ask the dealer also about articles and books you can read to add to this information. Some people on campus that you might talk to in preparing a speech are the security officer, for information on police and parking problems; the registrar, for data on student mix, entrance requirements, fees, and so on; the minority advisor, for information on special minority programs, affirmative action, and so on; the controller, for an explanation of the methods of giving out and accounting for university funds; and any professor as a subject-matter specialist in his or her area. Don't forget that there are also people in your community, especially those in government and public service, who are usually cooperative with students. Know what you want of an interviewee, however; be concise, and don't waste time.

PRINTED MATERIALS

The greatest single source of information for speeches is your college library. Knowing how to use it effectively is a great asset. The discussion that follows recommends a variety of tools within the library for tracking down information on a subject of your choosing.

First, there are indexes. The card catalogue is an index of available books. Unless you have a specific book or author in mind, the subject index will be most useful in researching a speech topic. For instance, suppose you wish to give an informative speech on the home-computer craze. Since you do not know of a specific book on this subject that you could look up by title or of an author whom you could investigate by name, you will have to turn to the subject index, looking under the heading ''computer'' and various subdivisions and cross-references listed under the heading.

Other indexes have specialized uses. Some of the more common ones, with the kinds of materials they reference, are listed in the following sections.

Periodical articles.   The *Reader's Guide to Periodical Literature* indexes articles appearing in 160 general-circulation magazines published since 1900. *Poole's Index to Periodical Literature* is a guide to periodicals published before 1900. The *Cumulative Magazine Subject Index 1909–1949* contains the volumes of the *Annual Magazine Subject Index* for the period indicated. The *Subject Index to Periodicals,* published from 1915 to 1961, and the *British Humanities Index,* published since 1962, list by author and subject articles from 250 periodicals. *Ulrich's International Periodical Directory* classifies approximately 55,000 periodicals and the sources in which they are indexed.

Specialized periodical indexes include *Art Index, Biological and Agricultural Index, Business Periodical Index, Social Sciences Index, The Humanities Index, Engineering Index, Index to Latin American Periodical Literature, Catholic Periodical Index, Index to Legal Periodicals,* and *Industrial Arts Index.*

Newspaper and current affairs indexes.   *The New York Times Index* and *The London Times Index* index by subject news events and features published in those newspapers since their beginnings. *Ayers Directory of Newspapers and Periodicals* lists American newspapers and periodicals. *Newspapers on Microfilm* lists about 4,600 foreign newspapers and 17,000 American ones. *Facts on File* is not strictly a newspaper index, but rather provides a brief, factual, chronological account of news events assembled in annual volumes.

General reference books.   Often it is useful to begin your research by referring to an encyclopedia. Encyclopedia entries provide a concise overview of the subject and a useful bibliography. The more common general encyclopedias are the *Britannica* and the *Americana,* but specialized encyclopedias exist and should not be neglected. Among them are the *Encyclopedia of the Social Sciences, Hasting's Encyclopedia of Religion and Ethics,* the *Encyclopedia of Educational Research,* the *Jewish Encyclopedia,* and the *Catholic Encyclopedia.*

Factual and statistical information can be found in such sources as *The World Almanac, Information Please Almanac, Statistical Abstract of the United States,* and *The Statesman's Year Book.* Hundreds of governmental documents, such as the *Census* and the reports of various federal departments, can be found in the documents room of your library.

Biographical dictionaries include *Current Biography, Dictionary of American Biography, Dictionary of National Biography, Who's Who, Who's Who in America,*

International Who's Who, and *Webster's Biographical Dictionary.* The *New York Times* also has a biographical index covering figures whose lives have been reported in the paper.

Literary references and quotations can be found in *Bartlett's Famous Quotations, Oxford Dictionary of Quotations,* and *Home Book of Quotations.*

RESEARCH

Researching a topic for a speech should be a learning process. You ought to approach it with an open mind, willing to throw out mistaken ideas if you are making an informative speech, and willing to change your mind on a controversial issue if you intend to make a persuasive speech. You have a responsibility to your audience: to provide them with accurate and timely data in any learning situation and, in a persuasive situation, to give them knowledgeable opinions that you can defend. In fact, in the persuasive situation one method is to inform the audience of opposing solutions to a problem and to rebut those alternatives. Research has shown that this method is more successful than concentrating solely on the solution that you think best, while ignoring all others. You should investigate with an open mind, then, all sides of a controversial topic. Make your research a learning process, not one in which you read selectively to confirm your own opinions.

Check the quality of your material in two ways. First, be critical of the reasoning processes used by the authors you read. In Chapter 5, we will discuss argumentation; learn the principles that will be presented and apply them to test the reasoning of your sources. Second, judge the qualifications of your sources and their probable reliability. Chapter 5 will give you methods for testing the reliability of sources. When speaking, you should be ready to cite your sources. Do not present ideas and information that come from others as your own. There is plenty of evidence that including sources in a controversial speech bolsters the speaker's image and ability to persuade.

Record the sources of your information accurately. Someone may ask you after a speech where you got your statistics on the number of unemployed persons in the United States in June of 1976. You should be able to answer exactly. This requirement means that you should note your evidence on cards (usually 3 by 5 or 4 by 6). You should also note the author, the title of the work, and where it can be located. Somewhere on one of the cards for that author, you should have a list of his or her qualifications.

Gene Lyons, "The Higher Illiteracy," *Harper's,* 253 (September 1976), 33–40.

"The business of the American English Department in a typical college or university is not the teaching of literacy; it is the worship of literature."

Figure 3.1   SAMPLE EVIDENCE CARD.
Note that the main idea of the article and complete source information are included on the card.

A typical note card is shown in Figure 3.1. This card contains what is essentially the main idea of Lyons's article. Other note cards would record the evidence Lyons presents to support his claim. For instance, one card would record the academic rank and privileges of those faculty members who teach composition compared with the rank and privileges of those who teach literature; other cards would compare the promotion and salary opportunities of the same two groups. On a separate card, you might record what *Harper's* offers of Lyons's qualifications: "Gene Lyons has taught English at state universities in Massachusetts, Arkansas, and Texas, and has contributed articles to many publications, among them the *New York Times Book Review, The New York Review of Books, Texas Monthly,* and *Harper's Bookletter.*"[1]

Other articles taking the same position as Lyons's should be read and relevant ideas and evidence recorded. Rebuttal articles should be sought to help you test Lyons's thinking and facts. All of the resulting note cards should be arranged and placed in a file to make them easy to find. You should begin to prepare the content of your speech only after this research process is completed.

PREPARING THE SPEAKING OUTLINE

Once you have located a subject, fixed your purpose, and gathered your materials, you must prepare yourself to present the speech. What

[1] Gene Lyons, "The Higher Illiteracy," *Harper's,* 253 (September 1976), 33–40.

follows are some general bits of advice to help you get started; more elaborate preparations will be discussed in future chapters. For the present, you need help in preparing your first speech assignments.

Select a single informative point or idea that you can illustrate in three or four minutes. Make it simple; do not attempt complex explanations or arguments. Some examples that might be used are:

> The federal income tax falls most heavily on the middle-income groups.
>
> Political interference threatens the continuation of the Olympic games.
>
> Cosmetics may be hazardous to your health.

Begin your speech with a purpose sentence identical in form to the sentences just listed. Amplify your purpose by giving three or four supporting examples, along with a few statistics or quotations from some respected authority. Make an outline like the following to speak from:

I. Purpose: Cosmetics may be hazardous to your health.
II. This claim can be supported in the following ways:
    A. Examples of hazardous substances contained in cosmetics.
       1. *Vinyl chloride*: Used in aerosol products such as hair sprays. Cite experimental studies showing damage to the livers of experimental animals from ingestion of vinyl chloride.
       2. *Mercury*: Used in skin bleaches and hair straighteners now banned by FDA.
       3. *Chloroform*: Used in toothpaste. Cite damaging effects.
       4. *Red dye no. 2*: Used in lipstick, rouge, and the like. Causes cancer in experimental animals. Banned by FDA.
    B. Examples of illness caused by the use of beauty products: Present an example of a woman or man made ill by chemicals in hair dye.
    C. Statistics: The FDA made a study of 10,050 households in 1975, covering a three-month period; 589 adverse reactions were reported, most of them produced by antiperspirant deodorants, soaps, or hair sprays/lacquers. These products are a $1.5 billion-a-year business.[2]

---

[2] Chris Wells, "Warning: Cosmetics May Be Hazardous to Your Health," *New Times*, June 25, 1976, pp. 42ff.

III. Purpose restated: So you see, there is substantial evidence to show that beauty products may be hazardous to your health.

The following outline was prepared by a student in a fundamentals of speech class in response to the suggestions just given. Read it carefully and criticize it in your mind; that is, try to evaluate what is good and bad about it.

Experimentation on Living Animals
Purpose statement: The unregulated use of living animals for scientific research has produced numerous abuses.

A. *Testimony*: "There is no valid justification for continued and duplicated experimentation on living animals, by professionals or by amateurs, which do not contribute to knowledge." ("The Case for Humane Vivisection," Paul W. Kearney, *Coronet.*)

B. *Hypothetical illustration*: Suppose you heard of an instance in which a surgeon was operating on a dog for a valid experimental reason. During the procedure he needs to check on a surgical technique. He clamps the dog's incision and studies materials for about half an hour leaving the animal strapped and awake. Would you sanction such a practice?

C. *Actual examples or illustrations*: In a New York laboratory doctors were trying to disprove or prove that tobacco containing glycol caused less damage to tissue than tobacco containing glycerin. They pumped smoke into the lungs of dogs and rabbits by means of an incision in the tracheas of the animals in order to see the lung damage. Only one doctor, of the twelve involved, anesthetized the animals he used. (*Lancet,* a British medical journal.)

In a "learned helplessness" experiment animals were taught rules for obtaining food and avoiding electrical shocks. The rules were then changed in inconsistent ways so the animal could not figure them out. Ultimately the animals simply lay down and passively endured repeated shocks. This experiment was supposed to reveal something about human depression. (Patricia Curtis, "The Case Against Animal Experiments," *New York Times Magazine,* December 31, 1979.)

D. *Statistics*: Figures prove that an enormous number of animals is experimented upon.
   1. A typical large laboratory may use 80,000 chickens, 1,000 dogs, 1,000 rabbits, 500 cats, 40,000 rats, 500 pigs, 5,000 guinea pigs, and 280,000 mice annually. (Kearney, *Coronet.*)
   2. Sixty-four to 90 million animals are used nationwide annually. (Curtis, *New York Times Magazine.*)
   3. Thousands of animals are used a year in amateur experiments. (R.M. Henning, "Animal Welfare Groups Press for Limits on High School Research," *Biological Science,* 29 [Nov., 1979]).
E. *Testimony*: British psychologist Richard Ryder says that scientists justify their use of animals by asserting they can transfer knowledge gained from animal experiments to human beings because human beings and animals are similar. But in moral justification they argue that animals are different from human beings, i.e., less intelligent, less sensitive, etc. "Suppose," says Ryder, "we were to be discovered by more intelligent creatures from elsewhere in the universe. Would they be justified in experimenting on us?" (Curtis, *New York Times Magazine.*)
F. *Purpose restatement*: Something must be done (other than the 1972 federal law which covers only 4% of laboratory animals) to prevent the misuse of animals in experiments.

The good things about this outline are that the student selected a topic that not only met the requirements of the assignment, but was also interesting and significant in its own right. Also, the claim in the purpose statement was supported by a good range of materials—testimony, examples or illustrations, statistics, and restatement. The outline falls down in its failure to identify its sources fully. The *Coronet* article is not fully documented and even the *New York Times Magazine* article lacks page numbers. The thesis restatement refers to a federal law that should have been introduced earlier and more fully explained.

DELIVERING YOUR FIRST SPEECH

There are many things that need to be said about effective delivery, that is, about the use of voice and body in projecting your message to an audience. As we said before, these matters will be discussed at length in separate chapters of this book. For the moment, however, you need a brief preview of how to handle your first speaking assignment. The sections that follow give you a few pointers.

DEALING WITH STAGE FRIGHT

Stage fright, the fear of making a formal public speech, appears to be a more specific fear than the general type of anxiety known as communication apprehension. *Communication apprehension* is the general fear of talking with another person or group of persons. Data collected at three large American universities show that between 15 and 20 percent of American college students suffer from communication apprehension to a degree that seriously affects their interpersonal relationships.[3] The same study reveals, however, that stage fright is experienced by the overwhelming majority of people and should be considered a "normal" reaction. It should also be comforting to know that students make significant gains in confidence as a result of taking a course in public speaking. The next three sections deal with three ways you can improve your level of confidence in speech making.

CULTIVATING THE RIGHT MENTAL ATTITUDES

Don't think that because you are afraid you are different or abnormal. Everybody experiences stage fright; it is both normal and desirable. Why desirable? To do your best in any activity, you have to be "psyched up" and ready to respond with more determination than usual. This means physical and emotional excitement. Stage fright is simply that: an appropriate physical and emotional peak for a challenging experience. Stage fright, then, can help you speak with distinction. If you were indifferent, you would undoubtedly do poorly.

Remember also that stage fright ordinarily doesn't show. Nobody knows how nervous you are. One study showed that not even speech teachers could tell how nervous a student was; in fact, they tended to underestimate rather than overestimate student nervousness. In another study in which three groups of judges (not speech teachers) rated the nervousness of 371 college freshman speakers, each group failed to judge

---

[3] James C. McCrosky, "Classroom Consequences of Communication Apprehension," *Communication Education,* 26 (1977), 28.

accurately the degree of stage fright as reported by the students themselves.[4] So even if you are nervous, your audience won't know it. They
will probably think you are confident and in control of the situation even if
you feel anxious and disturbed.

   You should look on a speech as an opportunity rather than a disagreeable task. If you regard your classroom speeches merely as assignments to
be gotten through, they will remain disagreeable tasks. But a speech can
become an enjoyable challenge if you see it as an opportunity to share
with others something in which you are vitally interested or about which
you have strong convictions. This thought means that your selection of
topic is vital. If you choose a topic that grows out of your own experience
(an interest in music or literature, perhaps) or one on which you have
well-formed opinions, like abortion, you will be able to speak with enthusiasm. Moreover, your attention will be focused on your message, rather
than on your own reactions to the speech situation. You will thus be able
to ignore symptoms of stage fright, and when they are ignored the
symptoms tend to go away. It is common for a speaker to feel nervous at
the outset of a speech and then to have that nervousness disappear as he or
she becomes deeply involved in the topic.

   Finally, don't be afraid to make mistakes before an audience. It is
impossible and unreasonable to believe that you can always state your
ideas accurately or that you can always avoid getting mixed up in
following your thoughts. Mistakes are only bad when you overreact to
them—when you allow them to fluster you. Be ready for the experience of
making mistakes, and respond to them normally and calmly. For example, say, "I'm sorry, I didn't express that the way I wanted to. Let me try
again," or, "I misread those statistics. Here's the way they are supposed
to be." If you can learn to accept mistakes and adapt to them intelligently,
your confidence level should rise.

PREPARING AND PRACTICING YOUR DELIVERY

   Good preparation makes for confidence. If you have an agreeable topic
and have collected and organized your material around a clear purpose,
you should have faith in your ability to deal with the situation. You can

---

[4] Caleb Prall, "An Experimental Study of Measurement of . . . Stagefright . . ." (Ph.D.
diss., University of Southern California, 1950), p. 181; and Paul D. Holtzman, "An
Experimental Study of Some Relationships Among Several Indices of Stagefright and
Personality" (Ph.D. diss., University of Southern California, 1950), *passim.*

help yourself feel in command by using notes intelligently. You should have two types of notes. First, you should have an outline of the major points of your speech. This outline should show key-words or key-phrases, not complete-sentences. It should be somewhat like the outline on cosmetics given earlier in this chapter. The purpose of this outline is to keep the *structure* of your speech before your eyes so you won't forget the progression of ideas. The outline should not tell you how to express your ideas, but simply what these ideas are. On this outline, you should indicate the location of the supporting materials you are going to use. These supporting materials are the other type of notes you may use. They consist of separate cards, each containing an example, quotation, statistic, or other data that make up a major part of the body of a speech. The information on these cards can be used, as indicated on the speech outline, to support individual points you want to make. Notes should be used inconspicuously. Lay them on the lectern where you can easily see them, and pick them up to read from only when and if necessary.

In using notes, you should strive for an extemporaneous, conversational style. *Extemporaneous style* means you decide on the actual language of the speech during the presentation itself. An extemporaneous speech is not memorized, nor is it read from notes or manuscript. It is carefully constructed with information, evidence and argument put together beforehand. The only thing that is not preplanned is the language in which the content is to be expressed. There is a good reason for using extemporaneous delivery. Memorized speeches or speeches read from a manuscript tend to sound stilted, artificial, and indirect, especially when attempted by inexperienced speakers. Such speeches are appropriate to some situations, and some speakers can handle them well, but as a beginning speaker you should plan to use the extemporaneous approach.

When you speak extemporaneously, you tend to be conversational and direct; and for most situations a direct, conversational style is best. You should not attempt to reproduce the style of conversation exactly; to do so encourages rambling, disorganization, and unsupported claims. The *quality* of good conversation, not its precise imitation, is what you are after: directness, animation, concern for the audience's reactions, a sense of talking with your audience. A conversational tone should show the confidence that comes from recognizing friendly listeners who are aware of and expect the normal mistakes and hesitations of everyday speech.

When you have prepared your speech, rehearse it several times, using your outline as a guide and speaking the speech aloud. Go through the speech completely each time you rehearse, overcoming stumbling blocks as you go. Don't stop when you experience difficulty in expressing your ideas. If you back up and start again, you are practicing something that you cannot do during the actual delivery of the speech. The advantage of rehearsal is that you can practice expressing yourself in connected speaking. By improving your ability to speak smoothly, you increase your confidence, which in turn improves your delivery. Also, practice will allow you to judge how much time the speech will take. Time limits are usually imposed in the classroom.

USING BODILY ACTIVITY CONSTRUCTIVELY

Physical activity helps to relieve tension; consequently, you should use as much action and as many gestures as possible, as long as they don't distract the attention of the audience from your ideas. Although you should use gestures freely, do not plan them; let them arise naturally, but don't inhibit yourself. Consciously attempt, without trying to use specific actions, to free yourself from self-conscious restraints that make you appear formal and wooden. You may practice certain gestures, such as the pointed forefinger or the open-palm gesture, but do not do so with the idea of using them at a given point in the speech. Practice them to develop muscular readiness, so that when you feel the impulse to gesture, a smooth rather than an awkward action may result.

Remember that all tension will not disappear from the speech situation. No one ever reaches the point of approaching a public speech as casually as speaking to a friend on the telephone. Public speaking involves a great responsibility. If you are to speak, for instance, to an audience of 500 persons for half an hour, you will be asking for 250 aggregate hours of someone else's time. You have a responsibility to say something appropriate and worthwhile to justify that expenditure of time and attention. Tension under such circumstances, as we have said, is appropriate and helps stir the speaker to communicate with distinction. Tension is bad only when it becomes a distracting anxiety that prevents you from thinking clearly and acting spontaneously.

SUMMARY

In selecting a speech topic you should consider not only the value of the subject matter to your audience, but also your own experience, knowl-

edge, and interests. Other factors in selecting a topic are its social usefulness, the availability and quality of material about it, and the amount of
time you have in which to speak. Speech purposes can generally be
classified into three categories: (1) to inform, (2) to persuade, and (3) to
stimulate.

Materials for speeches may be found in your own experience and
background of reading and in interviews. Another source is printed
materials such as books, periodicals, newspapers, and general reference
works, all of which are available in a library.

A simple outline will help you prepare for your first speech. It should
contain a single purpose statement that can be supported in two or three
minutes by examples, statistics, testimony, explanations, and the like. If
you experience stage fright you can reduce it to manageable levels by
cultivating the right mental attitude, by preparing and practicing your
speech, and by using bodily activity constructively as you speak.

Exercises

1. Go to the library and, using the resources and indexes described in
   this chapter, locate the following:
   a. The number of people in the United States who own their own
      home and the average cost of a new home in 1981
   b. A magazine article published before 1900 dealing with football
   c. Biographies of Thurgood Marshall and Alexander Haig
   d. A magazine article on pointillism
   e. A quotation from a prominent American supporting the aboli-
      tion of the electoral college
2. Select several topics from your major field of academic study, for
   example, psychology, English, or chemistry. Refine these from
   general purpose statements to specific-purpose statements. Indicate
   why you decided to speak informatively rather than persuasively, or
   vice versa.
3. Imagine you have been invited to speak to a real audience in your
   community—the Kiwanis Club, the Women's Club, a ministerial
   association, a Sunday school class, the PTA. Assume you were not
   assigned a topic. Choose a suitable topic and give a statement of
   your specific purpose. Justify the topic and purpose using the
   principles expressed in this chapter.

4. Make an estimate on a 7-point scale of your degree of nervousness during the first speech assignment. Have the audience rate you and give you their ratings so you can compare your feelings with those of the audience. Use a scale like this:

Very Calm   Average Nervousness   Very Nervous

Chapter Four
ORGANIZATION

OVERVIEW

The major divisions of a speech

Various patterns or orders by which the body of a speech may be organized

Outlines showing the overall structure of a speech

Transitional materials used to tie the parts of a speech together

---

Organization of the body of a speech is important to both the speaker and the audience. When organizing material, the speaker is forced to look at a speech as a pattern, with each part bearing a relation to each other part. Indeed, the meaning of a body of material may not be evident until such a pattern of relationships is seen. Thus, organizing is really thinking—a kind of thinking that reveals how the bits of a puzzle fit together to form a total picture. Organization forces the speaker to understand the meaning of the material as a whole, rather than as a collection of separate parts.

For the audience, organization is an aid to clear understanding and a help in remembering. As is true for the speaker, a pattern of organization aids the listener's understanding, and it also provides a convenient framework into which the listener may fit the details of the speech. Without an organizing framework, the audience would probably be less able to remember the evidence and arguments of a speech. Consider for example your ability to understand and remember the following sets of words:

inanimate, animate, plant, animal, invertebrate, vertebrate, dog, chow

thunder, butter, acorn, Chinese, small, purple, federal, plant

Which series of words could you remember more easily? Which series forms a sensible pattern revealing a perceived intention or purpose? Most people would choose the first set, because people prefer organized patterns of stimuli.

This chapter will discuss principles of organization in general, isolate the parts of a speech, indicate the functions of each part, and suggest applications of certain organizational patterns to informative, persuasive, and stimulating speeches.

Three major divisions generally characterize speeches: an introduction, which usually includes a statement of purpose; a body, or amplification of the purpose; and a conclusion. Not every speech has all of these parts. In fact, introductions and conclusions are often omitted; but every speech has a purpose (express or implied) and a body in which the purpose is elaborated. Let us look at each of these major divisions of a speech in some detail.

Although the following discussion proceeds in the sequence (1) introduction, (2) body, and (3) conclusion, you should not prepare a speech in that order. You should begin with the formulation of the purpose statement and then prepare the body of the speech. When you have completed the body of the speech, you should draw up the introduction and conclusion. All of this discussion assumes that the speech is prepared in advance and the structure is carefully thought out. If conditions call for it (if there is little preparation time or if you are speaking in a situation where several speakers are exchanging views), introductions and conclusions may be omitted, as we have said.

THE INTRODUCTION

An introduction to a speech serves several purposes:

1. It should gain the attention of the audience and focus it on the speaker's subject.
2. It should usually state the speaker's purpose (although sometimes the speaker may want to postpone disclosing the purpose until later).
3. It should recognize the audience and provide them with any definitions and background that may be necessary for full understanding of the subject.

An indirect benefit of a well-prepared introduction is that it allows the speaker to establish credibility with the audience and to adjust comfortably to the speech situation.

GETTING ATTENTION

The general principles of attention described in Chapter 2 may be applied in a number of specific ways in the introduction. The following paragraphs will demonstrate a few of these ways, but you should remember that these are merely some examples, and actually the ways of getting and holding attention are almost limitless.

A speaker may get attention in the introduction by *relating an anecdote or striking example that illustrates an aspect of the topic to be discussed*. In the following example, Ralph M. Baruch, chairman of the board of a large manufacturer of communications hardware, wanted to key his speech to the concept of continuous change. He began as follows:

Not too long ago, Walter Cronkite, the dean of American television newscasters, gave us the following quotation:

"It is a gloomy moment in the history of our country. Not in the lifetime of most men has there been so much grave and deep apprehension. Never has the future seemed so incalculable as at this time. The domestic situation is in chaos. Our dollar is weak through the world. Prices are so high as to be utterly impossible. The political cauldron seethes and bubbles with uncertainty. Russia hangs, as usual, like a cloud, dark and silent, upon the horizon; it is a solemn moment. . . . Of our troubles no man can see the end."

That quote was from an editorial that appeared in Harper's Weekly Magazine in October of 1857 . . . Over 120 years ago.

There is a school of thought that believes "the more things change, the more they stay the same." There is another school across the street that regards the dynamism of cultural and technological change as a very real force in shaping human destiny.

I got my diploma from that second school. I admit that I am addicted to the future. I see change not only as inevitable, but desirable.[1]

Having stated the view that change is not only inevitable, but also desirable, Baruch used several transitional sentences to move into a discussion of the great changes that have occurred in the communications industry over the past decade.

---

[1] Ralph M. Baruch, "Lifestyle Revolutions in the Television Age," *Vital Speeches of the Day*, 47 (1980–1981), 209. Reprinted by permission.

Some speakers use a *reference to the occasion* to arrest attention and get the speech started. In addressing the graduating class at Hartford College for Women on June 1, 1974, Mary Lou Thibeault used the occasion to reveal the central purpose of her speech:

Fellow celebrants of the graduating class and honored graduates! When you students invited me to be your Commencement speaker, I was surprised, honored, and worried. I was worried because I am so informal a speaker and I know that commencement addresses are supposed to be serious, profound, and pontifical.

The first one I ever heard was at my own commencement here at Hartford College seventeen years ago. I do not remember the speaker or anything he had to say (it probably was a ''he''), but it was in the familiar and traditional style. (One of our staff members calls such offerings ''encouraging noises.'') Two years later at Mt. Holyoke the same kind of speech was a little more memorable— perhaps because we had a woman speaker. Journalist Pauline Fredericks advised us to be ''uncommon women.'' The choice between being common and uncommon was not a difficult one to make, or so I thought at the time anyway.

I have listened to many commencement speeches since then. Typically, they commend the graduates for what they have accomplished thus far, warn them that there are obstacles ahead, but—the ray of hope—by applying what they have learned at college and facing the future with strength, determination, faith, and courage, they shall win professional and personal fulfillment.

My address will say the same thing.[2]

She then moved swiftly into a discussion of what sexual equality would mean for the graduates of Hartford College.

Another way of opening a speech is by the *use of humor* that focuses attention on the speaker's topic. Sometimes such humor is bitter, as in the case that follows. The statement was by James Farmer and represented the opening of his contribution to a debate before students of Cornell University's United Religious Work:

[2] Mary Lou Thibeault, ''The Hazards of Equality,'' *Vital Speeches of the Day*, 41 (1973–1974), 588. Reprinted by permission.

When the Freedom Riders left from Montgomery, Alabama to ride into the conscience of America and into Jackson, Mississippi, there were many persons who said to us, "Don't go into Mississippi, go any place you like, go to the Union of South Africa but stay out of Mississippi." They said, "What you found in Alabama will be nothing compared to what you will meet in Mississippi." I remember being told a story by one minister who urged us not to go. He said: "Once upon a time there was a negro who lived for a long time running from county to county. Finally he left the state and left it pretty fast, as Dick Gregory would put it not by Greyhound, but by bloodhound, and he went to Illinois to live, in Chicago. And unable to find a job there after several weeks of walking the streets unemployed, he sat down and asked God what he should do. God said, 'Go back to Mississippi.' He said, 'Lord, you surely don't mean it, you're jesting. You don't mean for me to go back to Mississippi. There is segregation there!' The Lord said, 'Go back to Mississippi.' The man looked up and said, 'Very well, Lord, if you insist, I will do it, I will go. But will you go with me?' The Lord said: 'As far as Cincinnati.' "[3]

One qualification with regard to the use of humor should be mentioned. Humor should be appropriate to the subject and the occasion. The speaker is not a stand-up comedian who uses humor for its own sake. Humor should contribute to the purpose of a speech; otherwise its effectiveness is reduced. It may even result in the speaker's being discredited.

A *reference to a recent event* is sometimes a good way to open a speech. An unusual happening in the news or even some striking theatrical production or new book may be used to good advantage. If you were to give an informative speech about sharks, the movie *Jaws* and the astonishing interest it created would certainly make a useful reference in your introduction. With a different topic, you might refer to a best-selling novel or an outstanding play, using the theme of such works as a lead-in to your own discussion. What follows is an illustration of how a student used a news event in the introduction of a classroom speech:

[3] James Farmer and Malcolm X, "Separation or Integration," *Dialogue Magazine* (May 1962), as quoted in Golden and Rieke, *Rhetoric of Black Americans* (Columbus, Ohio: Charles E. Merrill Publishing Co., 1971), pp. 422–423.

For the past few days, the newspapers have carried many articles about what they call the Philadelphia killer. The Philadelphia killer is a mysterious disease that recently struck more than 130 people and killed 25. All of the affected persons had attended the American Legion Convention in Philadelphia, July 21 to 24, and all had suffered the same symptoms—chest pains, high fever and lung congestion. Some called the disease the Legionnaire's disease, because it was confined only to persons attending, or in some way being associated with, the American Legion convention.

As soon as the Legionnaire's disease was recognized as an epidemic, the Center for Disease Control in Atlanta, Georgia went into action in an effort to determine its causes. The Center for Disease Control is an important part of the public health program in the United States. The U.S. Public Health Program is not well known to most citizens—it comes to their attention only sporadically in connection with such outbreaks as that of the Philadelphia killer. In the next few minutes I would like to tell you about the major features of the United States Public Health Program and what that program means to you.

There are many other ways of opening a speech. You may refer to a previous speaker or speakers, you may ask the audience a series of provocative questions concerning your topic, you may make a dramatic forecast about events to come, you may relate your topic immediately to some known need of the audience, or you may choose any of a number of other approaches that imagination and ingenuity may suggest.

STATEMENT OF PURPOSE

In the introduction, the speaker usually discloses his or her purpose. When the purpose is persuasive, a speaker may sometimes postpone the purpose statement, but this practice is not frequent, and its effectiveness is uncertain. The student speaker, therefore, should usually plan to reveal or at least suggest the purpose somewhere in the introduction. Usually a purpose statement comes at or near the end of the introduction.

The following is an example of a complete introduction that meets all the requirements we have described, including getting attention, recognizing the audience, and disclosing the purpose. This introduction is from a speech delivered by Robert Bunke, president of a telephone company, to the Louisiana Telephone Association.

Recognition of the audience and its needs; forecast of purpose

This morning I want to explore with you how small independent telephone companies can, in a changing world, not only survive but prosper if they will innovate and capitalize upon their smallness.

An unusual attention-getting story

We can all learn from the manager of a movie theater which was swamped with empty popcorn boxes after the Saturday matinee. An unimaginative manager would have just put up a sign asking the kids not to litter. But this manager was creative. He must have known something about small telephone companies. He numbered each box and held a drawing after the Saturday matinee. You can bet that the kids picked up every box after the show and filed by the manager to deposit their boxes in an official contest barrel. Wouldn't you agree that the prize he awarded each Saturday afternoon was well worth the saving in labor to clean up the theater—and the kids had fun with the contest too.

Title and further notice of special audience interests

The title of my talk is "Learning a Lesson from David" which is a Biblical reference relating squarely to our topic of survival. When I was invited to visit with you here in the South, I decided that a Biblical theme would be appropriate because I know the strong appeal the Bible has for the people of the South—as it has as well for some of us Yankees up North.

Purpose: to offer guidelines for survival rather than rules

I intend to suggest some guidelines you may wish to follow rather than handing you veteran telephone people several volumes of practices and procedures. In doing so, I heed the advice of Major General George S. Patton, Jr., who said:

> "Never tell people how to do things. Tell them what to do and they will surprise you with their ingenuity."[4]

---

[4] Robert Bunke, "Learning a Lesson from David," *Vital Speeches of the Day*, 43 (1977), 376. Reprinted by permission.

The introduction to a speech leads naturally into the body, where most of the content or subject matter is concentrated.

THE BODY

The subject and purpose of the speech tend to dictate the kind of organization used within the body. In an informative speech, the body will consist of the information you want the audience to know, organized to promote ease of learning. In a persuasive speech, the body is organized to present reasons and evidence in the order most likely to influence the attitudes and actions of the audience. Your choice of a particular pattern, then, will be influenced by how well it is suited to your general and specific purposes.

CHRONOLOGICAL ORDER

An informative speech dealing with the development of present social patterns (customs, dress, behavior, political institutions, and so on) would probably be organized in chronological order. So also would a speech dealing with processes like flight or with the evolution of legal interpretations such as those relating to pornography. A chronological pattern

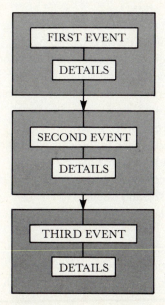

Figure 4.1 CHRONOLOGICAL ORGANIZATION.

simply begins at some point in time and moves forward to the present. (Of course, you can reverse the pattern if you like.) This type of organization is shown in schematic form in Figure 4.1. The following is a sample of the body of a speech organized chronologically:

Purpose: To support the claim that the establishment of slavery in America and its abolition required attitude changes spanning some 240 years

I.   The first blacks imported into this country came into Jamestown, Virginia, in 1619 as indentured servants.
II. Black indentured servants were quickly discriminated against by white society.
   A. In 1639 and 1643 laws were passed fixing limits to the terms of white indentured servants. The laws excepted blacks and Indians.
   B. Laws for the punishment of runaways discriminated against blacks. White runaways had their terms extended a year, blacks often for life.
   C. In 1661 a Virginia law provided that all blacks were to be ''perpetual servants.''
   D. In 1662 a law provided that the offspring of a slave mother were to be considered slaves.
   E. In 1670 a Virginia law provided that all bondmen coming to Virginia by sea ''shall be slaves for life.''
   F. A 1682 law provided that all ''non-Christians'' were to be permanent slaves.
III. Opposition to slavery grew slowly.
   A. Slavery was recognized in three provisions of the United States Constitution adopted in 1787.
   B. Slavery received political recognition in Congress in the compromises of 1820 and 1850.
   C. Abolition of slavery in the northern states was complete by 1820.
   D. Abolition societies for the elimination of slavery nationally began to function actively in 1835.
   E. Attempts to contain slavery or to abolish it continued from 1830 to 1860.

F. In 1860 the Republican Party was elected on a pledge to stop the spread of slavery.

G. In 1863 some slaves were freed, as a temporary wartime measure, by President Lincoln.

H. Slavery was permanently abolished by the Thirteenth Amendment to the United States Constitution in 1865.

Historical topics of this kind lend themselves easily to chronological development. Such things as the development of automobiles, airplanes, and space travel would also work well with such an organizational pattern. Persuasive topics may also, on occasion, be developed in a time sequence. For instance, a speaker might want to urge that incurably ill patients or their families should have the right to withdraw life-support systems so that those patients can accept death with dignity. That speaker might develop the argument chronologically by tracing the changing legal decisions having to do with a doctor's responsibility for prolonging life in various medical circumstances.

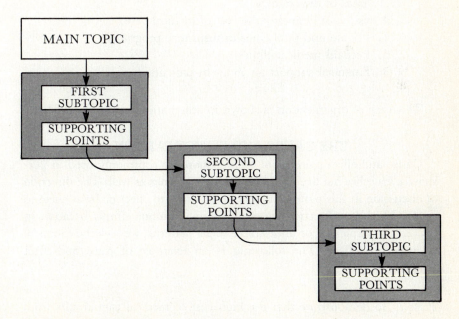

Figure 4.2 TOPICAL ORGANIZATION.

TOPICAL ORGANIZATION

Topical organization suits many kinds of informative-speech subjects. Topical organization divides the subject into major and subordinate topics and proceeds with an orderly discussion of these topics. For instance, a speaker might discuss the requirements of a good medical-care system through a set of subtopics as follows:

I. Good medical care requires at least the following:
   A. An adequate system of training and research.
      1. Medical schools must be numerous enough to ensure an appropriate doctor-patient ratio and medical personnel suitably trained in all medical specialties.
      2. The profession must have an aggressive, well-financed research program.
   B. An adequate system of delivering health care to the population.
      1. Enough hospitals must be available to meet requirements.
      2. Doctors and hospitals must be located so as to cover all areas of the country.
   C. A system of financing the cost of medical care.
      1. Private and public health insurance programs.
      2. Prepaid medical clinics.
      3. Financial support for indigent patients.

This type of organization is shown in schematic form in Figure 4.2.

THE CAUSE AND EFFECT PATTERN

Cause-and-effect patterns of organization are commonly used in persuasive speeches but are useful in informative ones as well. The direction of discussion in this pattern may be from cause to effect or from effect to cause. The latter direction is perhaps more common simply because, in explaining perplexing or undesirable social patterns, we seek the causes of an observed effect. The following is an example of cause-and-effect organization:

Purpose: To demonstrate that the high cost of medical care results from factors we could control

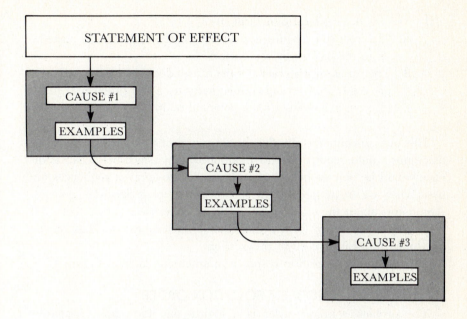

Figure 4.3 CAUSE AND EFFECT ORGANIZATION.

I. The medical profession has little reason to control costs.
   A. There is no fee competition among doctors. In fact, advertising of fees is considered unethical.
   B. The cost of expensive tests and treatments is borne by the patient; hence, the doctor has no reason to choose the cheaper of comparable procedures.
   C. Medical-insurance practices are heavily influenced by panels of medical advisors who stand to gain by increasing fees.
   D. The surgery-for-fee system results in many unnecessary operations: tonsillectomies, hysterectomies, appendectomies, and the like.
II. The drug industry, with the cooperation of doctors, uses expensive, cost-increasing practices.
   A. They encourage the use of brand-name drugs that are much more costly than equally effective generic ones.
   B. They sell drugs on the American market at costs substantially higher than on foreign markets.

III. Malpractice suits raise medical costs.
    A. Malpractice-insurance costs are extremely high and are passed
       on to the patient by the doctor.
    B. The threat of malpractice suits causes doctors and hospitals to
       use costly and perhaps unnecessary tests and procedures just
       to provide a defense for a potential malpractice suit.

This outline contains only the alleged causes of high medical costs. Its
assertions would require extensive supporting evidence before an audience would be able to believe them fully. Cause-to-effect sequences are
used when we try to predict the future impact of present-day policies.
Arguments about the effect of TV violence on viewers or the ecological
impact of aerosol sprays (and a whole class of such subjects) will usually be
developed in a cause-to-effect progression.
    This type of organization is shown in schematic form in Figure 4.3.

PROBLEM-SOLUTION ORDER
The problem-solution order is a logical one for many persuasive
speeches. The speaker simply divides the presentation into two major
divisions: a perceived problem and a recommended solution. Often the

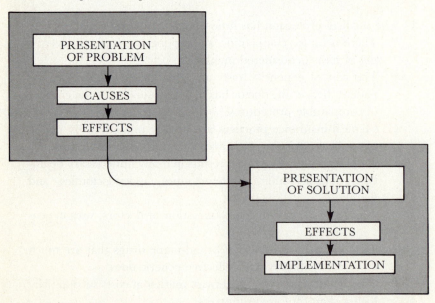

Figure 4.4 PROBLEM-SOLUTION ORDER.

problem portion of this pattern is developed in an effect-cause manner and is then followed by a recommended solution or solutions that will relieve the problem. For instance, the outline on medical costs might be used as the problem stage of a problem-solution speech. If so, it would be followed by the speaker's view of the undesirable effects of the situation on society and recommendations for dealing with the problem. In broad strokes, this section of the speech would probably look like the following:

I. The high cost of medical care results from:
   A. Lack of competition among doctors.
   B. Wasteful and expensive practices of the drug industry.
   C. Malpractice abuses.
II. The high cost of medical care produces undesirable results.
   A. It restricts medical care to persons financially able to bear the burden.
   B. Routine medical care absorbs too high a percentage of the income of low- and middle-class people.
   C. A catastrophic medical illness may completely exhaust the financial reserves of the victim.
   D. Increased medical costs deprive the elderly and persons on fixed incomes of adequate care.
III. The high cost of medical care can be reduced by the following:
   A. Allowing doctors to advertise.
   B. Modifying the fee system with prepaid health clinics.
   C. Allowing (or requiring) druggists to substitute generic for prescribed brand-name drugs.
   D. Placing legal restrictions on malpractice damage awards.

Figure 4.4 shows this type of organization.

THE MOTIVATED SEQUENCE

A structure that closely resembles the problem-solution order is the motivated sequence. The motivated sequence, according to its author, is "the sequence of ideas which, by following the normal processes of human thinking, motivates an audience to respond to the speaker's purpose." This sequence, as shown in Figure 4.5, has two major parts—need and satisfaction. But all the mental processes of the audience are recognized in other parts of the sequence, which follow:

1. *Attention step.* Here the speaker calls attention to the subject so that the audience will want to listen.

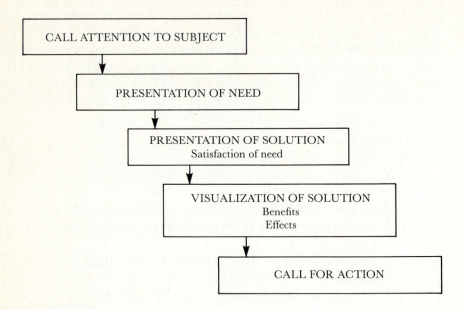

Figure 4.5 MOTIVATED SEQUENCE.

2. *Need step.* The speaker relates the topic to the wants and desires of
   the audience so they will see the usefulness of the message.
3. *Satisfaction step.* The speaker shows how the need may be satisfied
   by offering a solution to the problem.
4. *Visualization of step.* The speaker tries to visualize for the audience
   the advantages and satisfactions that will result from implement-
   ing the solution.
5. *Action step.* The speaker requests approval or action that supports
   the solution.[5]

Here is an outline for a persuasive speech organized on the pattern of
the motivated sequence.

Purpose: To arouse concern about wife beating and win support for a
proposed solution

---

[5] Alan Monroe and Douglas Ehninger, *Principles and Types of Speech*, 6th ed. (Glenview,
Illinois: Scott, Foresman and Co., 1967), p. 265.

I. *Attention step:*
   A. Case of Cora. She had been married for several years. One night during an argument her husband beat her with his fists, then pulled her by her hair across the living room and beat her across the shoulders, legs, and buttocks with a piece of fire-wood.
   B. The Bay County Sheriff's Crime Unit says that for every reported case of wife beating ten go unreported.

II. *Need step:*
   A. Wife beating is probably the most common "crime" in any given community. In Bay county it is estimated that ten thousand women are beaten annually.
   B. There is no specific law against wife beating. Cases are handled under assault and battery laws.
   C. Beaten wives do not know how to deal with the problem.
      1. They don't want to put their husbands in jail.
      2. They need counseling and a safe refuge.

III. *Satisfaction step:* A safe house or refuge house is needed where a woman can get counseling and 24–72 hours of shelter.

IV. *Visualization step:* In counties where safe houses or refuge houses have been established the results have been dramatic. Cite cases of rehabilitation and give statistics.

V. *Action step:* Urge your city commissioners to support the proposed refuge house for this county. Write or call them.

THE GEOGRAPHICAL OR SPATIAL PATTERN

Geographical or spatial patterns of organization are most often used in informative speaking but are occasionally appropriate for other speech purposes. The spatial pattern consists of proposals or topics arranged according to how their positions in space relate to each other. A speaker describing any number of mechanical devices, would most likely organize the material spatially. The space shuttle, for example, would probably be described from top to bottom and from outside to inside. A description of the control center that monitors space-ship flights would also probably follow a spatial order of some sort (for example, left to right, center to outside edges). More abstract topics may at times lend themselves to geographical order; for instance, a discussion of the impact of currency fluctuation on national economies might be discussed as follows:

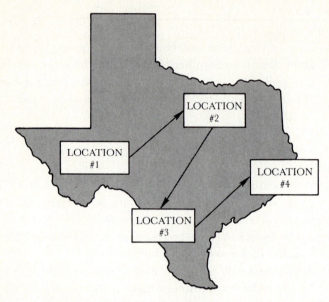

Figure 4.6 GEOGRAPHICAL OR SPATIAL ORGANIZATION.

I. Currency fluctuations are described in terms of a currency's dollar
   value.
   A. The English pound is worth $1.70.
   B. The French franc is worth about 14 cents.
   C. The Italian lira is about 1420 lira to a dollar.
   D. The German mark is about 2.50 marks to a dollar. [The
      speaker would, of course, substitute current values for those
      cited.]
II. Major changes in relation to the dollar cause internal economic
    problems.
    A. Problems created by changing value of the English pound.
    B. Problems created by changing value of the Italian lira.
    C. Problems created by changing value of the French franc.
    D. Problems created by changing value of the German mark.

So, as indicated, it is reasonable to divide the discussion of an economic
problem on a geographical basis. A speaker would probably do so if he or
she wanted to stress the effects of currency fluctuation on different countries. If the speaker wanted to stress the general economic principles
involved in varying currency values, he or she would probably use a
cause-effect or topical pattern of organization.

This type of organization is shown schematically in Figure 4.6.

THE CONCLUSION

The conclusion of the speech serves at least two main functions:

1. It summarizes the main ideas and arguments presented in the body of the speech.
2. It restates and reinforces the speaker's purpose and attempts to motivate the audience to respond positively.

If the purpose is informative, the speaker summarizes the major items of information and repeats the value of remembering and using the knowledge gained. In a persuasive speech, the speaker reviews the major issues and arguments and stresses how these should affect the belief and conduct of the audience. Conclusions may be of several types.

First, there is the *formal summary.* This is nothing more than a repetition of the major points of the speech outline, considerably condensed, followed by (in a persuasive speech) a summary of the solution step. Look back at the outline in the discussion of the problem-solution pattern of organization. A speaker using this outline might offer a formal summary somewhat like the following:

So you see, ladies and gentlemen, I have shown that the high cost of medical care results from lack of competition among doctors, wasteful and expensive practices of the drug industry, and abuse of malpractice claims. The undesirable social results of these high costs—such as denial of adequate medical care to elderly persons or to persons on fixed incomes—can be relieved by allowing doctors to advertise, by establishing prepaid health clinics, by more general use of generic drugs, and by controlling malpractice damage awards.

I hope you will support measures of this kind at every opportunity. You will be the one to profit from them.

In addition to the formal summary, speakers may *illustrate the advantages of their proposals* and paint an emotional picture of the rightness of their recommendations. John E. Jacob, then president-designate of the National Urban League, did this in a speech delivered early in 1981:

We've survived. We've survived because amidst the most terrible of the tragedies that ensnared us, we cared for each other. We fostered a spirit of pride and love that enabled us to overcome.

And on that base of mutual respect and support, we marched and demonstrated and fought for our rights until this nation, embarrassed by its own betrayal of its ideals of equality and awed by our determination to overcome, said:

"You are right. The Constitution is for everyone. The Bill of Rights is for everyone. This country has a place for everyone—black and white. Everybody deserves the chance to make it on their own."

Yes, it was black people that changed America. It was black people that joined hands with our white allies and helped turn this country around.

And now it is up to black people to do it again: To remind America that if racism was wrong in the sixties, it is wrong today; if civil rights was right in the sixties, it is right today; if equal opportunity was right in the sixties, it is right today.

So let us lift our voices and marshall our strength to help and nurture each other; to mute the pain and bring calming compassion to those in need. Let us lift our voices to remind America that we have fought and died for it; that we want our rightful share of our national heritage in the land we love.

Let us lift our voices to:

"Sing a song full of the faith that the dark past has taught us,
Sing a song full of the hope that the present has brought us,
Facing the rising sun,
Of our new day begun,
Let us march on till victory is won."[6]

John F. Kennedy's conclusion to his presidential inaugural address is a good example of the *inspirational* type of conclusion, in which the speaker calls on the audience to devote themselves to high ideals, forsaking self-interest for the welfare of all. Here are the last few lines of Kennedy's address:

[6] "New Realities, New Responsibilities," *Vital Speeches of the Day*, 48 (1981–1982), p. 256. Reprinted by permission.

And so, my fellow Americans: ask not what your country can do for you—ask what you can do for your country.

My fellow citizens of the world: ask not what America will do for you, but what together we can do for the freedom of man.

Finally, whether you are citizens of America or citizens of the world, ask of us here the same high standards of strength and sacrifice which we ask of you. With a good conscience our only sure reward, with history the final judge of our deeds, let us go forth to lead the land we love, asking His blessings and His help, but knowing that here on earth God's work must truly be our own.[7]

Another common device used in a conclusion is to *restate the purpose and support it with a quotation from a respected authoritative source*. The quotation is followed by an appeal for decision and action on the part of the audience. Here is an example of this type of conclusion, taken from a speech by William E. Simon, who was then Secretary of the Treasury of the United States:

Ladies and Gentlemen: America is still incredibly strong. Its mainspring is the largest and most dynamic marketplace in the world. We have the resources, and we know how to build our economy. The central question is whether we have the will and the courage to rescue ourselves from the relentless drift we have experienced in recent years.

It cannot be said too often that a centralized economy in America—the kind of economy we are now constructing—is the surest means we have of destroying the mainspring of our prosperity and our progress. In the United States today, we already have more government than we need, more government than most people want, and certainly more government than we are willing to pay for.

An epitaph written for ancient Athens and attributed to the pen of the historian Edward Gibbon is relevant for us now. "In the end," he wrote, "more than they wanted freedom, they wanted security.

[7] John F. Kennedy, "Inaugural Address, January 20, 1961," *Inaugural Addresses of the Presidents of the United States from George Washington 1789 to Richard Milhous Nixon 1969* (Washington, D.C.: U.S. Government Printing Office, 1969), pp. 269-270.

They wanted a comfortable life and they lost it all—security, comfort and freedom. When the Athenians finally wanted not to give to society but for society to give to them, when the freedom they wished for most was freedom from responsibility, then Athens ceased to be free.''

Whether the same will one day be said of America is the choice now before us. As leaders of the business community, each of you will have an important voice in deciding our country's direction and fate. Let there be no doubt of your choice for a free America.

Thank you.[8]

Whatever method you use, it pays to give thoughtful attention to the conclusion of your speech. A weak and aimless ending leaves a bad impression on the audience and may cancel out any favorable response you have gained. On the other hand, a strong conclusion may be the deciding factor in bending the audience to your purpose.

THE OVERALL ORGANIZATION OF A SPEECH

The preparation of an outline is valuable to speakers because it forces them to arrange their material in an orderly, thorough way. A complete speech outline will have three main divisions: introduction, body, and conclusion. Each of these divisions will be outlined in the standard outline pattern. Main heads are generally designated by roman numerals, major subheads by English capital letters, and further subdivisions by arabic numbers and lowercase English letters. The form of an outline is illustrated in the following:

Introduction

I. _____

_____

    A. _____

    B. _____

II. _____

---

[8] William E. Simon, ''Economic Concepts and Free Enterprise,'' *Vital Speeches of the Day,* 42 (1975–1976), 71–72. Reprinted by permission.

Body

I. _____

    A. _____

    B. _____

        1. _____

        2. _____

II. _____

    A. _____

        1. _____

        2. _____

            a. _____

            b. _____

        3. _____

    B. _____

Conclusion

I. _____

_____

    A. _____

    B. _____

II. _____

If you need further subheads beyond the lowercase letters, use Arabic numbers and then lowercase letters in parentheses, as follows:

I. _____

    A. _____

        1. _____

            a. _____

            b. _____

                (1) _____

                    (a) _____

        2. _____

    B. _____

In planning a speech outline, a speaker may elect to use one of two general patterns of development. The first is an *explicit disclosure pattern*, in which the purpose is stated in the introduction and is usually followed by a preview of the major points that will be covered in the body. This preview is sometimes called the *partitioning*, because it divides up, or partitions, the body of the speech into sections. As the speaker moves into the body of the speech, he or she specifically states the first of the major points or issues and follows up with the supporting materials. The speaker then moves to the second major point, and so on, until all the points have been covered. When the last point has been discussed, the speaker concludes with a summary and perhaps a statement designed to motivate action. Here is a sample outline organized in the explicit disclosure pattern, with major divisions and internal parts:

Introduction
I. *Attention-getting material:* Whale hunting is an inhumane practice.
  A. The whale is killed by a 200-pound, 6-foot-long iron harpoon, shot from a 90-millimeter cannon.
  B. The harpoon head contains a time-fused explosive that blows the whale's internal organs apart, leaving the creature in agony.
II. *Purpose statement and partition:* Today, I will show that this inhumane practice is unnecessary and, if continued, will within a few years result in the extinction of these magnificent creatures. I will also show how you can help prevent this tragedy from occurring.

Body
I. *First main point:* Whales are unique creatures that man should revere and not destroy.
  A. Whales are the largest creatures on earth. The blue whale:
    1. Is larger than 30 elephants.
    2. Weighs more than 2,000 people.
    3. Has a heart that weighs 1,200 pounds.
    4. Has a tongue weighing one-third of a ton.
    5. Has some arteries so large that a small child could crawl through them.
  B. Whales communicate with each other by producing high-pitched singing noises that can be heard for over 200 miles in open water.
  C. Whales are warm-blooded mammals that breathe air. They are gentle, playful creatures among themselves and around humans.
II. *Second main point:* In spite of the whale's uniqueness and appealing qualities, it is being slaughtered to extinction.

A. Whaling is big business.
   1. Whaling fleets roam the seas searching for their prey with sonar and helicopters.
   2. They can "process" an 80-foot whale into by-products in less than an hour.
B. The rate of killing in the last 10 years has been alarming.
   1. One whale is killed every 13 minutes.
   2. In 1976 Japan and Russia together killed more than 30,000 whales—almost 85 percent of the worldwide total.
   3. In 1976 almost 40,000 whales were killed.
III. *Third main point:* Whale hunting is completely unnecessary.
   A. Whales are killed for animal feed, industrial oils, fertilizer, perfume, soap, shampoo, gelatin, and other products.
   B. Inexpensive and plentiful substitutes exist for each of these whale by-products.
IV. *Fourth main point:* You can help stop this slaughter. Here's what you can do.
   A. Boycott products manufactured in Japan and Russia, two nations that have not joined an international moratorium on whale hunting. Economic pressure will help persuade them.
   B. Sign the petition circulated by the Whale Protection Fund, whose goal is to have one million signatures on a petition to the governments of Japan and Russia protesting the killing of whales.
   C. Send a tax-deductible one-dollar contribution to the Whale Protection Fund to help finance its program.

Conclusion

I. *Summary:* So, you see, these beautiful, unique creatures are being slaughtered by the thousands annually. They are being killed unnecessarily to provide products that we could develop from other inexpensive and plentiful substitutes.
II. *Motivation to action:* Join now in a concerted effort to save these unique and gentle creatures from extinction.
   A. Resolve to boycott Japanese and Russian products.
   B. Sign the petition I will circulate.
   C. Send a contribution to the Whale Protection Fund.[9]

[9] Adapted from a leaflet circulated by the Whale Protection Fund of the Center for Environmental Education, 2100 M Street, N.W., Washington, D.C., 20037. Reprinted by permission.

A second developmental pattern is the *implicit disclosure pattern*. This pattern differs from the explicit disclosure method in that the speaker does not use a partition or division of purpose and does not state the main points of the body of the speech until after the supporting materials (in the form of examples, testimony, statistics, and so on) have been presented. Speakers generally elect to use this pattern when they are speaking persuasively to an audience that will resist or actively oppose their proposals. The pattern is structured to reveal the evidence and argument for a belief before the belief itself is specifically stated. This approach assumes the audience will be more tolerant of the belief when it finally is stated because they will already have heard the justification for it. If the belief is presented first, they may tend to reject it without listening to the justification. The outline of a speech developed according to the implicit disclosure pattern looks like the following:

Introduction
   I. *Attention-getting material.*
  II. *Disclosure of problem area without explicit purpose statement.*

Body
   I. *First main point or issue:*
      A. Evidence and reasons supporting the issue.
      B. Statement of the issue.
  II. *Second main point or issue:*
      A. Evidence and reasons supporting the issue.
      B. Statement of the issue.

Conclusion
   I. *Summary.*
  II. *Motivation.*

   For instance, let's suppose you were trying to persuade an audience that the family of a clinically dead person should be allowed to withdraw life-sustaining equipment such as intravenous tubes and iron-lung machines. Knowing that your audience would probably be hostile to this idea, you might proceed as follows:

Introduction
   I. *Attention-getting material:* Hypothetical example of Madeline Brock, who, as a result of taking an overdose of drugs, destroyed the

consciousness and thinking areas of her brain but was kept alive by medical procedures for five years. She never regained consciousness and ultimately died.

II. *Purpose statement* (not an explicit disclosure of intent): Cases like that of Madeline Brock exemplify a social problem that has a serious impact on society and on the families of stricken people.

Body

I. *First main point:*
   A. There are thousands of cases like that of Madeline Brock in the United States today. [This statement would be followed by statistics on the number of cases, how long they stay in hospitals, the cost in dollars of providing the procedures that keep them alive, and so on.]
   B. Statement of first major point: Many of these cases cause an intolerable financial burden on the families involved, and they increase hospital costs substantially for other patients.

II. *Second main point:*
   A. Cases like that of Madeline Brock adversely affect the welfare of the patients' famlies. [This would be followed by evidence that the stress of such a catastrophic illness may cause emotional disturbances in the family that lead to physical illness, mental illness, divorce, or in some rare cases, to suicide.]
   B. Statement of second major point: By unnecessarily prolonging the life of a clinically dead person, doctors place a destructive emotional burden on the family.

III. *Summary of first, second, and other main points and explicit statement of purpose:* Families of clinically dead people should have the right to withdraw life-sustaining equipment.

Conclusion

I. *Summary and restatement.*
II. *Motivation and appeal for positive response.*

TRANSITIONS

Transitions are sentences that mark the speaker's movement from one unit or subunit of the speech outline to another. Thus, there will normally be a transition between the introduction and the body of the speech and between the body and the conclusion. Such statements as the following may be used:

> Since my purpose is to . . . , I would like to give you my first reason for believing as I do. [between introduction and body]
> Now that I have given you a variety of reasons for believing that . . . , I would like to make a few final observations. [between body and conclusion]

Internal transitions are also needed within the major parts of the speech. If you begin a speech with an example or illustration, you need a transition into your purpose sentence. Something like what follows will do:

> This illustration is evidence of a significant problem with which we must deal. I feel we must deal with it as follows: [statement of purpose]

Other kinds of transitions and their uses are briefly illustrated below:

> These statistics are not the only evidence of the problem; experts maintain . . . [to tie separate pieces of evidence together, in this case statistics and the testimony of experts]
> One issue raised by the high cost of medical care is its impact on fixed-income groups, a matter we have just discussed. Another issue is. . . . [to move from one reason or issue to another]
> Selecting the proper cord is only the first step in preparing to make a macrame pot hanger. After the cord is selected you must. . . . [to pass from one step in a process to another step]
> Although this point is important, the . . . is even most important. [to help establish relative emphasis among ideas]
> What is the next step/or issue to be considered in the matter? [to move from point to point by means of a question]

Good transitions are useful to the audience because they clarify the thought patterns of the speaker and how evidence relates to the conclusion it supports. In the form of internal summaries, good transitions help the audience recall and understand the speaker's material.

SUMMARY

Speeches are usually divided into three main parts: the introduction, the body, and the conclusion. The introduction should gain the audience's attention and disclose the speaker's purpose. The body of the speech should be organized in a way that suits the subject and purpose. Common organizational patterns are: chronological order, topical organization, the cause and effect pattern, the problem-solution order, the motivated sequence, and the geographical or spatial pattern. The conclusion of the speech should summarize the main ideas and arguments and repeat and reinforce the speaker's purpose. The outline of a speech should follow a pattern that usually begins with roman numerals for main heads, capital letters for first-level subheads, arabic numerals for second-level subheads, and so forth. Transitional sentences and phrases are needed to tie the parts of the outline together.

Exercises

1. Read the chapter of the textbook dealing with persuasion and try to make an outline of it. After doing this discuss the following questions with classmates. Is it difficult to distinguish main headings from subheadings? Is the method used chronological? Spatial? Topical? Psychological? Does the author seem to have a reason for his choice of method? Does the chapter have an introduction, body, and conclusion? After this experience, how many details do you think you should put into an outline from which you plan to speak?

2. Make an outline of a speech you intend to give in class. Cut the outline apart by headings: I, A, 1, 2, B; II. A, 1, 2, B, and so on. Then mix the headings up. Exchange this scrambled outline with one prepared and scrambled by a classmate. After you have both tried to reconstruct the outlines, discuss the problems revealed about correct outlining.

3. Make an outline for your next speech assignment and hand it in to the instructor. Revise it according to the instructor's comments. After you have given the speech, revise the outline again to reflect changes you think would have made the speech better.

4. Go to a source like *Vital Speeches of the Day* and bring to class examples of introductions and conclusions you think are superior. Read some of these to the class for analysis and evaluation.

Chapter Five
CONTENT

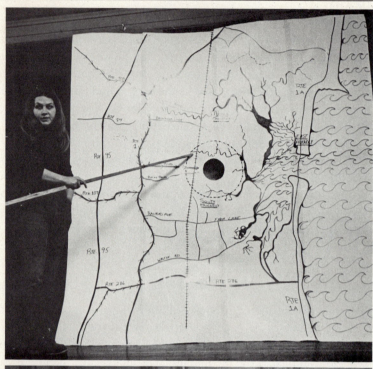

OVERVIEW

The content of a speech is heavily influenced by its purpose. After they have completed their research, speakers select from among the available materials those items that logically and psychologically fit their communication goals. In classical rhetorical theory, this process was called *invention*, a term intended to stress that speakers do not merely use whatever materials come to hand. Rather, they select critically, guided by what they hope to achieve and by what they think will work with the audience. Thus, when the purpose is to inform, the speaker will try to transmit knowledge clearly, forcefully, and accurately; when it is to persuade, the speaker will strive for these same outcomes but will also try to justify or prove the opinions and proposals being advocated.

We indicated earlier that speakers should investigate all sides of their subjects. This means gathering not only material that supports their proposals, but also information that disputes or suggests modifications in their proposals. Thus, when speakers have completed their research, they should look again at their purposes before selecting their materials. Perhaps the speaker will want to change the purpose at this point or even abandon it. Certainly speakers should not continue to advocate a proposal when the knowledge they have gained does not support it. One student, for instance, decided to make a speech attacking the Alaska oil pipeline as an ecological disaster. On completion of the research, he felt that the evidence did not support his earlier position. Accordingly, he decided it would make more sense to give a speech on the precautions that were used in the construction of the pipeline to avoid damaging the ecology of the area. So, as this case illustrates, the material selected should not only fulfill the speaker's purpose and the psychological needs of the audience; it should also accurately and honestly reflect the subject.

Matthew Arnold, a great English poet and educator, once observed that a good education should expose a student to the "best that has been thought and said in the world." While this statement may be idealistic, it can reasonably be applied to speech preparation: A speaker's aim should be to reflect the best that has been thought and said about the topic he or she is discussing. In the following section, we will describe the kinds of supporting materials that go into the body of the speech and make up its content. As we talk about examples, comparisons, illustrations, statistics, and so on, there may be a tendency to forget we must judge the quality of these elements. The essence of invention—the selection of speech content—is not just the discovery of resources, but the discovery of the *best* resources available.

SUPPORTING MATERIALS

DESCRIPTIONS AND EXPLANATIONS

In almost any speech, objects must be described and processes and ideas explained. For instance, if you were to give an informative speech on the use of torpedoes in naval warfare, you would first have to describe a torpedo, explain how it works, and outline the strategies that govern its use in an attack. Descriptions and explanations should be vivid and accurate and, if possible, should be enhanced by the use of models, pictures, or diagrams. Most of the time, however, you will have to rely on clear and accurate language. The following passage is an example of clear and accurate explanation. The subject was how to read your airline ticket: what it entitles you to and what obligations it places on the carrier. The author was explaining a consumer right that some people know little about.

Thanks to regulations of the C.A.B. and the International Air Transport Association, the airlines' responsibility for getting you to your destination goes well beyond ... "best efforts" and "reasonable dispatch" (of the Warsaw Convention).

There's something called denied boarding compensation, for instance—some people refer to it as bump insurance. If you've got a confirmed flight reservation and the airline can't take you on because it has oversold the flight, then it has to pay you a penalty equal to the fare of the flight for which you're checking in, but not less than $25 or more than $200. That's a penalty, remember, not a refund—

your ticket is still valid. The airline doesn't have to pay you, though, if it can put you on another flight that will get you to your destination within two hours of your originally scheduled arrival time, if it's a domestic flight, or within four hours on international flights. But to be entitled to the payment if you're bumped, you have to be at the checkout counter on time. This varies with the airline and the location, but it's generally between ten and twenty minutes before scheduled departure.[1]

The explanation is clear and precise. All conditions and qualifications are noted. As a result, consumers should understand their "bumping rights" fully.

COMPARISON AND CONTRAST

Speakers use *comparison* to show similarities between something known to an audience and some new thing being discussed by the speaker. It is sometimes called *analogy*. We will discuss comparison here as it is used in informative speeches. Later we will further discuss comparison as a form of proof or argument. Speakers use *contrast* to try to make a topic or point clear and meaningful by showing how it differs from some other concept or thing. A simple comparison would be a statement like the following: "An electrical capacitor is like an air compressor: It stores up electricity, like air in a compressor tank, to be released later with increased quantity and force." A simple contrast statement would be: "A nail is a fastener that works by being tightly wedged between the wood fibers of a board, whereas a screw has grooves on its shank that burrow their way into the wood fibers." A more complex example of comparison follows. It was used by Claude Cox, president of a public relations and advertising firm, to help the audience understand Cox's concept of changing trends in American society.

Just imagine that standing here in front of you is one of the ornate old grandfather clocks. It's beautiful walnut, has a hand painted face, and a full glass front. You look though the glass to see a hand tooled

[1] Richard Joseph, "Getting There. How to Read Your Airline Ticket," *Esquire,* 86 (September 1976), 44.

and engraved brass pendulum. The pendulum is slowly swinging from left to right, right to left. You notice that the pendulum only stops twice during a cycle. When it swings all the way left, it pauses only a moment before starting to the right. Then on the extreme apex of the right swing, the pendulum stops momentarily to begin its methodic and monotonous travel in the opposite direction. You also note that the pendulum does not—I repeat does not—stop in the middle of the swing. That is, not unless the total function of the clock also ceases, and the hands no longer show the correct time of day.

Due to my vocation and education, I have been asked to speak on understanding today's youth. I believe that the topic is so complex and so multifaceted that my telling you how to understand today's youth is very presumptuous. I don't even understand, and sometimes try not to understand, my own teen age daughters, 16 and 18 years old. I say try not to understand them because it often is better to not attempt to apply logic and reason to analyzing their actions, and just accept them as individuals.

Now you are asking yourself what I was doing explaining all that grandfather clock business. You're going to find out right now. The pendulum theory is a valid approach to analyzing each generation of youth . . . and adults too. In most of the world the pendulum theory today works . . . at least in the progressive societies of the world.

Let's compare the pendulum to contemporary society and trends. Our American society swings like a pendulum . . . from one extreme to another . . . only pausing when one extreme is attained, and turning around to race to the other extreme. I speak of fads, lifestyles, fashions, trends, economy, and other elements of daily life. In most cases these elements that seem to comprise so much of our daily lives go as far as acceptable in one extreme, then pause, and begin a direct 180 degree reversal to the opposite extreme. If you will, let me nudge your memories, and review a little bit prior to speaking of the future.[2]

A good illustration of the use of contrast can be seen in Lawrence W. Reed's speech, "Liberty and the Power of Ideas: Five Ideas of Socialism." Reed, a professor of economics, structures his entire speech on a

[2] Claude Cox, "One Extreme to Another," *Vital Speeches of the Day*, 43 (1976–1977), 74–75. Reprinted by permission.

contrast between the basic ideas of socialism and those of liberty. Socialism, he says, is based on "The Pass a Law Syndrome," "The Get Something for Nothing Fantasy," "The Pass the Buck Psychosis," "The Know-It-All Affliction," and "The Envy Obsession." In "stunning contrast," liberty rests on creative ideas of "Self-reliance," "Personal responsibility," "Respect for life and property," "Voluntary assistance for the needy," and "Limited government."[3] By contrasting the social impacts of these ideas, each in several paragraphs, Reed constructs his entire speech.

EXAMPLES, ILLUSTRATIONS, AND ANECDOTES

Examples, illustrations, and anecdotes are commonly used to explain or enlarge the ideas presented in a speech. An *example* is an instance. An *illustration* is the same. An *anecdote* is an example or illustration told in the form of a story, often with dialogue and drama. Here is a sample from a speech by James N. Sites, Vice President for Communications of the Chemical Manufacturers Association, in which a single example is used to support the claim that news reports often misrepresent events associated with the chemical industry:

"The Valley of the Drums" is another sad case. When that story first broke out of Louisville, Kentucky, an EPA staff person was asked on the scene to make an estimate of the number of barrels of chemicals on the site. His guess of 100,000 drums was picked up by reporting services, and that's what you've seen again and again throughout the nation. Even a normally reliable publication like the *Congressional Quarterly* used this as an illustrated cover story—further adding to the pressure for new controls on industry.

Well, the state of Kentucky finally counted the drums. It found 11,000 empty barrels and 5,000 full ones, with half of the full ones containing solids. So down goes the count to 2,500 barrels that could have been hazardous—*not* 100,000. We still haven't seen any news corrections of this. But we live in hope that someone somewhere someday *will* try to set this record straight.[4]

[3] Lawrence W. Reed, *Vital Speeches of the Day,* 47 (1980), 19–21.
[4] "Chemophobia, Politics and Distorted Images," *Vital Speeches of the Day,* 46 (1979–1980), 153. Reprinted by permission.

Businessman Howard E. Kersher used examples effectively to show how ancient civilizations contributed to their own ruin by inflating their currencies:

Ancient Egypt was once a prosperous country. Business, art, medicine, literature—all flourished and prospered for many centuries until the Pharaohs became extravagant and began to spend more than their incomes, to put their friends on the payroll, and to increase the quantity of debt. Looking around for some way to get more money with which to pay their bills, they hit upon the scheme of melting down the coins of gold and silver and recasting them with a large portion of some base metal. They then decreed that a coin that was 90 percent lead and 10 percent gold or silver was worth as much as a coin that was all gold or silver. This, of course, is a lie. And it violates the Commandment, "Thou shalt not bear false witness. . . ." No one and no nation has ever been able to violate the moral law of God without paying the penalty.

Here we have the first well known example of Gresham's Law, which says that bad money always drives out good money. The gold and silver left ancient Egypt, driven out by the debased coinage, and Egyptian civilization declined, never to recover its grandeur.

The same thing happened in Greece and again in Rome.[5]

Examples often add interest and excitement to a presentation and may be chosen for that reason, but the choice should not sacrifice accuracy and correctness. Logical requirements for choosing examples will be discussed later in this chapter.

DEFINITIONS

Whenever a speaker uses unfamiliar terms or concepts or familiar terms whose meaning is unclear, like *poverty*, they must be defined. The following are some common methods of definition: (1)tracing the origin of the word (etymology); (2)classifying the term in a category known to the audience; (3)giving examples; (4)explaining the function or purpose of the concept; and (5)explaining how the concept is similar to and different from related ideas.

[5] Howard E. Kersher, "Stop Inflation and Depression Now," *Vital Speeches of the Day,* 42 (1975–1976), 12. Reprinted by permission.

Concrete things are generally easier to define than abstractions. The definition of a theodolite, for instance, might be handled in the following way:

A theodolite is a surveying instrument [classification] that sits upon a heavy tripod like a camera [comparison]. It measures horizontal and vertical angles [purpose] by means of a telescope that is calibrated to horizontal and vertical scales [function].

An abstraction like the term *standard deviation* is much more difficult to define. A glance at the dictionary (in this case, *The American Heritage Dictionary*) will show how inadequate usual definitions are: ''A statistic used as a measure of dispersion in a distribution, the square root of the arithmetic average of the squares of the deviations from the mean.'' The trouble with such a definition is that only experts in the field of statistics can understand it. To make the concept understandable, one should use an example that employs lay terms rather than the vocabulary of experts:

If you measured the height of a typical sample of American males, you might find that the average height was 5 feet 9 inches. But not everyone in the sample would be of that height: some would be much taller (some basketball players are seven feet tall or more), and some would be much shorter (some men are little more than five feet tall). The standard deviation is a number that tells us to what extent people in a typical sample will vary from the average. The standard deviation allows us to compare the expected height variation of a typical sample with the height variation in another sample that may or may not be typical. If the height variation in a comparison sample differs from the standard deviation, we know that, for some reason or other, the height of that group as a whole is not ''normal.'' It is not a typical group as far as height is concerned.

Standard deviation is an example of an abstraction that has a fixed, agreed-upon meaning. Many abstractions relating to social life and institutions are much less fixed and agreed upon. What does *democracy* mean, or *justice,* or *fairness,* or *morality*? When confronted with such terms, a speaker often tries to define them in a way that will help achieve his or her purpose. If the speaker succeeds in getting the audience to accept that definition, it may be eaiser to persuade them of other claims or proposals. Richard M. Nixon, in his famous "Checkers" speech, used this tactic in defending himself against the charge that he was wrong in using an $18,000 fund collected for him by friends:

I am sure you have read the charge, and you have heard it that I, Senator Nixon, took $18,000 from a group of my supporters.

Now, was that wrong? And let me say that it was wrong. I am saying, incidentally, that it was wrong, not just illegal, because it isn't a question of whether it was legal or illegal. That isn't enough.

The question is, was it morally wrong? I say that it was morally wrong—if any of the $18,000 went to Senator Nixon, for my personal use. I say that it was morally wrong if it was secretly given and secretly handled.

And I say that it was morally wrong if any of the contributors got special favors for the contribution they made.[6]

Having laid out his definition of the term *morally wrong,* Nixon then proceeded to show (at least to the satisfaction of many) that he had not used the money personally, that the money was not given or handled secretly, and that the contributors received no political favors. Therefore, the fund was not morally wrong by his definition.

An ethical point is evident here. We should not build definitions solely to serve our own purposes. As we noted earlier, free speech imposes a responsibility to be fair and honest, and if a definition does not seem an honest and fair one, it should be rejected.

STATISTICS

Statistics are examples expressed in numbers. The simplest kind of statistic is the percentage. Percentages make possible quicker and more accurate comparisons than could be made by citing examples. Note how President Ronald Reagan, in February, 1981, used statistical comparisons in his "State of the Nation's Economy" address:

---

[6] Richard M. Nixon, "My Side of the Story," *Vital Speeches of the Day,* 19 (1952), 11–12. Reprinted by permission.

Twenty years ago in 1960 our Federal Government payroll was less than $13 billion. Today it is $75 billion. During these 20 years, our population has only increased by 23.3 percent. The Federal budget has gone up 528 percent.

We have just had two years of back-to-back double digit inflation—13.3 percent in 1979, 12.4 percent last year. The last time this happened was in World War I.

In 1960 mortgage interest rates averaged about 6 percent. They are two and a half times as high now, 15.4 percent. The percentage of your earnings the Federal Government took in taxes in 1960 has almost doubled. And finally there are seven million Americans caught up in the personal indignity and human tragedy of unemployment. If they stood in a line—allowing three feet for each person—the line would reach from the coast of Maine to California.[7]

Two of the simplest and most useful statistics are the average and the median. The *average* is a figure derived by adding together a number of separate scores or other figures and dividing the sum by the number of items that were added together. For instance, if you knew that five workers in a single department of a factory earned annual amounts of $5,800, $5,750, $6,200, $6,500, and $6,350, you would find the average annual salary by adding these figures together and dividing the sum by 5; that is, $30,600 divided by 5 equals $6,120. The average often gives a false impression of the facts, because it tends to suggest that every item in the sample is near the average; for example, it might be assumed in this case that all workers are making $6,120 a year, or very near that figure. In fact, however, the salaries of two workers are well below that figure, and the salaries of two are well above it. The false picture given by the average would be more obvious if, in the series given above, the last worker made $10,500 instead of $6,350. The total of all salaries would then be $34,750, and the average would be $6,950. But this figure is $400 more than the second-highest-paid worker gets and $1,200 more than the lowest-paid worker gets. If the company reported that the average worker in the department earned $6,950 per year, the figure would give a false impression.

[7] *Vital Speeches of the Day,* 47 (1980–1981), p. 290. Reprinted by permission.

Table 5.1 MEDIAN MONEY INCOME OF YEAR-ROUND FULL-TIME WORKERS
WITH INCOME, BY SEX AND AGE: 1970 TO 1979

[Age as of March of following year. Refers to civilian workers. 1970 not strictly comparable with later years due to revised procedures;
see source. For definition of median, see Guide to Tabular Presentation]

AGE	WOMEN			MEN			RATIO: WOMEN TO MEN		
	1970	1975	1979	1970	1975	1979	1970	1975	1979
Total with income	$5,440	$7,719	¹ $10,550	$9,184	$13,144	¹ $17,514	.59	.59	¹ .60
14–19 years	3,783	4,568	² 6,719	3,950	5,657	² 7,494	.96	.81	² .90
20–24 years	4,928	6,598	8,575	6,655	8,521	11,477	.74	.77	.75
25–34 years	5,923	8,401	11,151	9,126	12,777	16,798	.65	.66	.66
35–44 years	5,531	8,084	11,190	10,258	14,730	20,052	.54	.55	.56
45–54 years	5,588	7,980	10,937	9,931	14,808	20,464	.56	.54	.53
55–64 years	5,468	7,785	10,868	9,071	13,518	19,415	.60	.58	.56
65 years and over	4,884	7,273	10,678	6,754	11,485	16,125	.72	.63	.66

¹ For the year 1979, restricted to 15 years old and over.   ² For the year 1979, restricted to 15 to 19 years.
Source: U.S. Bureau of the Census, *Current Population Reports,* series P-60, No. 129, and earlier issues.

Another simple statistic, the median, is less deceiving. The *median* is a figure that stands exactly in the middle of a range of figures so that, of the remaining figures, half are above the median and half below. This figure is often used to compare and contrast groups. To prove that employed women are paid less than employed men, median annual incomes of men and women might be compared as shown in Table 5.1.

More complex statistics than the average and the median may be used to establish relationships among variables like attitudes toward women and certain personality traits. For instance, a sample of individuals may be given two kinds of tests—one a test of stereotyped sex attitudes and the other a test of political conservatism. The scores may then be compared, by what is known as a *coefficient of correlation,* to discover whether people who score high on stereotyped sex attitudes also score high on political conservatism. If such a relationship is found (with appropriate statistical safeguards), we may quote such evidence to support the claim that politically conservative people tend to be conservative in their attitudes toward women. Just such a study was done some time ago by Susan Hesselbart, an assistant professor of sociology at Florida State University. She discovered that "political conservatism" and "authoritarianism" scores were the best predictors of a person's tendency to display conservative sex-role stereotyping.[8]

Statistics like the coefficient of correlation and tests of the differences between the mean scores of various groups appear most often in scientific surveys and experimental studies. Measures of the differences between the means (such as Chi-square, analysis of variance, and so on) are used in

[8] Susan Hesselbart, "Attitudes Toward Women, and Their Implications. . . ," *Governmental Research Bulletin,* 12 (June 1975), 1–4.

experimental studies that try to link some characteristics of a speech with a subsequent outcome in a dependable way. For instance, if you were testing the hypothesis that women are more easily persuaded than men, you would probably go about it as follows: You would test the attitude of a group of men and that of a group of women on some topic, such as belief in the truthfulness of a political candidate. You would have, as a result, the average score or mean score for each group. Then you would expose each group to an identical speech attacking the candidate's trustworthiness. Following their exposure to this speech, you would test each group again; these test results would give you a difference between the mean score of the men before listening to the speech and their mean score after listening to it and the same value for the women. The first thing you would want to know is whether the difference between the "before" and "after" mean scores for each group was really significant; that is, whether the difference resulted from listening to the speech or was just an accident occurring by chance. Statistical tests would tell you this. You would also have a difference between the change in mean score of the men and the change in mean score of the women after exposure to the speech. This would be your critical difference. If statistical tests showed a significantly greater change in mean score for the women than in mean score for the men, this finding might be used to support the hypothesis that women are more easily persuaded than men.

This kind of statistical evidence is becoming more and more important in present-day discussions of political and sociological matters. A good speaker must know where to find and how to use such material. All statistics like averages and percentages need to be interpreted for the audience, but statistical measures like coefficients of correlation and differences between the means must be interpreted with special care. For instance, a high correlation does not necessarily mean that one thing *causes* another. It would be unwise to argue, in the example discussed earlier, that political conservatism causes conservative sex-role stereotyping. The reverse might be true. Moreover, both political conservatism and sex-role stereotyping might be the result of some other, as yet unknown factor.

In applying the results of an experiment involving measures of the difference between means, one must be careful not to generalize too much. That women may change their attitudes more than men when subjected to persuasion in one situation does not necessarily mean that they would do the same under other circumstances. Such uncertain and restricted findings may be worth noting, but they are not conclusive.

TESTIMONY

Examples, illustrations, and statistics are ways of presenting an audience with facts that can be observed and verified. *Testimony* is a way of establishing facts secondhand (as when a witness tells what he or she saw at the scene of an accident) and of giving opinions on matters where facts are not available (as when a medical examiner testifies about the probable time of death of a body that was not immediately discovered). Here is an example of the use of testimony. The speaker is Lisa L. Golub, a freshman at the University of Wisconsin, speaking on the topic, ''The neglect of the elderly is a serious social problem.''

According to Senator Charles H. Percy in *Growing Old in the Country of the Young,* one out of three of our elderly live in substandard housing. In addition, the quality of life decreases with each increase in inflation. In Percy's book, one aged person offers this testimony:

> ''I am 74 years old and living in a building 70 years old. I moved here 9 years ago and paid $90 a month for rent. Then the building was sold. The first two years, my rent was raised $4 each year. Then I got a $10 increase. Now, $20 more. I get $141 social security. Rent is $130. Plus gas, plus utilities, plus telephone. How can I eat?''

While Social Security was not designed to provide sole or adequate support, it now struggles to provide at least 90% of the total income for more than four million of our older people. The battle is being lost.[9]

In Golub's example, the quotation taken from Senator Percy's book is called *lay testimony.* In this kind of testimony, the person relates personal experience without making any authoritative judgments about events. Speakers may also use *authority* or *expert testimony* to support their ideas. In the example that follows, the speaker is R. R. Allen, a professor at the University of Wisconsin. By using expert opinion he tries to show that one reason many college students write poorly is that English teachers do not want to teach composition.

[9] Wil Linkugel, et al., eds., *Contemporary American Speeches* (Dubuque, Iowa: Kendall/Hunt Publishing Co., 1982), pp. 230-231.

I think we all know that English teachers have failed to promote basic skill development in students for three very obvious reasons.

First, secondary school English teachers are not interested primarily in basic skill development. In the September 1975 issue of the *English Journal,* Stephen Dunning, then President of the National Council of Teachers of English, noted:

> . . . basic literacy hasn't been our central aim as English teachers. Few of us prepared to teach English from passionate interest in basic skills. Most of us came to English teaching from the study and love of literature.

Adrian Peetoom, writing in the May 1975 issue of the *English Journal,* reinforced this perception by speaking nostalgically of the time, not so distant past, when English teachers reigned supreme:

> English teachers did not only teach literature. They had to teach grammar and composition, perhaps spelling and speech. But no one was under any illusion as to where these activities ranked—they were slaves of literature.

Thus, most secondary school teachers of English come to their profession not to promote basic student skills in the use of the English language, but rather, to share their love and enthusiasm for literature written in the English language. Gordon M. Pradl, calling for a new definition of English in the April 1976 issue of the *English Journal,* provided one: "English," he wrote, "is the experience of literature."[10]

This is a typical use of expert authority. Note that Allen gives the qualifications of one of the authorities, at least briefly. The qualifications of the others are implied by their being published in the *English Journal.* This speaker is thus able to show his audience the authority of expert opinion, instead of trying to convince them solely with his own opinion.

Quotations from experts are useful in other situations, too. For instance, if you were discussing the probable economic impact of wealth piling up in the hands of people in oil-rich countries, you would certainly want to inject the opinions of economic experts. So, too, if you were discussing some complex technical problem, such as the probable effect on

---

[10] R. R. Allen, "Do You Really Want to Know Why Johnny Can't Write?" *Vital Speeches of the Day,* 42 (1975–1976), 149. Reprinted by permission.

human beings of traveling through space for periods as long as two or
three years, you would be wise to use the opinions of trained scientists.
Your own experience would not give you the necessary knowledge to
make reasonable predictions.

QUOTATIONS

Testimony appears in the form of quotations, of course; but as used
here the term *quotations* means examples quoted from literature. Such
quotations are usually used to add feeling and strength to ideas rather
than to prove them. Quotations are often used in the introduction or
conclusion of a speech, but they may appear anywhere in the body also.
They often fit well in speeches of tribute, welcome, farewell, introduction,
and so on, in which the speaker aims to sharpen and heighten feelings
rather than change them.

Winston Churchill used quotations appropriately and well. In a wartime speech on May 19, 1940, he concluded with a stirring quotation. He
had taken the helm of Britain just at the moment when the Germans
broke through the Maginot Line of fortifications in France and were
threatening to destroy both the French and the British armies. Having
noted the gravity of the situation, he concluded his call for sacrifice and
courage with the following words:

Today is Trinity Sunday. Centuries ago words were written to be a
call and a spur to faithful servants of truth and justice.
  "Arm yourselves, and be ye men of valor, and be in readiness
  for the conflict, for it is better for us to perish in battle than to
  look on the outrage of our nation and our altars. As the will of
  God is in Heaven, even so let Him do." [11]

Literary quotations may, on occasion, be used to illustrate a persuasive
argument. Harold Macmillan, then prime minister of England, in a
speech before the Parliament of the Union of South Africa on February 3,
1960, demonstrated this kind of use. He had been arguing the point "that
in this modern world no country, not even the greatest, can live for itself
alone." He uttered a brief quote from the Bible (Romans 12:5): "We are
all members one of another." He then followed with this paragraph:

[11] As quoted in James McBath and Walter Fisher, *British Public Address, 1828–1960*
(Boston: Houghton Mifflin, 1971), p. 497.

What Mr. John Donne said of individual men 300 years ago is true today of my country, your country, and every other country in the world:

> *Any man's death diminishes me,*
> *Because I am involved in mankind.*
> *And therefore never send to know*
> *For whom the bell tolls:*
> *It tolls for thee.*

All nations now are interdependent upon one another. This is generally recognized in the Western World, and I hope that in due course the countries of communism will recognize it too.[12]

REPETITION AND RESTATEMENT

A speaker can emphasize and enhance an idea merely by repeating it in the same words: "If we put our hearts to the task, we can turn the enemy back. I repeat: If we put our hearts to the task, we can turn the enemy back." This tactic cannot be used frequently, for it tends to become distracting. Moreover, research has shown that a speaker gains little effectiveness by repeating an idea more than three times when using the same words.

A more effective form of repetition is restatement. *Restatement* means expressing the same idea in words that are partially or wholly different. Often the speaker will repeat a key phrase word for word and follow that with reworded versions of arguments used previously. If properly done, such restatement can have immense impact. William Lloyd Garrison, the famous nineteenth-century foe of slavery, was a master of repetition for emphasis. Consider the passage from a speech he delivered in the Broadway Tabernacle in New York City on February 14, 1854. He had just given twelve common reasons said to justify slave holding and then attacked them as unacceptable.

If they are valid, in any instance, what becomes of the Declaration of Independence? . . . *If they are valid,* then why is not the jesuitical doctrine, that the end sanctifies the means, and that it is right to do

---

[12] Ibid., p. 82.

evil that good may come, morally sound? *If they are valid,* then how does it appear that God is no respecter of persons, or how can he say "All souls are mine?" . . .

But they are not valid. They are the logic of bedlam, the morality of the pirate ship, the diabolism of the pit. They insult the common sense and shock the moral nature of mankind.[13]

Martin Luther King used a similar tactic in his famous "I Have a Dream" speech delivered in Washington, D.C., in 1963. Several times King repeated the phrase "I have a dream" with dramatic effectiveness. Then, in the conclusion, King skillfully repeated the words "Let freedom ring" nine different times. His speech ended amid tremendous applause that showed the deep emotional involvement of his audience.

VISUAL AIDS

Visual aids make it possible for an audience to see as well as hear the explanation of a concept. Description and explanation are thus taken in through two sensory channels and, presumably, the impact on receivers is more vivid. For instance, if you were trying to explain to an audience how a rotary engine works, you would find your task much easier if you could produce a simple working model of the cylinder of such an engine. Visual aids also help to maintain the audience's attention and interest.

Visual aids may be of several types. First, there are *actual objects* or *models of objects.* If you were trying to show that some product containers are more misleading than others, you might produce two liquid-detergent bottles. You would show how one, because of its shape, is made to look much larger than the other, although both hold the same amount. Size limits the use of actual objects. Small things such as the bottles just mentioned can be handled easily, but large objects cannot be carried or moved around well. Scale models may work when one wants to present large objects visually. Models can also be built so that they show the workings of internal parts. Some models can be taken apart to help explain construction and function.

If a three-dimensional model is not available, a two-dimensional drawing is often useful. Such drawings must be large enough so that the audience can see them, and parts must be clearly labeled. A good example

---

[13] William Lloyd Garrison, "Garrisonian Abolitionism," in *American Forum,* ed. Ernest Wrage and Barnet Baskerville (New York: Harper and Brothers, 1960), pp. 172–173.

THE HYDROLOGIC CYCLE

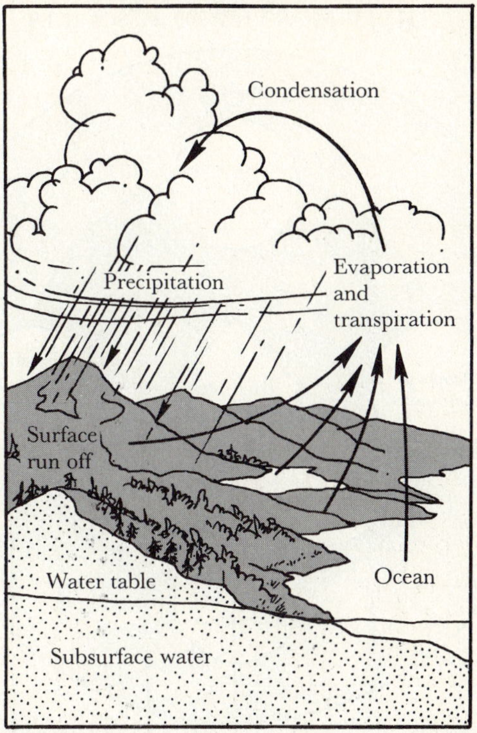

Figure 5.1 A DRAWING AS A VISUAL AID.
Redrawn from Joseph S. Weisberg, Meteorology: The Earth and Its Weather, *2nd ed. (Boston: Houghton Mifflin Company, 1981), p. 80.*

of this type of presentation is shown in Figure 5.1. A mere verbal explanation of the earth's water cycle would be far less effective than an explanation supplemented with this drawing. Models are even more useful when they can be used to illustrate abstract concepts. Figure 5.2 illustrates clearly the multi-faceted idea of how a business affects and is thus viewed by the society it operates in.

Charts and graphs make up a second category of visual materials. These can be of many types. Students need only to look at texts in economics, sociology, government, and other such fields to be aware of the kinds available. A few of the most common varieties will be illustrated here. First is the line graph, which shows how several factors are associated with each other. The authors who used Figure 5.3 were trying to show the relationship between age and participation in the work force for women between 1900 and 1978. As the graph shows, there has been a

THE FIRM AS VIEWED BY SOCIETY

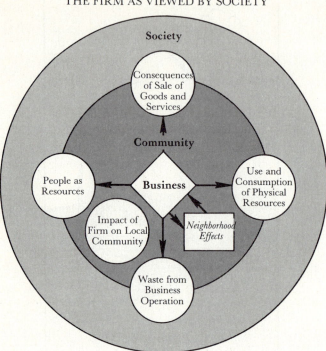

Figure 5.2 A DIAGRAM OF AN ABSTRACT CONCEPT.
Redrawn from George C. Sawyer, Business and Society: Managing Corporate
Social Impact *(Boston: Houghton Mifflin Company, 1979), p. 163.*

significant, overall increase in the participation in the work force by
women of all ages. However, the age of peak participation, mid-twenties,
seems to be consistent.

Another common type of graph is the bar graph. It is especially useful
for comparing units with one another to see how they relate in size or
quantity. A typical bar graph is shown in Figure 5.4. This graph was
designed to show the amount of energy consumed by different parts of the
world between 1968 and 1980.

A common kind of diagram is the pie diagram. It is generally used to
show how a total unit is broken into subunits and to show the size of each
unit relative to the others and to the whole. For instance, Figure 5.5
illustrates the possible breakdown of a sample of 400 television households
to establish the ratings of certain programs.

FEMALE PARTICIPATION
IN THE LABOR FORCE,
BY AGE,
1900–1978

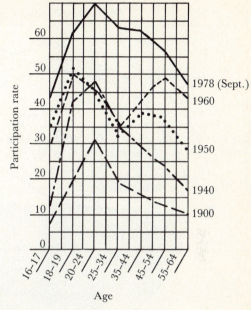

1978 (Sept.) ———
1960 – – –
1950 ••••••
1940 — · —
1900 — — —

Figure 5.3   A LINE GRAPH.
Redrawn from Sheila Ruth, Issues in Feminism: A First Course in Women's
Studies *(Boston: Houghton Mifflin Company, 1980), p. 333.*

PERCENTAGES OF
ENERGY CONSUMED
BY SELECTED PARTS
OF THE WORLD

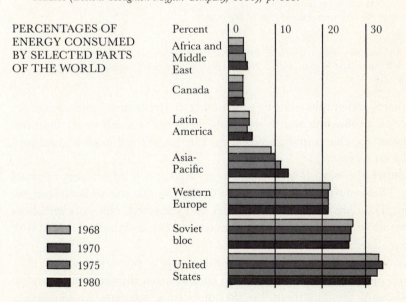

1968
1970
1975
1980

Figure 5.4   A BAR GRAPH.
Redrawn from Keith Young, Geology: The Paradox of Earth and Man *(Boston:
Houghton Mifflin Company, 1975), p. 46; data from the tables in W. A. Bachman,
et al,* "Forecast for the Seventies," *Oil & Gas Journal, 67 (1969), 162–164.*

BROADCASTING IN AMERICA

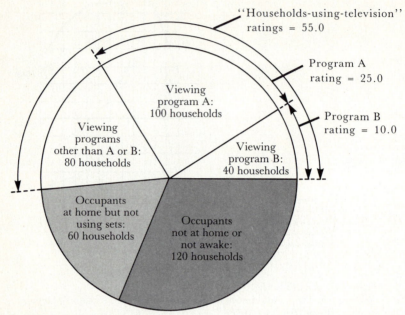

"Households-using-television" ratings = 55.0

Program A rating = 25.0

Program B rating = 10.0

Viewing program A: 100 households

Viewing programs other than A or B: 80 households

Viewing program B: 40 households

Occupants at home but not using sets: 60 households

Occupants not at home or not awake: 120 households

Sample: 400 television households
Universe: All television households in the market

Figure 5.5 A PIE CHART.
Redrawn from Sydney W. Head, Broadcasting in America: A Survey of Television and Radio, *3rd ed. (Boston: Houghton Mifflin Company, 1976), p. 233.*

Charts and graphs must be prepared on poster boards large enough for everyone in the audience to see. If the audience is much larger than two dozen or so, charts and graphs should be transferred to slides and projected on a screen.

Photographs, maps, sketches, and cartoons make up a third category of visual aids. These must be blown up large enough so that the audience can see them. They are best placed on slides and projected. Not only are slides more visible, but they may be arranged in order and thus presented with ease.

Certain precautions should be taken when preparing visual aids. Charts and graphs should not be so complex that they cannot be understood easily. Simplify them, but do not sacrifice accuracy. Avoid distracting elements, and display only one visual aid at a time. Coordinate your visual aids with your verbal presentation. When a visual aid is no longer in use, remove it from the audience's view (this is easily accomplished with slides but less easily with prepared charts and graphs). Don't distribute leaflets to an audience unless you plan to go over the contents in detail. Otherwise, the audience will be distracted from your message. And, finally, make sure that the room in which you will speak has the facilities necessary for the use of your visual aids. An easel may hold your chart, whereas a blackboard trough may not. Electrical plugs may be spaced so as to require an extension cord for your projector (don't forget an extra projector bulb). A screen may not be available. Neglecting such matters can seriously disrupt your speech.

JUSTIFYING MATERIALS—LOGICAL PROOF

The essence of persuasive speaking is offering reasons for what the speaker recommends. Reasons are often referred to, in a general way, as proof. As used with respect to persuasive speaking, the term *proof* does not mean exact, irrefutable, scientific demonstration. Rather it means those matters in the speech that cause the audience to believe. Audiences may be led to believe a claim if the speaker offers facts or evidence and then reasons carefully to show the significance of that evidence. Such proof is called *logical* proof. But the speaker may also offer other kinds of reasons that are not wholly logical. One kind is *emotional* proof, which springs from our desire to believe whatever promises to satisfy our needs and desires. A third kind of proof is referred to as *ethical* proof, a term that may be somewhat confusing because it seems to suggest a moral dimension. *Ethical* in this sense, however, does not mean grounded in morality. Rather, it refers to the inclination to believe a statement solely on the basis of the speaker's personality. A modern-day term used to signify this kind of tendency is *credibility*. We will reserve a discussion of emotional and ethical proof until later, when we discuss persuasive speaking more fully. At this point, we will confine our discussion to logical proof.

Logical proof consists of judgments or conclusions drawn from evidence. If, for instance, you observe that your neighbor's car has a large dent in the fender and that one of the posts lining the neighbor's driveway is broken off, you would probably come to the conclusion that your neighbor ran into the post. The *evidence* in this case is made up of the dented fender and the broken post; the *conclusion* is that your neighbor ran into the post. You don't know this for certain, but you do know that dents in automobile fenders usually are caused by the car running into something (or being run into by something). You also know that broken driveway posts generally get that way from being struck by an automobile. So you reason as follows: Since autos usually get dented by running into something, and since driveway posts usually get broken by being struck by an auto, it is probable that my neighbor ran into the post.

This is a very simple illustration of reasoning, but it shows clearly that reasoning consists of drawing conclusions from evidence. The illustration should also make clear that the quality of a conclusion depends, in part, on the quality of the evidence. If the evidence is false or invalid, then the conclusion drawn from it is likely to be false also. In the preceding example of reasoning, the evidence consisted of directly observable, physical objects. But this type of evidence is not usually available to you when you are preparing a speech. If, say, you wished to use as evidence the annual number of automobiles that collide with stationary objects (such as the driveway post in your neighbor's yard), you could not directly observe all instances of such crashes. You might find such evidence in reports from your state's bureau of highway safety or a similar agency that keeps track of automobile accidents. Or you might read a magazine article dealing with automobile insurance in which the author cites the statistics you need. Or you might find data in an almanac or the *Statistical Abstract of the United States*. But you would have to find your evidence in some such written source. You could not go out and find it by personal inspection.

KINDS AND QUALITY OF EVIDENCE

Evidence falls into two broad categories. The first kind is facts in the form of examples or statistics; the second kind is testimonial evidence or statements of opinion as to what is, has been, or will be true in a given case. Testimonial evidence is used when no facts are available for judgment. It is needed when someone wishes to make a prediction about what will happen in the future as a result of taking some present action. For example, if we place a seven-cent federal tax on gasoline and plan to increase it annually, what will happen to the consumption of gasoline, to the petroleum industry, to the development of alternative energy sources? Here we would have to rely heavily for answers on the testimony of so-called experts.

The quality of factual and testimonial evidence must be judged by the characteristics of the source from which the evidence comes. Here are several tests that may be used to gauge a source's reliability.

1. *Objectivity and accuracy record*   Some sources have a reputation for objectivity and accuracy, while others do not. Governmental agencies like the Census Bureau and the Department of Labor Statistics are generally considered to have a good record. The executive branch of the government does not. It too often releases distorted information or information that is simply false. Many newspaper columnists are unreliable sources because of extreme political bias.

2. *Expertise and knowledge of facts*   In the case of testimonial evidence, a person's expertness and experience in a field are crucial. In fields such as criminology, medicine, economics, foreign affairs, and nuclear science (and other scientific fields), the opinions of persons with appropriate education and experience are to be trusted over the opinions of lay persons. When reporting observed facts, however, a lay person may be just as reliable as an expert as long as he or she is in a position to acquire the facts and has a record of objectivity and accuracy.

3. *Consistency*   This test has two aspects. The first is internal consistency; for example, does a source contradict itself in reports spread over an extended period of time or within the same report? Secondly, is the information given by a source consistent with other sources? If not, someone is mistaken, and the evidence needs to be confirmed in some fashion before it is accepted as reliable.

Two professors of communication, Robert and Dale Newman, have applied the above tests to sources generally used by students in their speeches. Their observations may be paraphrased as follows: Information released by the executive branch of the government is mostly biased. Members of Congress who have made themselves experts in chosen fields are good sources, but watch out for bias in their statements caused by pressure from voters or financial backers. Newspapers are more reliable by far than government sources, but some have a strong political bias. Most reporters, however, are conscientious and careful. News magazines vary in reliability. *Newsweek* is most accurate and reliable. *Time* and *U.S. News and World Report* tend toward bias and inaccuracy. *Reader's Digest* publishes many articles that are frankly propagandistic. Pressure groups like the American Medical Association and the Tobacco Industry Research Council have strong biases; information from them should be carefully evaluated. In general, you should confirm pressure-group evidence from other sources before using it. Scholars in academic institutions are acknowledged experts and are generally good sources, but watch out for exceptions. If they hold rich government contracts or if they are consultants for business and government, they tend to become biased.[14]

These judgments are, of course, open to dispute. Your experience with the sources evaluated by Newman and Newman may have been different. But the Newmans' assessments were based on systematic study over a long period. So you may wish to approach the sources whose reliability they question with the idea that confirmation from other sources might be desirable.

Statistical evidence deserves consideration on its own. Darrell Huff's book *How to Lie with Statistics* demonstrates the many ways in which statistical evidence can be used to misrepresent a situation. For instance, different sets of statistics that apparently measure the same thing may not really be comparable if the definitions used in collecting the statistics were different. What is an automobile accident, for instance? Is it a dented fender? A crash that injures someone? A crash that involves $200 worth of damage? The way in which opinion surveys are conducted also illustrates a potential weakness of statistics. The sample may be biased because of small size and improper selection, and the questions may be worded in such a way that they influence the responses. Newman and Newman, after reviewing the weaknesses of statistical evidence, offer the following advice:

There are no specific tests of credible statistics, but three questions can help guide an evaluation of statistical evidence:

1. *Objectivity:* Who wants to prove what?
2. *Authenticity:* What do the figures really represent?
3. *Carefulness of generalization:* What conclusions do the figures support?[15]

---

[14] Robert P. Newman and Dale R. Newman, *Evidence* (Boston: Houghton Mifflin, 1969), p. 198.
[15] Ibid., pp. 206, 224.

We have indicated the kinds of materials that make up evidence. Specifically, they include factual examples (including illustrations and comparisons or analogies), statistics, and testimony. Evidence provides a basis for reasoning—for drawing some conclusion suggested by the evidence. We will now discuss the kinds of conclusions that can be drawn.

INDUCTIVE REASONING

The generalization.   *Inductive* reasoning is the process of drawing a general conclusion about a class of things from observation of a number of examples from that class. These examples make up a sample. The conclusion drawn from the sample is called a generalization. A generalization is valid if the examples used are a fair sample of the class, that is, if there are enough of them and they are typical of the whole.

Ordinarily, a speaker gives three or four examples, perhaps along with some statistics, to back a claim and assumes that the audience will accept the sample as typical. In the following case, note that the generalization with which the speaker begins is supported by statistics and by seven specific examples. The passage is from a speech by Ralph Ablon, chairman of the Odgen Corporation:

Corporations which do not adapt to a changing environment—like the dinosaurs—become extinct.

If you consider the one-hundred largest corporations in the United States at the end of the First World War, you will find that fifty-two have disappeared entirely and many others are either no longer important or simply names which are not pertinent to their original business.

Look at what has happened to Baldwin Locomotive, U.S. Woolen, Packard, Pennsylvania Railroad, The New York Central Railroad—and others such as Studebaker or Curtiss-Wright who have changed their form or lost their dominance.[16]

Once a generalization is established, the speaker will apply it to some specific situation by saying something like, "So, you see, if *your* corporation does not adapt to changing times, it too will become extinct."

Sometimes a person will support a generalization with a much more elaborate array of examples. This is generally done when the speaker or

---

[16] Ralph Ablon, "Financing of the Corporate Structure for the 1980's," *Vital Speeches of the Day,* 43 (1976–1977), 399. Reprinted by permission.

writer fears that there will be strong resistance to the general statement he
or she seeks to prove. In the previous case, the generalization was almost a
truism, and the speaker felt little need for elaborate proof, but in the case
that follows, the advocate knows that many people will resist the conclusion she will draw; hence, she takes pains to support it fully. The writer,
Betty Friedan, is supporting the generalization that women in American
society have been conditioned by educators and the press to accept the
idea that their fulfillment should come from the role of wife and mother
and that their whole self-concept should revolve around this image. A
glance at three chapters of Friedan's book will suffice to show what kind of
evidence she accumulates to support her generalization:

> Chapter 2, "The Happy Housewife Heroine": Friedan surveyed
> popular woman's magazines, such as *Ladies Home Journal, McCall's,
> Good Housekeeping,* and *Woman's Home Companion,* to see how they
> portrayed the ideal woman. She cites examples of stories and articles
> from the period 1939–1960 to support her generalization.
> Chapter 6, "The Sex-Directed Educators": Friedan reports the
> results of her conversations with girls at Smith College, with whom
> she lived for a week, and then the results of interviews with "girls
> from colleges and universities from all over the United States."
> Quoted examples support her claim that educators have convinced
> college girls to think of little but the wife-mother role.
> Chapter 9, "The Sexual Sell": Friedan interviewed Dr. Ernest
> Dichter, head of the Institute for Motivational Research, and cites
> his opinions. She examined a large sample of Dichter's studies,
> which were done to provide advertisers with marketing strategies.
> Her examples show that in their messages, advertisers reinforce the
> wife-mother role as the ultimate fulfillment for women.[17]

The strongest kind of generalization about large groups is one supported by valid statistics. If a sample is carefully chosen and systematically
surveyed, very precise generalizations may be drawn. Use college librarians as an example. From your own experience, you could generalize that
most college librarians are women. But you can generalize much more
precisely if you have a statistical base. The Bureau of Labor Statistics'
report, *Library Manpower—A Study of Demand and Supply,* reveals that in
academic libraries in 1970 there were 6,600 male employees as compared
to 12,900 female employees. These figures show 34 percent males and 66

[17] Betty Friedan, *The Feminine Mystique* (New York: Dell Publishing Co., 1970).

percent females. Other figures from the same report, however, showed that only 8 percent of head librarians were female.

A generalization should be evaluated on the quality of the examples used to support it. The number of examples used is not necessarily critical. National polling agencies can make predictions about the presidential voting behavior of the entire nation on the basis of a few thousand interviews—predictions that are accurate within a few points. Thus, it is the representativeness of the examples, not their number, that makes the generalization acceptable. Nevertheless, it is wise to be wary of a very small sample, unless some other evidence (manner of selection, authoritative opinion) is presented to ensure that the examples are typical.

Causal generalizations.   A causal generalization establishes a cause-effect bond between two events. The statement, "Excessive cigarette smoking causes lung cancer," is a causal generalization. When establishing a causal generalization, a person will usually use either the *method of agreement* or the *method of difference*. These techniques, which were pinpointed by John Stuart Mill, one of nineteenth-century Britain's great philosophers, may be explained as follows.

The method of agreement consists of examining a series of examples in which a given effect is observed and selecting a single relevant factor that the examples have in common. This relevant factor is assumed to be the cause of the effect. Dr. Karl Menninger, a well-known psychiatrist provided the following illustration in a speech:

The fourth observation I wanted to make is that some patients may have a mental illness and then get well, and then may even get "weller"! I mean they get better than they ever were. They get even better than they were before. This is an extraordinary and little-realized truth—and it constitutes the main point of my talk today. Take an instance familiar to all of you. Abraham Lincoln was undoubtedly a far more productive, a far bigger man, and a far broader and wiser man after his attack of mental illness than he was before. Prior to it he had seemed to fail at everything—in his profession, in politics, in love. After his terrible year of depression, he rose to the great heights of vision and accomplishment for which we all know him. And Lincoln is not the only one; there are many others, but he is a conspicuous one. Now I ask you, does this occur in physical illness?[18]

---

[18] Karl Menninger, "Healthier Than Healthy," in *A Psychiatrist's World* (New York: Viking Press, 1959), pp. 637–38.

In this case, a single example is used to show an attack of mental illness that improved a prominent person emotionally and mentally. We are then assured by the speaker that there are many other examples of this type to support his generalization.

A fully developed cause-effect argument based on the method of agreement would cite many examples. The relevant factor or factors common to all of them would be pointed out. Then the conclusion would be specifically stated. For instance, such an argument might be phrased as follows: Each time, in recent years, that a commercial aircraft has crashed on landing in the United States, there have been two factors present: bad weather and poor pilot judgment. These factors were present in the recent crash at A airport, and they were also present in crashes at B, C, and D airports. It seems evident, then, that bad weather and pilot error are primary causes of air accidents. Schematically the situation looks like this:

Crash A	*Crash B*	*Crash C*	*Crash D*
Thunderstorm	Low visibility	Strong cross winds	Freezing-rain storm
Pilot error	Pilot error	Pilot error	Pilot error

Therefore, bad weather and poor pilot judgment are responsible for landing crashes.

When using the method of difference, a speaker may compare a single example in which an effect is observed with other examples where the effect is not operating. For example, a speaker may argue that a particular man has lung cancer because he smoked two packs of cigarettes a day for twenty years, while cancer-free men did not smoke at all. Or the speaker may compare the same example with itself, describing one condition when the effect was not operating and another after the effect became evident. For instance, the speaker may argue that the man just referred to did not get lung cancer until after he started to smoke heavily. Thus, the method of difference allows us to say, in effect, that when we change something and different behavior begins to take place, the change has caused the different behavior. An example will probably make this clearer. Here is talk in which the speaker argues that job enrichment can cause improved productivity. His method is to compare the productivity of a corporation after a program of job enrichment with the productivity of the same company before job enrichment. The speaker is T. C. McDermott, vice president of Rockwell International.

A different approach is job enrichment. I am sure you are familiar with this one. It is essentially a program to allow the employee to enlarge his job assignment either horizontally, vertically or both. In an assembly line example, the worker performing a single operation might expand his activities horizontally to include a series or group of related operations.

In another case, the employee might enrich his job vertically by assuming the responsibility for planning his work and material requirements or other management-type tasks.

This approach, too, obviously provides the employee with an opportunity to feel greater creativity and involvement in his work.

Perhaps one of the most unusual ... and successful ... new developments took place a year or so ago at the U.S. Elevator Corporation.

The business was in a bad way with high costs and inefficiencies leading to heavy losses.

To find a way out, the director of manufacturing operations turned to the application of Transactional Analysis techniques.

His approach was to cure the crisis by treating the workers as adults, laying out the problem and asking their help in solving it. He met with groups of workers and told them that he knew the solutions to the problems were in their heads; that they ... not he ... knew all about building elevators, and that he was not going to solve the problem, they were.

I don't have the time now to describe all of the innovations that resulted, but the bottom line is that same year there was a 45 percent improvement in factory operations, a 15 percent improvement in shipping operations, a 50 percent decline in field complaints on quality problems, and an 80 percent reduction in overtime.

I would term that successful.[19]

Another common way of establishing cause-effect relationships is simply to refer to the opinions of authorities. Here is how Jenkin L. Jones, editor and publisher of the *Tulsa Tribune,* traced the cause of what he felt was a breakdown in values among young people:

Dr. Robert E. Cavanaugh, writing in a recent issue of *Psychology Today* magazine says, "The failure of the home, the school, the church to transmit a sound and solid value system further heightens the student identity crisis. Today's student lacks a strong parental figure or a deeply indoctrinated sense of values to give him polarization."

---

[19] T. C. McDermott, "The Human Dimension in Productivity," *Vital Speeches of the Day,* 43 (1976–1977), 307. Reprinted by permission.

In his book, *Ancient Rome, Its Rise and Fall,* Philip Van Ness Myers says, "First at the bottom, as it were, of Roman society and forming its ultimate unit was the family. The most important feature or element of this family group was the authority of the father. It was in the atmosphere of the family that were nourished in Roman youth the virtues of obedience, deference to authority, and in the exercise of parental authority, the Roman learned how to command as well as how to obey."

Then what happened? Jerome Carcopino in his book, *Daily Life in Ancient Rome,* said, "By the beginning of the second century A.D., Roman fathers, having given up the habit of controlling their children, let the children govern them and took pleasure in bleeding themselves white to gratify the expensive whims of their offspring. The result was that they were succeeded by a generation of wastrels." I might point out that after the generation of wastrels came Attila, the Hun.[20]

In this case, Jones called upon authorities from the fields of psychology and history to show that a breakdown in family discipline is linked to a decline of values among children.

Cause-effect arguments relating to complex social phenomena, such as crime, unemployment, war, inflation, and so on, are not easy to establish. Usually, no single, simple cause can be pinpointed; rather, a number of factors are responsible, and each contributes to the effect. Take inflation, for instance. Some economists argue that excessive federal spending causes inflation; others say high wages cause it; some say excessive increases in money supply; some say reductions in labor productivity; and so on. The point is that all of these factors are probably related to inflation in some way, so no one should try to blame inflation on a single factor.

APPLYING THE GENERALIZATION—DEDUCTION

In simple *deductive* arguments, a person uses a generalization as a basis for reasoning and concludes that what is proposed in the generalization would be true of a specific case to which the generalization can be applied. The whole argument would consist of evidence to establish the generalization, plus the application step, as follows:

---

[20] *Vital Speeches of the Day,* 40 (1973–1974), p. 475. Reprinted by permission.

Inductive evidence

I. Examples of tooth-cavity rates in communities where drinking water contains fluoride and where there is no fluoride.

Generalization

II. Persons who drink fluoridated water have significantly fewer cavities.

Deductive application

III. If New York City adds fluoride to its drinking water, its people will experience lower rates of tooth decay.

Below is an actual example of deductive argument taken from a debate at the West Point National Debate Tournament of 1966. The speaker is a student, Michael Denger, of Northwestern University:

Now, the second problem created by giving primary responsibility to attack organized crime to local officials is that the syndicate leaders can escape prosecution by living outside the jurisdictions where their illegal operations exist. William G. Hundley, Chief of the Justice Department Organized Crime and Racketeering Section, wrote in the 1963 *Notre Dame Lawyer* that, "Artificial jurisdictional boundaries that divide state from state, county from county, and city from city, prevent local law enforcement officials from pursuing a criminal whose operations are conducted within his jurisdiction, but who remains outside of it." Thus Milton Russell, the Assistant Attorney General wrote in 1961, "By committing crimes within only local jurisdiction, prosecution can be splintered into a large number of local districts, and the syndicate leaders thereby effectively insulate themselves from vigorous law enforcement." Tampa Police Chief Neil Brown indicated this problem of splintered jurisdiction in his 1963 testimony before the Senate Committee on Government Operations. He reported that, "The Tampa Police Department has been unable to do anything about the activities of Santo Troficanti, a major Florida racketeer, because it has no jurisdiction over his affairs elsewhere in central Florida." Now, clearly, by making all organized criminal offenses violations of state and federal laws as well as local law, our proposal will remove these jurisdictional barriers to effective law enforcement.[21]

---

[21] As quoted in Glen Mills, *Reason in Controversy* (Boston: Allyn and Bacon, 1968), p. 341.

In this case, the speaker cites evidence to establish the generalization that artificial jurisdictional boundaries make it possible for organized criminals to escape prosecution. He argues that if the United States eliminated jurisdictional boundaries by making all organized criminal offenses state and federal crimes, it would make for better law enforcement.

A contemporary English philosopher, Stephen Toulmin, in his book *The Uses of Argument,* provides a way of looking at deductive argument that differs from the one just given.[22] Toulmin begins by offering several

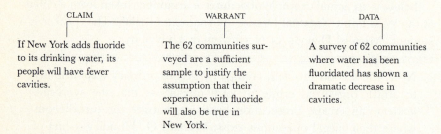

CLAIM	WARRANT	DATA
If New York adds fluoride to its drinking water, its people will have fewer cavities.	The 62 communities surveyed are a sufficient sample to justify the assumption that their experience with fluoride will also be true in New York.	A survey of 62 communities where water has been fluoridated has shown a dramatic decrease in cavities.

Figure 5.6   TOULMIN MODEL OF ARGUMENT.
The relationships of *claim, warrant,* and *data* in the fluoridation-tooth decay argument.

CLAIM	RESERVATIONS	WARRANT	DATA
Increasing domestic production of oil will reduce foreign oil imports into the United States.			We are able to produce domestically only 80% of the oil we consume. We must import 20% of it.
	Provided there is no increase in oil consumption. Provided oil companies can make as much profit on domestic oil as they can on imported oil.	We would prefer to use our own oil rather than foreign oil.	

Figure 5.7   TOULMIN MODEL OF ARGUMENT.
The insertion of *reservations* in the argument for increasing the production of domestic oil.

---

[22] Stephen Toulmin, *The Uses of Argument* (Cambridge, England: Cambridge University Press, 1958), Chapter 3.

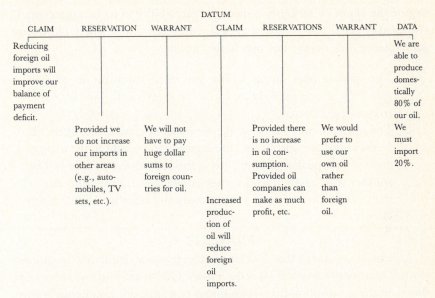

CLAIM	RESERVATION	WARRANT	DATUM CLAIM	RESERVATIONS	WARRANT	DATA
Reducing foreign oil imports will improve our balance of payment deficit.						We are able to produce domestically 80% of our oil.
	Provided we do not increase our imports in other areas (e.g., automobiles, TV sets, etc.).	We will not have to pay huge dollar sums to foreign countries for oil.	Increased production of oil will reduce foreign oil imports.	Provided there is no increase in oil consumption. Provided oil companies can make as much profit, etc.	We would prefer to use our own oil rather than foreign oil.	We must import 20%.

Figure 5.8 TOULMIN MODEL OF ARGUMENT.
How the *claim* in Figure 5.7 may become the *datum* for another claim about
the U.S. balance of payments.

concepts that he thinks characterize argument. These are claim, data, warrant, and reservation. A *claim* is the conclusion that a speaker wishes the audience to accept. *Data* are the pieces of evidence that support the claim. The *warrant* is the connecting link that establishes the bond between the data and the claim. These relationships are shown in Figure 5.6 for the fluoridation-tooth decay argument that was presented a few paragraphs ago. The concept of *reservation* is inserted between the warrant and the claim. A reservation is any factor that could prevent the operation of the warrant, which must be accepted to justify the conclusion drawn from the data. Figure 5.7 shows an example of how reservations fit into the argument.

In complex arguments, the claim of one chain of reasoning may become a *datum* for an additional claim. Figure 5.8 shows this relationship, using and extending the example from Figure 5.7.

Toulmin's model of deductive argument is useful because it calls attention to the importance of having supporting evidence when drawing a cause-effect generalization. Also, his concept of reservations introduces an element that is not generally thought of in the traditional deductive model, where reservations tend to be ignored entirely. Since reservations may negate the claim or seriously reduce the probability of its being accepted, the speaker should be prepared to deal with reservations when addressing an audience. He or she has two basic options:

1. The speaker may simply ignore any reservations on the ground that they are so unlikely as not to be significant. This course is frequently chosen.
2. The speaker may mention the reservations and refute them. If reservations are serious and are logically important to the acceptance of the speaker's claim, this is the best course to follow. The speaker may argue that the reservations are unlikely to occur or that, if they do, they will not seriously weaken the validity of the claim.

ANALOGY

A form of argument that is neither inductive nor deductive (or at least doesn't exactly fit these forms) is the *analogy*. Conclusions from analogy are based on the assumption that if two things resemble one another in known ways, they will also resemble one another in ways that cannot be observed. Analogies are of two kinds: figurative and literal. The *figurative* analogy compares things across categories, whereas the *literal* analogy compares things within the same category. Thus, if you said that a factory resembles a beehive in its organization and distribution of labor, you would be using a figurative analogy. If, on the other hand, you said that the Ford assembly plant in Marietta, Georgia operates like the Oldsmobile assembly plant in Lansing, Michigan, you would be using a literal analogy. When used to explain and clarify, analogies are generally called comparisons. We have already discussed this type of use.

Analogies may also be used as argument, however. In such use, the speaker concludes that what has happened in one case will also happen in a similar case. The following passage is an example of a figurative analogy used as argument. It comes from a speech by Theodore Parker, a New England Congregational minister. Its provocative title is ''The Transient and Permanent in Christianity.'' One of Parker's points was that the Christian religion consists of a set of ethical and moral principles independent of Christ, whose name is used to identify them. To support this point, Parker said:

Almost every sect that has ever been makes Christianity rest on the personal authority of Jesus, and not the immutable truth of the doctrines themselves.... yet it seems difficult to conceive any reason why moral and religious truths should rest for their support on the personal authority of their revealer any more than the truths of science on that of him who makes them known first or most clearly. It is hard to see why the great truths of Christianity rest on the personal authority of Jesus, more than the axioms of geometry rest on the personal authority of Euclid or Archimedes. The authority of Jesus, as of all teachers, one would naturally think must rest on the truth of his words, and not their truth on his authority.[23]

In this passage, Parker uses a figurative analogy to make a cross-category comparison between religion and mathematics.

An example of the use of a literal analogy as argument can be seen in the following excerpt from a speech by Henry George, a nineteenth-century popular economist, who believed that all government—local, state, and national—should be supported by a single tax on land. Note how he draws an analogy between the experience of San Francisco and what would happen in other cities if they did the same thing:

. . . we could, from the value of land, not merely pay all the present expenses of government, but we could do infinitely more. In the city of San Francisco, James Lick left a few blocks of ground to be used for public purposes there, and the rent amounts to so much, that out of it will be built the largest telescope in the world, large public baths, and other public buildings, and various costly monuments. If, instead of those few blocks, the whole value of the land upon which the city is built had accrued to San Francisco, what could she not do?

So in this little town [where George was speaking] where land values are very low as compared with such cities as Chicago and San Francisco, you could do many things for mutual benefit and public improvement did you appropriate to public purposes the land values that now go to individuals. You could have a great free library; you could have an art gallery; you could get yourselves a public park, a magnificent public park, too. . . . You might make on this site a city that it would be a pleasure to live in.[24]

---

[23] Quoted by Perry Miller in *The American Transcendentalists* (Garden City, N.Y.: Doubleday Anchor Books, 1957), p. 120.

[24] Henry George, "The Crime of Poverty," Wrage and Baskerville, p. 254.

In this analogy, George predicts what would happen in Burlington, Iowa, the town in which he was speaking, by observing the experience of San Francisco. The two cities are assumed to be enough alike so that whatever happened in San Francisco would also happen in Burlington.

SUMMARY

A speaker selects the content of a speech from a large body of available materials so that the speech will suit both the purpose and the audience. In general, the following kinds of content will be chosen: descriptions and explanations; comparison and contrast; examples, illustrations and anecdotes; definitions; statistics; testimony, both lay and expert; quotations, and repetition and restatement. Visual aids in the form of models, photographs, slides, charts, and graphs are also useful.

Some supporting materials, consisting of evidence and argument, are used to support persuasive proposals. Evidence consists of reports of fact and opinion. Its source must be tested for reliability: for its objectivity and accuracy record, its expertise, and its consistency. Arguments are generally classified as inductive and deductive. An inductive argument uses examples or statistics to establish a common characteristic or a cause-and-effect relationship among a class of things. Once established, generalizations are applied deductively to specific cases to specify their nature or predict their behavior. The Toulmin model of analyzing a deductive argument uses the concepts of claim, warrant, data, and reservations to test the argument's quality. Finally, analogies, both literal and figurative, are used to support the prediction that, since a particular outcome occurred in one situation, it will probably occur again in a similar situation.

Exercises

1. Read a speech like Newton Minow's "Television: The Vast Wasteland" [in *Voices of Crisis,* Floyd W. Matson, ed. (New York: Odyssey Press, 1967), pp. 250–262]. Identify the supporting materials used in this speech. Discuss the supporting materials. Were they used effectively? Could other types have been used? What types? Where?
2. Examine several persuasive magazine articles in journals such as *Harper's, Atlantic Monthly,* and so on. Find examples of (1)generalizations and the evidence used to support them, (2)analogies, (3)cause-

and-effect generalizations, and (4)deductive arguments. Bring these to class. Compare them with examples found by classmates and evaluate their quality.

3. Prepare and deliver a speech in which you establish a single claim of cause and effect by the use of statistics, testimony, and the method of agreement.

4. Each member of the class should give a short speech using audio-visual aids. Each speaker should illustrate the subject fully with charts, models, pictures, slides, tape recordings, and so on. Discuss each person's effectiveness in using these aids.

5. Locate in magazine articles, books, or speeches examples of arguments that may be analyzed using the Toulmin model. Diagram some of these arguments on the blackboard as a basis for class discussion.

Chapter Six
DELIVERY:
NONVERBAL COMMUNICATION

OVERVIEW

The role of bodily movement in speaking
The use of various kinds of gestures
Principles of good gesturing
Appearance as a form of nonverbal communication
Voice formation and use

To assume that verbal content transmits all the meaning in a speech would be a mistake. Certainly words carry the bulk of a message but, in a sense, a speaker gives two speeches, one with words and the other with nonverbal bodily actions. This body language supplements the verbal meaning and reveals the speaker's attitudes toward the audience and the topic. It reveals the speaker's interest, indifference, or boredom, and his or her emotional involvement (anger, elation, fright, disgust, and so on).

The behavior of poker players illustrates the extent to which body language carries meaning. A good player learns to read the strength of the hands of careless players from certain bodily signs. He or she "notices whether they sit close to the table or lean back, place their bet quickly or slowly, put their chips in the center of the pot or closer to themselves, and so on."[1] In addition, a clever observer may read meaning into the tension or relaxation of the voice with which a player makes a bet. A good player avoids revealing his or her own strength by putting on a "poker" face (one without expression) and by carefully controlling all bodily movements and vocal inflections.

Whereas the poker player wants to conceal meaning, the public speaker wants to supplement and enrich meaning and therefore uses body language as an additional channel of communication. When we speak of delivery, we mean the use of bodily action and nonverbal voice cues as a back-up communication code to supplement the verbal one. More specifically, delivery can be broken down into the following components: facial expression, gestures, posture, eye contact, appearance, and nonverbal vocal signs such as pitch, rate, volume, and inflection.

---

[1] Philip Zimbardo and Floyd Ruch, *Psychology and Life* (Glenview, Ill.: Scott, Foresman, 1975), p. 159.

FACIAL EXPRESSION

A speaker reveals emotions to the audience by facial expressions that show the speaker's attitude toward the subject. A speaker who is angry or indignant, and wants the audience to feel that way too, can use facial signs to show the emotion. By sympathetic reaction, those signs tend to draw out the same emotion in the audience. Charles Darwin, in his book *The Expression of the Emotions in Man and Animal* (1872), argued that emotions were expressed in inborn ways, such as showing the teeth in anger. Darwin implied that the facial signs accompanying emotions like rage, fear, and grief were the same among individuals and across cultures. Later investigators showed that this was not the case. Crying, for example, is associated not only with grief, but with other emotions as well. Anger is expressed by different facial movements across different cultures and even among different persons in the same culture. Nevertheless, most people can tell whether a facial expression indicates pleasantness or unpleasantness, rejection or acceptance. This holds true even in the absence of any confirming details (that is, when someone is just looking at a picture of a face). When the circumstances provoking a facial expression are revealed, an observer is able to describe the emotion expressed with even more accuracy.

Since the causes of a speaker's emotions are clearly revealed in the public-speaking situation, the audience will be able to read facial expressions well. If a person describes a circumstance that calls for anger and indignation, and his or her face fails to reflect this emotion, the audience might doubt the speaker's sincerity; at the least, they would consider the lack of emotional reaction strange. On the other hand, a speaker who shows appropriate facial expressions can communicate concern to the audience with greater impact and urgency.

HAND GESTURES

Hand gestures are usually of two types: emphatic and descriptive. *Emphatic gestures* are used to add stress or emphasis to portions of the speech the speaker considers especially important. If you say, for instance, "We must not allow such a tragic event to happen," you may reinforce the statement with a pointed forefinger, a clenched fist, or some other hand movement that seems natural to you. Such a determined statement will not seem convincing unless accompanied by appropriate bodily action.

Descriptive gestures are conventional hand movements whose meanings are commonly understood. A police officer raises a hand at shoulder height with palm held forward—a gesture we understand to mean stop. A football referee swiftly signals the kind of infraction for which a penalty is called. Gestures of this nature can often help you in speaking. The police officer's halt gesture, for instance, may be used to indicate rejection of an idea or as a signal to stop thinking about a particular course of action.

Other descriptive gestures imitate closely what they represent. Such gestures are called *mimetic*. When you are describing kinds of movement in space, mimetic gestures almost always occur. For example, imagine how difficult it would be to illustrate the difference between a forehand and a backhand in tennis without the use of descriptive gestures. Descriptive gestures may also show the relationship of objects to one another in space, or they may actually serve like a picture as you sketch a figure in the air.

Some research suggests that teachers who gesture regularly get better results from their students than those who do not. One explanation for this difference might be ''that frequent gesturing has been found to be a part of a general affiliative style that conveys positive feelings (Mehrabian). Such a style tends to elicit reciprocal liking and cooperation from other people. Thus, a teacher who uses many gestures . . . is probably expressing a positive feeling for his students leading to their greater involvement in the class.''[2] If teachers improve their effectiveness by gesturing, it seems reasonable to assume that public speakers will also be more effective if they gesture frequently.

Whatever gestures you use you should keep certain principles of effective movements in mind:

> To be effective, hand gestures should be spontaneous. They should spring from the impulse to communicate and you should not plan them deliberately (although in practicing a speech you might do so).

> Effective hand gestures involve the entire body not merely the hand and arm. If not accompanied by movements of the head,

---

[2] Paul Eckman and Wallace Friesen, ''Hand Movements,'' *Journal of Communication*, 22 (1972), 159.

shoulders, and trunk, a hand gesture looks mechanical, not like a coordinated action of the whole person.

Hand gestures should not be too abundant or too exaggerated. Gestures support your verbal message; they should not detract from it by drawing undue attention to themselves.

Effective gestures have a purpose. They contribute to the impact of your message by illustrating it or by emphasizing its importance.

MOVEMENT AND EYE CONTACT

Some bodily actions help a person adjust to a communication situation. A speaker tends to be only partially conscious of these actions. Shifting weight from one foot to another, adjusting your glasses, and wiping away perspiration are examples of such actions, which are called *adaptors*. If your adaptors suggest that you are ill at ease or nervous, they will distract from your message. You should recognize your adaptors and try to control them if necessary.

Eye contact (looking directly into the eyes of another person) helps establish psychological involvement. On the other hand, if you wish to show lack of interest in another person or to signal negative feelings, you avoid eye contact or resort to furtive glances. In a restaurant, for instance, you do not look directly at persons occupying the next table; glances are quick and hesitant. If eyes do meet directly, the people involved become embarrassed and look away at once. People do, though, tend to look directly at individuals they like or are interested in. Such eye contact signals a positive relationship. Under other circumstances, however, staring at another person is considered bad manners and can make the person stared at uneasy or even angry. Monkeys and apes tend to look directly into the eyes of an individual whom they are ready to challenge or attack, just as people often stare in anger when offended. Thus, it seems eye contact can signal either positive intentions or negative ones, depending on the situation.

In public speaking, good eye contact consists of looking at the audience without staring at a particular individual. The speaker's eyes do not remain fixed but move from one area of the audience to another, so that all the people feel the speaker is directly and positively involved with them. Lack of eye contact makes the audience feel that the speaker is not interested and is not coping well with the communication situation.

APPEARANCE

A person's general appearance is another form of nonverbal communication. Consider what your appearance may reveal about you. Take your hair, for example. If you are a man with long hair that hangs below your shoulders, some people may think that you belong to a rebellious subculture. They may view you favorably or unfavorably because of this impression. If you have a beard, it also conveys a nonverbal message about you. The same is true of your clothing. If you are a woman and wear a cloth coat, you show something about yourself that differs from what a woman in a mink coat shows. Whether you wear a lot of make-up or a little also creates an impression. In general, your dress and overall grooming can and do reveal a lot of information about you such as the following:

1. *Socioeconomic class* A blue-collar worker may dress informally. A professional person, such as a doctor or a lawyer, will almost always dress more formally (except that some high-status people deliberately try to dress informally). The style and quality of a person's clothes can indicate income level or the level a person seeks.

2. *Personality* Dark, conservatively cut clothing will suggest a personality that is conservative, or at least cautious. A person wearing bright, stylish clothing will probably be thought of as more liberal and adventuresome.

3. *Status* Some garments clearly indicate status: the robes of a judge, for instance, or the academic gown of a scholar. In general, people perceive a person who wears expensive, well-tailored clothes and accessories as being of higher status than one who does not.

4. *Affiliation* Grooming and clothing may well distinguish a particular group of people. Extreme examples are the shaved heads and orange robes of the Hare Krishna cult and the long hair, studded leather jackets, and boots of some motorcycle gangs. But people also have more subtle ways of revealing their affinity for certain groups through their appearance.

Clearly, then, your appearance is important, and people will use it to form positive or negative images of you. You should be alert, therefore, to dress appropriately for the occasion and for yourself as a person.

VOICE FORMATION AND NONVERBAL VOICE CUES

We speak words with our voices, but a voice conveys additional meaning beyond what the words signify by themselves. The nonverbal part of the voice—its quality, pitch, rate, volume, and inflection—is a language in itself that helps listeners interpret the words we speak. Nonverbal cues usually supplement and enhance verbal meanings but, on occasion, words may say one thing and nonverbal voice cues something different. Sarcasm is a good example of inconsistency between word meaning and voice meaning. A person may say, for instance, ''I just love classical music,'' using a distasteful tone of voice that makes quite clear a meaning just the opposite of what was said. For the remainder of this section, we will discuss the voice: how it is formed and used and what meanings it can convey. A speaker must be able to control nonverbal voice cues and, to do so, must understand how the voice is produced, amplified, and articulated.

THE DIAPHRAGM

The diaphragm is a muscular membrane that separates the lungs from the abdomen. With the help of the chest muscles, the diaphragm causes our lungs to expand and contract, allowing us to breathe. The primary purpose of breathing is to provide oxygen for the blood, not to furnish energy for making sounds. Voice production, however, depends on a breath stream that activates the vocal folds. Gradually relaxing the diaphragm causes a steady stream of air to pass between the vocal folds, producing the voice. Thus, control of the diaphragm is critical for speech. We won't discuss the various exercises for controlling the diaphragm that exist. But if you have breathing troubles, such as breathlessness or problems controlling your breath stream, ask your instructor for help.

PHONATION

Phonation is the production of sound by vibrations of the vocal folds as air passes between them. The vocal folds produce sound in much the same way that sound can be made by closing the lips and forcing air out between them. Unlike the lips, however, the vocal folds are joined only at one end and are pulled together by various muscles along their edges. The action is much like closing the V-shaped gap formed between the extended thumb and forefinger.

The vocal folds' length and thickness largely determine the pitch of the sound that they produce; men generally have lower-pitched voices than women because men's vocal folds are longer and thicker. However, tension placed on the vocal folds also affects pitch, forcing it higher than it would be with a relaxed throat. You should experiment at speaking with a relaxed throat to learn your most comfortable pitch level.

As a person speaks, there may be changes in pitch from one word or sentence to the next, but there are also sliding changes known as *inflections*. Pitch changes and inflections add, through emphasis, to the meaning that words suggest. These changes also create a pattern in the voice that may affect how the audience views the speaker. Such changes may make the speaker sound enthusiastic, timid, bold, pushy, limp-wristed, powerful, and so on; and these impressions may influence credibility with the audience.

RESONATION

After phonation, the voice is *resonated*. Resonation means that the basic pitch pattern is amplified and picks up overtones. These overtones give the voice's tone a unique character called voice quality. A note played on a cello sounds different from the same note played on a violin. The difference is caused by the different resonating chambers of the two instruments. In voice formation, the resonating chambers are the pharynx, the mouth, and the nose. The pharynx is a chamber that lies immediately above the larynx (or voice box) and connects it with the oral and nasal cavities. As the vibrating air passes through these three chambers, certain overtones are amplified, and the voice acquires a distinctive quality. If much of the air column passes through the nose, the voice may acquire a nasal quality. This may be pleasant or unpleasant, according to its degree. If most of the air column goes through the mouth, bypassing the nose, the result may be a denasal quality, which tends to make the voice flat and uninteresting. By experimenting with pitch and with control of the resonating chambers, an individual may make substantial changes in voice quality. Figure 6.1 illustrates voice formation.

An agreeable voice quality seems to be an asset in communication. Some studies have shown that a good voice increases liking for and confidence in a person:

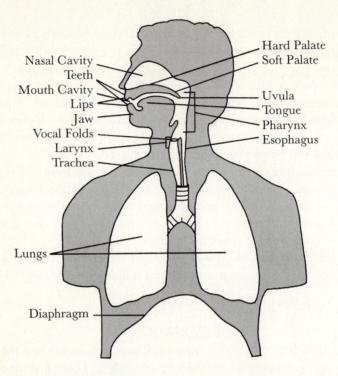

Nasal Cavity
Teeth
Mouth Cavity
Lips
Jaw
Vocal Folds
Larynx
Trachea

Hard Palate
Soft Palate
Uvula
Tongue
Pharynx
Esophagus

Lungs

Diaphragm

Figure 6.1 VOICE FORMATION.
Sound is produced when the diaphragm forces air from the lungs over the
vocal folds. As the vibrating air stream moves upward it emerges from both
the mouth and the nasal cavities, both of which resonate the tone. In the
mouth, vowels are formed by the shaping of the tongue and consonants by
pressure of the tongue on the teeth and gum ridge.
Redrawn from Edward Strother and Alan Huckleberry, The Effective Speaker
(Boston: Houghton Mifflin Company, 1968), p. 243.

High school and college graduates with clear, intelligent-sounding
voices have a much better chance of landing a job than those with
harsh or hard-to-understand voices .... A college on Long Island
... kept track of scores of job hunting graduates and established that
students who had participated in college dramatics, debating and
politics, and had cultivated good voices, landed jobs much more
quickly than other students.[3]

[3] Paul Green and Cliff Cochrane, ''Your Voice is Your Fortune,'' *This Week,* January 15,
1950, p. 8.

The study just quoted did not rule out factors other than voice that might have contributed to the success of the dramatics, debate, and political students. The results do, though, tend to support those of later studies showing that, in interpreting the meaning of messages, receivers place over five times as much importance on nonverbal cues as on the verbal message itself.[4]

The importance of emphasis to the interpretation of meaning can be illustrated by considering a single sentence: "I believe you are right." Note the different meanings of this sentence that can be created by placing the primary emphasis on different words:

I believe you are right (though nobody else seems to).

I *believe* you are right (but I'm not yet sure).

I believe *you* are right (not your opponents).

I believe you *are* right (although everything up to now has pointed to the contrary).

I believe you are *right* (I will now change my belief and act upon yours).[5]

Changes in emphasis and in the pattern of pauses will radically transform the meaning of the following unpunctuated sentences:

You hope she said too much (Who is speaking this sentence?)

A man called while you were out to lunch with your wife (Were you out to lunch with your wife?)

The teacher says the principal is a fool (Who is the fool: the teacher or the principal?)

Woman without her man would be a savage (Is man or woman the savage?)

What do you think I will let you drive my new car (Will I be permitted to drive it or not?)

---

[4] Albert Mehrabian, *Silent Messages* (Belmont, Calif.: Wadsworth, 1971), *passim.*

[5] Alma Sarett, Lew Sarett, and W. T. Foster, *Basic Principles of Speech* (Boston: Houghton Mifflin, 1966), p. 85.

If the above sentences were punctuated, we would know their meaning because the punctuation would provide clues as to what words are to be emphasized and where the pauses are to go. When one *hears* such sentences, however, the meaning is conveyed entirely by nonverbal cues.

ARTICULATION AND PRONUNCIATION

Articulation, or the production of correct vowel and consonant sounds, and *pronunciation* are the final stages of voice production. As the breath stream moves through the mouth, it is altered by the tongue and teeth to produce vowel and consonant sounds. Correct articulation and pronunciation are important in conveying meaning. If words are not properly articulated and pronounced, they may be confused with other words and the speaker's message may be misinterpreted. Articulation and pronunciation are also extremely important in helping the audience form impressions of the speaker's background and competence. In America, systematically poor articulation and pronunciation are associated with the speech of persons who do not know English well. Foreign and regional accents may add interest and attractiveness to speech, especially if they distort the language only slightly. Heavy accents, however, may seriously disrupt communication and cause listeners to become hostile toward the speaker. Native speakers of English whose articulation and pronunciation are nonstandard may seem undereducated, or even incompetent, except among groups where similar nonstandard pronunciation prevails. Persons who say *liberry* for *library, swaller* for *swallow, hunert* for *hundred,* and so on, lose the credibility and respect of many listeners. Their ability to communicate suffers accordingly.

VOLUME AND RATE

Changes in volume are necessary for emphasis and for correct pronunciation, but the speaker should also pay attention to his or her general loudness. Now that electronic amplifiers are readily available, speakers tend to neglect the ability to project the unamplified voice throughout a large auditorium. Sometimes, such speakers need a microphone even in smaller assemblies where the unamplified voice could easily be heard. You should practice speaking without a microphone in various situations until you learn to adjust your volume to audiences and halls of various sizes. This ability will make for better volume control even when the voice is amplified.

The normal rate of speech is between 150 and 185 words per minute. Rate is controlled by the duration of syllables and by pauses between individual words, phrases, and sentences. Short speeches delivered in an experimental setting by speakers who exceeded 185 words per minute (up to 275) did not cause the audience to understand less. A speaker going on for forty or forty-five minutes at that rate, however, probably would cause the audience to lose some of the message.

Changes in the rate of speaking are a common form of emphasis. A speaker who has been proceeding at a fairly rapid rate can underscore ideas by slowing down and speaking at an even pace. When noise is a distracting factor, increasing syllable duration definitely aids understanding. Sarett, Sarett, and Foster sum up the importance of the speaker's being able to control rate as follows: "In any case, variations in rate are essential to effective communication. Speech that sounds like either a buzz-saw or a metronome defeats its purpose."[6]

TIPS FOR EFFECTIVE USE OF BODY AND VOICE

As we said earlier, it is not easy to work the voice and body consciously to achieve a preplanned effect. Even an actor can't create grief, indignation, anger, or other emotions automatically. Actors learn their art by applying certain principles of effective acting. In the same way, speakers will find that bodily action and nonverbal voice cues are most effective when they spring spontaneously from the application of certain principles.

1. *Nonverbal cues should spring from a genuine desire to communicate.*
   Persons who really want to communicate become centered on their message: their attention is focused on what they have to say and on how the audience is receiving the message. They are not concerned with themselves or with the impression they are making. They do not see themselves as performers, but as agents for the transmission of ideas. This focus results in a lack of self-consciousness that allows body and voice to respond naturally and spontaneously to the message. It is from such an orientation that good nonverbal messages grow.

---

[6] Sarett, Sarett, and Foster, p. 366.

2. *Nonverbal cues should be appropriate to the topic, the audience, and the occasion.* Some topics demand greater action than others. Likewise, some audiences expect more nonverbal cues than others—an audience of entertainment personalities, for instance, or an audience of children. Finally, different occasions make different demands. A keynote speaker at a political convention is expected to gesture vigorously and to speak in an excited, compelling tone; a preacher at a funeral, however, moves slowly and solemnly and speaks with deliberate, impressive tones.

3. *Nonverbal cues should be appropriate to a conversational style of speaking.* In some ways, this rule is misleading, for it tends to suggest that a good speech should be delivered in the same way as good conversation. In fact, it means that good speech delivery should have the best characteristics of conversation while avoiding the bad ones. Some aspects of conversation that are *not* desirable are the conversationalist's lack of organization, which results in rambling and repetition, the frequently sloppy articulation, and the overuse of slang and colloquialisms. On the other hand, the spontaneity, directness, liveliness, and emphasis of conversation are desirable, and these qualities form the basis of the conversational style.

GENERAL STYLES OF DELIVERY

As a speaker delivers a speech, he or she must draw on the materials and ideas gathered during preparation. How is this best done? Politicians, ministers, lecturers, and other professional speakers have used three general ways of handling material, each of which has a distinctive influence on style. One way is to write out the speech and memorize it; the second is to write it out and read it; and the third is to speak extemporaneously. Let us consider the advantages and disadvantages of each of these methods in turn.

Carl Schurz, the nineteenth-century Republican politician, wrote out and memorized all of his speeches. Since on many occasions he spoke for over an hour, he had to spend countless hours in preparation. This is one of the great disadvantages of the memorized speech. Another is the lack of flexibility in manner of expression: many people lose spontaneity and vocal inflection when delivering a memorized speech. Likewise, they are unable to adapt readily to audience feedback or to any adjustments that may be needed during the course of the speech. Nevertheless, some speakers use this style effectively. Schurz, for instance, was credited by his contemporaries with being a graceful and persuasive speaker. His rapport and effectiveness with his audiences did not seem to be unfavorably affected by his use of memorization.

Reading from a written manuscript is an extremely common form of delivery among professional speakers. Its advantages are many. One can precisely control the length of a speech so that it fits into the allotted time frame for a TV presentation or other tightly structured format. One can also carefully word comments on sensitive subjects, as is often necessary for politicians, whose smallest remarks may stir public controversy. A speaker can release remarks to the press prior to delivery time to obtain more accurate and thorough coverage. President John F. Kennedy used this style of presentation, as have most recent presidents. All of President Abraham Lincoln's best speeches, including the inaugural ones and the Gettysburg Address, were written out and read. This form of preparation allowed Lincoln to polish his style and expression far more than he could when speaking extemporaneously.

There are several difficulties with writing out and reading a speech. Most people find it difficult to preserve a conversational tone, with its spontaneity and ease. Many people have trouble reading a speech without losing desirable variety and flexibility of voice. Nevertheless, this useful form of delivery has its advantages. You should experiment with it and try to master it.

In Chapter 3, we briefly described the extemporaneous style of delivery. The term *extemporaneous* should not be confused with *impromptu*. *Impromptu* means speaking off the cuff without formal preparation, although the speaker may have had much experience with the topic and may have given it some thought. For extemporaneous speeches, however, speakers research the topic, give it systematic thought, exercise judgment in selecting materials, and give careful thought to organization. They simply do not use a manuscript, nor do they memorize. They make up the language of the speech (not the evidence and ideas) as they deliver it. United States Representative Barbara Jordan of Texas used this style of speaking very effectively in the Nixon impeachment committee hearings. Many other figures in politics, religion, and public affairs use it, as well. The advantages are many. Speakers usually can be spontaneous, direct, and free in expression. They also learn to adapt to audience feedback and to compress or expand their speech to fit time limits. Best of all, they are usually able to express themselves naturally, without sounding studied and prerecorded, as people who memorize or read a speech often do. You should practice the extemporaneous method; of the three styles, it usually conveys the greatest command of the speaking situation.

SUMMARY

Nonverbal bodily actions and use of the voice convey a lot of information. Bodily actions include not only hand gestures, but also facial expression, posture, moving on the platform, and semiconscious movements that help the speaker adjust. Facial expression is one primary means by which the speaker shares feelings and attitudes with the audience. Hand gestures are used for emphasis and description. They should be spontaneous and should involve the entire body. A speaker should use them with a clear purpose and avoid excessive or flamboyant movement. Some bodily movements, called adaptors, help the speaker adjust to the situation; but avoid inappropriate movements, such as constantly playing with your glasses or wiping your brow.

Personal appearance—hair, clothing, general grooming—gives the audience clues about your socioeconomic class, your personality, your status, and sometimes your affiliation with a particular group.

Your voice tells much about your personality, but it is also an invaluable aid in enhancing your verbal messages. You need to learn to control it by understanding how it is produced. Sound begins with the vibration of the vocal folds and is resonated and given a unique quality by passage through the nasal and oral cavities. Articulation of the vowels and consonants takes place when the tongue is changed in shape or pressed against the teeth and gums.

In general, speeches are delivered extemporaneously, read from manuscript, or spoken from memory. The extemporaneous style is helpful to beginning speakers because, by using it, they are usually able to achieve spontaneous, direct, and free expression.

Exercises

1. Record one of your classroom speeches delivered extemporaneously from notes. Record the same speech as read from manuscript.

Compare the effectiveness of your delivery, especially your vocal variety and emphasis. Practice improving your delivery by making additional recordings.

2. Pantomime a simple task before the class. Select a task that requires several operations to complete, such as changing an automobile tire; fastening a wire to a picture and hanging it on the wall; fixing a camera on a tripod, posing a subject, and taking a picture; opening a closet, getting out a vacuum cleaner, running it over the floor, and putting it away; and so on. Ask the audience to identify what you are doing and to evaluate your effectiveness.

3. Observe people who talk with one another in conversation and describe the kinds of bodily activity they show. Observe your own behavior when you are speaking un-selfconsciously. Note any kinds of behaviors in yourself or others that could be transferred to the public speaking situation.

4. Make a speech that requires the description of a process. Practice the description in front of a mirror, watching to see if you can illustrate the process with appropriate actions. Use action freely and often.

5. Look up and practice the correct pronunciation of the following frequently mispronounced words:

athlete	just
attacked	larynx
comparable	length
drowned	mischievous
genuine	nuclear
grievous	preferable
infamous	sterile
impious	virile

Chapter Seven
STYLE

OVERVIEW

The nature of style: role of denotation and connotation
The elements of good style: clarity, vividness, forcefulness, and
  appropriateness
How to achieve the elements of good style
Speaking style vs. written style

Style is the individualistic way a person uses language. Two people, given the task of describing an old woman's face, would certainly word their descriptions differently. One might say, "She has fine, but heavily wrinkled features." The other might say, "Her little face is wrinkled like a walnut shell." While both of these expressions convey roughly the same image, there is a substantial difference in their impact on an audience. That difference arises from each person's own preferences in the use of language.

Language is the basic means of human communication. We transmit ideas and feelings to others through language, words, and sentences, and it is language that stirs up ideas and feelings in the brains of listeners. Thus, the two verbal descriptions of an aged face just given do not convey exactly the same idea; they could do so only if they were worded and spoken identically.

DENOTATION AND CONNOTATION

Although two words that are labeled "synonyms" are commonly supposed to mean the same thing, this is not so. Words have both denotative and connotative meanings. A synonym, while conveying a similar denotative meaning, must always have a slightly or even substantially different connotative meaning; that is, it must have different implications and associations. Take the word *contemporary*, for example. If you say that a man's dress is contemporary, you mean that it is of the period in which he is living. If, however, you were to use *modern* as a synonym for *contemporary*, you would suggest that his clothing is faddish or stylish in addition to being contemporary. It is possible for the man's clothing to be contemporary but not modern.

Thus, word choice is also a choice of image or meaning. Good speakers and writers know this and select words that suggest precisely the meanings they want. Careless communicators, on the other hand, use words as if they were interchangeable currency. Such people cannot distinguish the difference between *gift* and *present, drink* and *imbibe, shout* and *yell, sing* and *chant, laugh* and *chuckle,* and hundreds of other pairs. Such persons are inexact stylists, which is another way of saying that they are poor communicators.

STYLE AND WHAT IT ACCOMPLISHES

Many people think of style as an adornment, like jewelry. Such people make a distinction between manner of expression and substance. They believe that style may adorn without affecting the substance. This is comparable to saying, for instance, that a picnic table is the same as an oak dining-room table. We have already indicated that style is inseparable from substance, that a change in style is also a change in meaning. We may grant that a picnic table and an oak table are both tables, but they are not the same. Their style has changed the way in which people will regard them.

It is the same with language. Two messages may deal with essentially the same substance, but the messages will be considered distinctive by their receivers because of their stylistic elements. Good style is clear, vivid, forceful, and appropriate. Poor style is vague, dull, weak, and ill suited to its audience. In the sections that follow, we will discuss how to achieve the elements of good style.

CLARITY

To communicate successfully, a speaker must stir up ideas in the minds of the audience that are the same as the speaker's own ideas. Clarity in style accomplishes this goal. To achieve it, the speaker must use concrete rather than abstract words, simple rather than involved words, and correct rather than incorrect words.

Abstractions are by their very nature vague. Abstractions blur individual characteristics to make a single term cover countless specifics. The word *animal,* for instance, does not create a concrete image at all. At best, it allows the mind to imagine some living thing that is not a vegetable. As words become more concrete, images become clearer. If you say *reptile,* clarity improves, because now we know that mammals, birds, and insects are not included. But still the image is not clear. A reptile might be a snake, a turtle, or an alligator. Use of the word *snake* creates a concrete image that can be made even more concrete by use of the words *boa constrictor* or *rattlesnake*.

Consider how the following sentences become clearer and sharper when concrete and specific terms replace abstract words or expressions.

Professor Smith is a good teacher.
Professor Smith delivers well-organized, interesting, and sometimes humorous lectures.

She bought a lot of things at the store.
She went to Maas Brothers and bought a pink skirt, a white blouse, and a set of pearl earrings.

The senator has been dishonest in the past.
The senator lied about his expense account and denied he held any stock in ITT when, in fact, he owned 2500 shares.

He has a big, flashy car.
He owns a Lincoln Continental with a red vinyl top, a glossy black body, and mag wheels.

The preceding examples of abstractions all refer to objects or observable human actions. A different form of abstraction is involved in terms like *justice, love,* and *brotherhood,* which really represent rules for behavior that arise from specific human transactions. *Justice,* for instance, implies the application of certain principles in the treatment of people by their government and by one another. Not everyone agrees on the nature of the rules that underlie the concept of justice. Clarity of style thus requires that such terms be clearly defined, especially through examples, if there is a chance of disagreement. When people speak out of the same culture or subculture, however, a definition may not be needed; there may be substantial agreement among people of that culture about what justice is. Under these circumstances, the use of such abstractions can be a powerful, emotional force that emphasizes the unity of the group and blocks out differences. The American Declaration of Independence is a good example of the use of emotionally unifying abstractions.

Clarity of style also comes from using simple terms. English tends to be a language composed of one-syllable words. Words of more than one syllable that stand for commonly used concepts tend to be shortened by English speakers to one syllable; for example, *gasoline* is shortened to *gas, automobile* to *car, laboratory* to *lab,* and *telephone* to *phone.* Lincoln's Gettysburg Address consisted of 272 words, 190 of which had one syllable and 56 of which had two syllables. Some of the most effective novelists in the English language show a preference for simple words. Of the words used by Somerset Maugham, Kathryn Mansfield, John Galsworthy, Sinclair Lewis, Thomas B. Macaulay, Robert Lewis Stevenson, and Charles Dickens, 70 to 78 percent were of one syllable.[1]

University professors frequently speak and write in violation of the rule to use simple words. In certain technical fields, complex words are needed for accuracy, but often communications seem deliberately loaded with difficult terms. In the following passage, a professor is writing in a textbook for college students about experiments in which scientists applied electrical stimulation to the brains of rats:

In these explorations during voluntary activity of the animal two electrovital fields were tapped at the same time and from them both synchronous and isomorphic and asynchronous and anisomorphic action-current patterns of a suggested informative distribution were recorded. It was observed that the degree of synchronization and isomorphism of the patterns varied in direct proportion to the propinquity of the compared contralateral homologous fields. Thus, the directly apposed motor fields afforded the greatest fidelity in synchronization and isomorphism, and the auditory and more disparate of the compared contralateral homologous fields afforded the least fidelity in synchronization and isomorphism.[2]

This passage could have been written in simpler terms without sacrificing accuracy.

Government officials also have a preference for complex rather than simple terms. During World War II, a civilian defense official sent a letter to federal agencies concerning blackout preparation. The letter read:

[1] G. G. Williams, *Creative Writing for Advanced College Classes* (New York: Harper and Brothers, 1954), p. 106.

[2] Lee E. Travis, *Speech Pathology* (New York: D. Appleton & Co., 1931), p. 162.

Such preparations shall be made as will completely obscure all federal government buildings and non-federal buildings occupied by the government during an air raid . . . from visibility by means of internal or external illumination. Such obscuration may be obtained either by blackout construction or by termination of the illumination . . . ; in buildings in which production must continue during the blackout, construction must be provided so that internal illumination may continue. Other areas may be obscured by termination of the illumination.[3]

It is said that Franklin Roosevelt rewrote the memorandum as follows: "Tell them that in buildings where they have to keep the work going, to put something across the windows. In buildings where they can afford to stop working for a while, turn out the lights." Roosevelt's translated version is certainly much clearer than the original, and much briefer, too.

Clarity of language is difficult to achieve without using words correctly. Language is a code that consists, in a given culture, of a set of agreed-upon meanings. Thus, *horse* is the agreed-upon term for a certain four-footed mammal. It cannot be called *mule,* although a mule may resemble a horse in some ways. The same is true of the grammatical structure of the language: incorrect tense or faulty subject-verb agreement may result in muddy, inaccurate communication. Here are a few examples of inaccuracy in the use of words and grammatical constructions:

Irregardless	Regardless
Could of	Could have
Him and me went	He and I went
The TV media	The TV medium
Data is	Data are
Us Americans	We Americans
It does not effect me	It does not affect me
Sit it there	Set it there
You can't hardly see	You can hardly see
Punishment will learn him	Punishment will teach him
Aggravated	Irritated
Leave me think	Let me think

[3] See W. Norwood Brigance, *Speech: Its Techniques and Disciplines in a Free Society,* (New York: Appleton-Century-Crofts, 1961), p. 301.

These terms not only cloud the clarity of communication, they also convey negative impressions of the speaker, resulting in loss of credibility. Most people associate such inaccurate usages with lack of education, low socioeconomic status, lack of self-esteem, and perhaps stupidity. All of these perceptions are negative and work against the speaker's ability to influence listeners.

VIVIDNESS

By using figures of speech, especially similes and metaphors, speakers can add vividness to their styles. A simile is a comparison between two things in which the word *like* or *as* is used. The following sentences, for instance, are similes: "The diamond was as small as a grain of sand." "He fumed like a volcano." Similarly, a metaphor presents two things as being the same, but does so without using the word *like* or *as*. The above examples would be transformed into metaphors as follows: "The diamond was a mere grain of sand." "He was a volcano of irritation." Figures of speech should not be overused. Nor should straining for picturesque effect be too obvious. Used carefully, however, figures of speech can be remarkably effective. Note the following examples:

Abraham Lincoln: "A house divided against itself cannot stand." I believe this government cannot endure, permanently half *slave* and half *free*.

Martin Luther King: But one hundred years later, the Negro still is not free. One hundred years later, the life of the Negro is still sadly crippled by the manacles of segregation and the chains of discrimination.

One hundred years later, the Negro lives on a lonely island of poverty in the midst of a vast ocean of material prosperity. One hundred years later, the Negro is still languished in the corners of American society and finds himself an exile in his own land. So we have come here today to dramatize a shameful condition.

In a sense we have come to our nation's capital to cash a check. When the architects of our republic wrote the magnificent words of the Constitution and the Declaration of Independence, they were signing a promissory note to which every American was to fall heir.[4]

[4] Quoted by Roy Hill in *Rhetoric of Racial Revolt* (Denver: Golden Bell Press, 1964), p. 371. Reprinted by permission.

Ralph Zimmerman: Medical authorities agree that a hemophilic joint hemorrhage is one of the most excruciating pains known to mankind. To concentrate a large amount of blood into a small compact area causes a pressure that words can never hope to describe. And how well I remember the endless pounding, squeezing pain. When you seemingly drown in your own perspiration, when your teeth ache from incessant clenching, when your tongue floats in your mouth and bombs explode back of your eyeballs; when darkness and light fuse into one hue of grey; when day becomes night and night becomes day—time stands still—and all that matters is that ugly pain. The scars of pain are not easily erased.[5]

Similes and metaphors of this kind visualize and strengthen ideas and give them greater intensity. To use figures of speech effectively, you should avoid trite and overused comparisons. To say "as sweet as a rose," "as pretty as a picture," or "as blue as the sky" is ineffective because these terms have been so frequently used that they have lost the power to excite vivid images.

Overused adjectives and adverbs fill everyday speech. To some people, everything is "nice" or "interesting." They had a *nice* time, received a *nice* gift, thought it was a *nice* day, and so on. Other overworked words are *real* or *really*, as in the sentence *It was a really good show; very*, as in *very* good, *very* pleased, and so on; and a whole group of similar expressions: *cool* behavior, *awfully* happy, a *funny* experience, a *lovely* dress, a *cute* dress, *most* unusual. These words fail to create any sharp images and are excess weight in the sentences in which they occur.

Finally, vividness (and also correctness) comes through using words that have colorful connotative meanings. For instance, transforming a *rope* into a *noose* suggests all the imagery of a hanging; referring to a *house as a hovel* draws an image of broken-down poverty; and calling a woman *slender* rather than *skinny* changes the perception of that woman from unhealthy to stylish. You should take care that the connotative meaning of words conveys the impression you want. To describe the Supreme Court of the United States as a *gang* of judges may be fine if you intend to condemn them, but it is a disastrous choice if you plan to praise them.

---

[5] Ralph Zimmerman, "Mingled Blood," in *Contemporary American Speeches*, ed. Wil Linkugel, et al. (Belmont, Calif.: Wadsworth, 1969), p. 202.

FORCEFULNESS

The next element of good style that we will discuss is forcefulness. A good way to be forceful is to use simple sentence structure. Simple sentences or compound sentences joined by conjunctions tend to be more forceful than complex sentences or compound-complex ones. One example should be enough to illustrate this. Someone might say, "The tree, which stood before the ancient house, shed, every fall, its colorful leaves in a thick carpet upon the lawn." The impact of this sentence would be improved by saying, "The tree stood before the ancient house. Each fall it shed its colorful leaves in a thick carpet on the lawn."

Forceful expression can also be achieved by repeating a grammatical structure. Winston Churchill told the English people of the British government's determination to resist invasion by German forces as follows: "We shall fight them on the beaches, we shall fight on the landing grounds, we shall fight in the fields and in the streets, we shall fight in the hills; we shall never surrender." The repetition of the words *we shall fight* gives force to this passage. Its simple sentences expressed in simple terms add still more to its impact.

Another quotation from Martin Luther King's "I Have a Dream" speech will illustrate how repeating a grammatical structure enhances forcefulness:

And so let freedom ring from the prodigious hilltops of New Hampshire.

Let freedom ring from the mighty mountains of New York.

Let freedom ring from the heightening Alleghenies of Pennsylvania.

Let freedom ring from the snow-capped Rockies of Colorado.

Let freedom ring from the curvaceous slopes of California.

But not only that.

Let freedom ring from Stone Mountain of Georgia.

Let freedom ring from Lookout Mountain of Tennessee.

Let freedom ring from every hill and molehill of Mississippi, from every mountainside, let freedom ring.

And when this happens, and when we allow freedom to ring, when we let it ring from every village and hamlet, from every state and city, we will be able to speed up that day when all of God's children—black men and white men, Jews and Gentiles, Catholics and Protestants—will be able to join hands and to sing in the words of the old Negro spiritual, "Free at last, free at last; thank God Almighty, we are free at last."[6]

Another form of sentence structure that resembles the above passages is called *antithesis*. Antithesis involves coupling opposite concepts in grammatically parallel sentences for the purpose of contrast. Here is an example drawn from a speech by Malcolm X. Note how Malcolm contrasts being American with being a victim of America and sees the American dream as the American nightmare:

No, I'm not an American. I'm one of the 22 million black people who are victims of Americanism. One of the 22 million black people who are victims of democracy. . . .

I'm speaking as a victim of this American system. And I see America through the eyes of the victim. I don't see any American dream; I see an American nightmare.[7]

Often antithesis consists of coupling nouns or adjectives of opposite meaning in short sentences, as in the following: "The proposal is not wisdom but folly. It will bring not security but war." Antithesis can be overdone and should be used sparingly in speech. If used too frequently it tends to make a speech appear showy and stilted.

Rhetorical questions also give forcefulness to speech. Questions create tension as the audience awaits the answer. Used properly, questions can create excitement and emotion in the listener. In his 1775 "Liberty or Death" speech, Patrick Henry, speaking to the Virginia Colonial legislature, answered the argument that the colonies were too weak to resist Great Britain with a paragraph of rhetorical questions:

They tell us, sir, that we are weak; unable to cope with so formidable an adversary. But when shall we be stronger? Will it be the next week, or the next year? Will it be when we are totally disarmed, and

---

[6] Hill, pp. 374–375. Reprinted by permission.
[7] *Malcolm X Speaks*, ed. George Britman (New York: Grove Press, 1965), p. 26.

when a British guard shall be stationed in every house? Shall we
gather strength by irresolution and inaction? Shall we acquire the
means of effectual resistance by lying supinely on our backs, and
hugging the delusive phantom of hope, until our enemies shall have
bound us hand and foot? Sir, we are not weak, if we make a proper
use of the means which the God of nature hath placed in our power.

Another type of sentence structure that adds to forcefulness is known as
climatic arrangement. This structure usually consists of a series of dependent
clauses that build up to, and complete the argument for, the claim made in
the independent clause. Examine, for instance, how the following sentence, again from Patrick Henry's "Liberty or Death," builds to a
climax:

If we wish to be free—if we mean to preserve inviolate these
inestimable privileges for which we have been so long contending—
if we mean not basely to abandon the noble struggle in which we
have so long engaged . . . we must fight! I repeat it, sir, we must
fight!

A final rule about forcefulness in style is that a speaker should use active
rather than passive voice. Passive voice reverses a sentence so that the
direct object (receiver of the action of the verb) becomes the subject, and
the actor (performer of the action) becomes the predicate. Here are several
sentences written in the passive voice, coupled with their active-voice
counterparts. Note how the active-voice version gains in forcefulness (and
is also shorter):

The book was torn by him.
He tore the book.

Slavery is regarded by them as a moral, social, and political wrong.
They regard slavery as a moral, social, and political wrong.

Tax problems, unemployment, inflation, and international relations
were some of the topics commented on by the president.
The president commented on tax problems, unemployment, inflation, and international relations.

APPROPRIATENESS

Appropriateness means fitting your language to the occasion and the audience. The football coach, speaking to a local quarterback club, will use informal language highlighted with slang and references to the special vocabulary of sports. He may also use language that would be considered indecent or offensive in a more formal circumstance. In contrast, a minister preaching a eulogy at a funeral will use formal diction that fits the sober mood of the event. Below are a few factors to keep in mind for choosing appropriate language.

Audience knowledge of topic.   Professional people have difficulty communicating at times because they use terms that are familiar to them but unknown to a general audience. The lawyer who speaks to an ordinary audience and sprinkles his sentences with terms such as *voir dire* and *certiorari* will not be understood. Doctors, professors, computer specialists, and others who are in highly specialized types of work need to tailor their vocabulary to audience knowledge of the topic.

Audience attitude toward the topic.   The use of inappropriate language could inflame an audience with strong attitudes on a controversial topic. If you describe an audience's known position as ''foolish'' and ''ill considered'' you are likely to provoke anger and make the task of changing minds more difficult. If you say, however, that a position is one that many people may disagree with, you might get an audience to listen without arousing hostility. There may be occasions when you do not care to speak moderately, when you want to express your conviction without concern about your listeners. If so, speak as bluntly as you like, but if you really want to influence people's views, beware of insulting them with harsh evaluations of attitudes unlike your own.

Commonality of experience.   To illustrate your ideas, choose examples that involve persons who are like members of your audience. If an example is about persons from the same city, region, or occupation as the audience, it may appeal to them more strongly than if it involves strangers. If possible, use the experience of local bankers when speaking to bankers, not the experience of automobile mechanics. Also, you can refer to common cultural experiences you share with the audience. For instance, events or themes from recent movies and TV programs are a source of such material. Another source is personal examples based on experiences common to you and your audience. You might say, for instance,

---

Every one of us has had a costly experience with a product that doesn't give us the service we have the right to expect. Recently I bought a new Toyota and drove it to Atlanta. It was four weeks old and had only 1600 miles on it. Outside Macon the camshaft broke, disabling the car. It sat in the repair shop for three weeks because parts were not available. During that time I was out the expense of a rental car less the meager $75 that Toyota allots under such conditions. The consumer movement, about which I have been speaking, is one of the few sources you can turn to that will try to influence legislation to protect people who have such problems.

Finally, by using personal pronouns such as *you, we, us,* and *our,* you can build a sense of identity with persons in the audience.

Offensive and taboo expressions.   In highly emotional confrontations, such as occurred in the civil rights movement of the sixties, speakers have been known to use four-letter obscenities. However, use of such words generally brings negative reactions and, ordinarily, should be avoided. Even mild forms of swear words, such as *damn,* should be used with caution. Dan Rothwell, after studying the effects of obscenities in the speeches of agitators, concluded that four-letter words turn the majority of Americans against an agitator's cause. Such words cloud the issues by calling undue attention to themselves. They also arouse a spirit of counterattack and increase the opposition of listeners.[8]

Ethnic, racial, or religious slurs are inappropriate for much the same reasons that obscenities are. If you refer to persons as *wops, kikes, niggers, hillbillies,* and so on, you provoke anger and aggressive reactions that shift attention from the issue you are discussing to the language itself. The audience will tend to reject your proposition not on its merits but because of the language used.

---

[8] Dan Rothwell, "Verbal Obscenity: Time for Second Thoughts," *Western Speech,* 35 (1971), 231-242.

Similar considerations apply to the use of sexist terms. Speakers often unintentionally offend a part of their audience by using insulting sexual reference such as: "That's an old wives' tale" or "He acts like an old woman" or "He has the mind of a girl." But often sexual slights are more subtle. One talks of fire*men,* repair*men,* police*men,* post*men,* and so forth, as if these occupations were the special preserve of men. Even chair*man* suggests that women don't have the ability or opportunity to preside over a meeting. The generic terms *man* and *mankind* identify the species only in the male gender. Finally, the use of male pronouns, while grammatically correct, may be offensive to women. Consider, for instance, the following sentence: "The research professor stands at the frontier of knowledge; he is the pioneer of new ideas; his discoveries underlie the technology used by industry." Clearly, male pronouns here suggest that university research is done by men not women.

The sexual implications of words and expressions like those mentioned can be avoided if you substitute such terms as chairperson, police officer, humankind, and the like, for the potentially offensive terms. Frequently, you can avoid undesirable pronoun references simply by rewording the sentence as plural: "Research professors stand at the frontier of knowledge; they . . ."

It is difficult to avoid all sexist expressions. They are deeply imbedded in our language. But by being aware of their presence and consciously checking their use, we may avoid some of their unfortunate implications.

SPEAKING STYLE VERSUS ORAL STYLE

Speaking style can be and usually is different from writing style. Effective oral style is tuned to the ear rather than the eye, and thus has its own peculiar rules. In 1936, Gladys Borchers, of the University of Wisconsin, summarized eighteen characteristics of oral style:

1. In oral style the sentences should be shorter.
2. There should be greater variety in sentence structure in oral style.
3. Sentences are less involved in structure in oral style.
4. Personal pronouns are more numerous in oral style.
5. Oral style requires more careful adaptation to the speaker.
6. Oral style requires more careful adaptation to the audience.

7. Oral style requires more careful adaptation to the occasion.
8. Oral style requires more careful adaptation to the subject matter.
9. Fragmentary sentences may be used in oral style.
10. Slang may be used in oral style.
11. Contractions are used more often in oral style.
12. Indigenous language should be more predominant in oral style.
13. Oral style is more euphonious.
14. Repetition is more necessary in oral style.
15. Concrete words should be used more often in oral style.
16. Effusive style or copiousness is more predominant in oral style.
17. Vehement style is more predominant in oral style.
18. The rhythm of oral style is different from the rhythm of written style.[9]

Borchers offered these observations as hypotheses to be confirmed by experimentation. Later investigators have confirmed some of them. After analyzing selected, prepared, written and spoken messages of speech students, Gibson, Gruner, Kibler, and Kelly concluded that

The spoken style was significantly more readable, more interesting and contained a simpler vocabulary than the written style, tending to confirm the supposition of some speech textbook writers that spoken style is different from written style on certain variables.[10]

Other investigators have found that oral communication contains more short, easy words, more personal pronouns, more self-reference terms, and more verbs and adjectives. It is, in general, less abstract than written communication.[11]

---

[9] Gladys Borchers, "An Approach to the Problem of Oral Style," *Quarterly Journal of Speech,* 22 (February 1936), 115–116.
[10] James Gibson, Charles Gruner, Robert Kibler, and Francis Kelly, "A Quantitative Examination of Differences between Oral and Written Style," *Speech Monographs,* 33 (1966), 451.
[11] Joseph DeVito, *The Psychology of Speech and Language* (New York: Random House, 1970), p. 11.

One writer, Rudolf Flesch, analyzed many samples of written language to determine those characteristics of style that make for ease of understanding. While Flesch dealt with written communication, his findings support the generalizations that we have made about the nature of oral style. Flesch found that comprehension was improved when

Sentences were composed of relatively few words. In general, a short sentence was more easily understood than a long, involved one.
Words were composed of few syllables. Long words of many syllables were difficult to understand. The meaning of a passage made up of short words of one or two syllables was much more easily grasped.
Personal words and sentences were frequent. If a passage contained many personal pronouns, such as *you, us,* and *we,* it was more easily understood than if it contained many impersonal or abstract terms.

Flesch created a method for estimating readability by counting the length of sentences, the average number of syllables per word, and the number of personal words in a passage. This method has been used by a number of investigators in the field of communication and has been found to support what experts judge to be an oral as opposed to a written style.[12]

The latest study to confirm the commonly accepted differences between oral and written style was done by Lois Einhorn, of Indiana University, in 1978. She contrasted seven stylistic features in samples of oral and written messages and arrived at the following conclusion:

. . . in comparison to written style, oral style uses significantly more personal references, more personal pronouns of the first- and second-person singular and plural, shorter thought units, more repetition of words, more monosyllabic words, and more familiar words. No significant difference was found for variety of thought unit length.[13]

The difference between an oral and a written style of expression can be seen in the following two passages. The first passage is from a speech by

[12] Rudolf Flesch, *The Art of Plain Talk,* (New York: Harper and Row, 1946), *passim.*
[13] Lois Einhorn, ''Oral and Written Style: An Examination of Differences,'' *Southern Speech Communication Journal,* 43 (1978), 302.

Herbert S. Richey, chairman of the board of the U.S. Chamber of
Commerce, called "The Real Cause of Inflation." Read it and try to
identify those elements that make for the direct, conversational quality of
oral style.

Why is the private sector starved for capital?

The finger of suspicion points to the public sector, the government. Think of it this way: Suppose that all economic growth is
caused by a magic powder which I'll call "growth stuff." Before
growth can occur, this powder must be sprinkled over the place
where growth is wanted—just like fertilizer.

This magic powder is difficult and time-consuming to make, so
the supply cannot be expanded rapidly. The manufacturing facilities
for the powder are all in the private sector of the economy.

If you controlled the supply of this powder, you could decide how
the economy would grow. But you would have to make choices:

Sprinkle it evenly over both the public and the private sectors
and each grows slowly.
Sprinkle it over the public sector alone and the public sector
grows rapidly while the private sector stagnates.
Use it on the private sector alone and that grows while the
public sector marks time.

Looks like six of one, half-dozen of the other, doesn't it? But there
is a very important difference. If you use all of the growth stuff on
the public sector, then the production of everything slows down in
the private sector, including the production of growth stuff itself.

On the other hand, if you use most of the growth stuff on the
private sector, then the production of growth stuff speeds up. Eventually you'll have more to spread around; more for the public sector,
too. But it takes time.[14]

Things you may have noted are shorter and uncomplicated sentences,
fragmentary sentences, use of the personal pronoun *you* to involve the

[14] Herbert S. Richey, "The Real Cause of Inflation," *Vital Speeches of the Day*, 43
(1976–1977), 388. Reprinted by permission.

audience, a simple vocabulary, and very concrete words. If you did, you picked out some of the things that make for good oral style.

Now read and analyze the following selection from a speech by E. Bartell, president of Stonehill College. In the speech quoted, he was commenting on the loss of public respect for colleges and universities.

The timing of this slip from heroic virtue has happened to coincide with a major increase in government activity to effect within the institutions of our society through traditional powers of taxation and regulation an historically increasing range of public goals and purposes whose time has perceptibly arrived. So it is not strange that the active intervention of the government, federal, state and local, in the affairs of colleges and universities has suddenly become for administrators in higher education a dominant source of preoccupation and worry. Government regulation of business has a long enough history to have already become canonized in undergraduate courses and textbooks. However, the deflowered maiden of higher education, so long accustomed to be the spokesperson of public virtue in society, finds herself uneasy in her new status, so recent and sudden that she is not yet sure whether she has been publicly ravished or has become the innocent but willing partner in a morally ambiguous affair with social power, wealth and influence.[15]

You probably noted the absence of almost all of the characteristics of Richey's speech. The sentences are long and complex, there is no use of *you*, the vocabulary is complex, and the whole passage is very abstract, except for a single metaphor in the last sentence. In spite of the fact that the passage is from a speech, it has many of the characteristics of written style.

When a speaker elects to use oral style, his or her speech shows the characteristics that we have noted. Oral style is, thus, probably the most appropriate for the speaker to use and, generally, the most satisfying for audiences to hear. But many occasions, including funeral orations, eulogies, and sermons, require very solemn and formal speech style. Moreover, many speeches must be written out to ensure accurate expression

[15] E. Bartell, "Higher Education and Government," *Vital Speeches of the Day,* 43 (1976–1977), 389. Reprinted by permission.

and to hold to time limits. Such speeches may not display the language characteristics typical of oral style, but they may be just as effective.

Thus, as a general rule the best course is probably to talk with the simplicity and spontaneity of conversation. You should remember, however, that an elevated, more complex and elaborate style may occasionally be required.

SUMMARY

Style is the individualistic way a person uses language. To use language effectively a person must distinguish between what a word denotes and what it connotes. The elements of good style are clarity, vividness, forcefulness, and appropriateness. Clarity is achieved by the use of specific and concrete words and from the use of simple words and sentences. Vividness comes from the use of figures of speech, especially similes and metaphors. Forcefulness, like clarity, comes from the use of simple, concrete terms and from sentence structure that has elements like repetition, antithesis, or climax. Appropriateness fits language to the audience's knowledge of the topic and to their attitude toward it. Citing experiences that are common to the audience and the speaker can enhance a speech. An appropriate speech will respect the audience's sensitivity to obscenity and to ethnic, racial, religious, and sexist insults.

Speaking style differs from written style because it is more direct and informal and is made up of sentences that are shorter, less complicated, more inclined to be fragmentary and sprinkled with personal pronouns.

Exercises

1. Write out a three-minute speech in manuscript form on a subject of your own choosing. Deliver the same speech extemporaneously from notes. Record the latter. Listen to the speech played back and compare the language you used with that used to express the same ideas in the manuscript.
2. Select six or eight paragraphs randomly from a speech by black activist Jessie Jackson. Compare the paragraphs' sentence structure, word usage, and so on, with several randomly chosen paragraphs from Martin Luther King's speech ''Love, Law and Civil Disobedience.'' What conclusions can you draw?

3. Make a recording of one of your classroom speeches and analyze your use of language. Watch especially for trite, overused words. Make a list of them and come up with alternative expressions. List what you can do to improve the vividness and forcefulness of your sentences. Reword some sentences to see how much improvement you can make.

4. Select a speech from a recent issue of *Vital Speeches* that seems effective to you. Prepare to describe the language techniques used in it to the class. Comment on sentence structure, use of figures of speech, word choice, and other aspects of style that have been discussed in this chapter.

Chapter Eight
LISTENING

OVERVIEW

Listening is the counterpart of speaking. The speaker transmits a message that flows across a channel, as was indicated in Chapter 1, to its destination: a person who listens, understands, thinks about the message, and responds. A flow of reactions, or feedback, returns from the listener to the speaker, who responds, thus starting another cycle of communication. So speaker and listener are linked together, each reacting to the other in a joint effort at understanding.

Listening is the most common communication activity for most people. It has been estimated that the average person spends about 70 percent of his or her waking hours in some form of communication: 9 percent of the time is spent in writing, 16 percent in reading, 30 percent in speaking, and 45 percent in listening.[1] Much of a person's knowledge of current political and social events comes from listening. Also, many attitudes and beliefs are based on information and ideas that have come through listening.

It would appear, therefore, that listening is an activity that everyone ought to be aware of and good at. Unfortunately, few people ever think about their listening ability. Fewer still ever make a serious effort to improve that ability. We will try in this chapter to help you avoid that situation by analyzing the nature of the listening process and by giving you some suggestions on how to improve your own listening.

KINDS OF LISTENING

An easy way to classify the kinds of listening is by the kind of communication that is taking place between speaker and audience. Accordingly, we can distinguish three basic types: (1) listening for pleasure; (2) listening for

---

[1] Elizabeth Andersch and Loren Stats, *Speech for Everyday Use* (New York: Rinehart and Company, 1960), p. 164.

understanding; and (3) listening for persuasion. When people attend a symphony concert, a movie, or a Broadway production, they listen to enjoy. This does not mean that listening for pleasure excludes all elements of understanding and evaluation. These elements are present, of course. But the understanding and evaluation in such situations help to explain and enhance the enjoyment offered by the experience. A full discussion of listening for pleasure is beyond the scope of this book. We will concentrate on the remaining two types.

LISTENING FOR UNDERSTANDING

As students, you often have to listen to understand meaning. Every time you attend a lecture on the social criticism implied in some literary work or on the impact of the frontier on American culture, you are placed in a situation where understanding the material is of primary importance. You have to understand what the professor is talking about to pass the course with a decent grade. Listening for understanding will continue to be very important after you leave your college or university. Regardless of what job you find yourself in, you will have to listen to explanations of policies and programs and participate in carrying them out. The ability to listen carefully and precisely will be invaluable to you. Rewards like promotions and salary increases often depend on efficient listening.

LISTENING FOR PERSUASION

As citizens, you will frequently listen to proposals for changes in policy, procedures, beliefs, and attitudes. These proposals will be accompanied by reasons for what is wrong with present practices and predictions of what proposed changes will do. You will listen for understanding to these arguments, of course, but beyond that you will listen to evaluate and criticize. In this context, to criticize does not mean to find fault for the sake of finding fault. Rather, it means to test: to weigh and consider the quality of reasons given for change, and to judge the probable consequences if a change is made. As a critic of speaking, you will listen to evaluate a communicator's motives, sources, and thought processes. By doing so, you will decide how you will react to the speaker's attempts at persuasion.

STEPS IN LISTENING

To listen well, you must make a series of responses to a communication. The first step is *attending* to or tuning in the message. Many listeners are weak at this stage. They seem unable to concentrate on the message for more than a few moments. The second step is *understanding*, being able to take in accurately what the message means, with all its implications. The third step is *assimilation* of the material. Assimilation means relating the message to your previous knowledge and evaluating it in terms of your present stock of beliefs, attitudes, and needs. The fourth step is *reaction*, deciding what kind of response to make to the message. Is the knowledge conveyed useful to you in some way? How? Are the proposals recommended something you approve of and will support? If so, how? Perhaps the entire speech has nothing to do with you, and you wish only to forget it. In some way, however, you will respond; and your response will be useful feedback to the speaker.

IMPROVING LISTENING

Not a lot is known about efficiency in listening. Several studies have been done in which the traits of good listeners were compared with the traits of poor listeners. The results have shed some light on the factors that make for good listening. One of the best studies was published in 1948 by Ralph Nichols, and later studies have added very little to Nichols's findings. According to Nichols, good listeners

1. Have superior language skills as shown by their ability to read well, to use English grammar correctly, and to use a large vocabulary.
2. Have the ability to detect organizational patterns in discourse, and to fit supporting materials in a message to main points.
3. Have the ability to draw inferences about the import or meaning of the material.
4. Have an interest in the subject and ability to see its significance.
5. Are able to adjust emotionally to the speaker's topic.
6. Are not physically fatigued or debilitated.[2]

It takes time to improve listening skills. Inspection of the above list shows that good listeners have skills that they have developed over a long period. Their linguistic ability, for instance (reading ability, grammatical

[2] Ralph Nichols, "Factors in Listening Comprehension," *Speech Monographs,* 15 (1948), 154–163.

correctness, large vocabulary), did not develop overnight. Neither did their ability to detect organizational patterns or to draw conclusions from the material. These abilities are the result of continuous attention and sustained effort. You should understand, then, that a program to improve listening must continue indefinitely. There are some things you can do, however, that will bring immediate improvement.

1. *Adopt practices that will improve your concentration and ability to pay attention.* First of all, try to avoid external distractions when you listen. Sit away from windows where you might see distracting things outside. Try to adjust the room temperature so that it's comfortable. Choose a seat from which you can both see and hear well. Often such measures, while not crucial, are helpful.

   Try also to avoid internal distractions. Consciously put away thoughts about other classes, upcoming examinations, or dates, and other matters. Don't have a heavy meal immediately before listening, since that will make you sluggish. Wear comfortable clothing.

   Try to have a frame of mind favorable to listening. Learn something about the speaker and the topic. Try to understand what the talk might offer you that would be worthwhile. Examine all the fine points of the speaker's topic. How will it relate to you? Don't dismiss it out of hand as irrelevant. Maybe it will be relevant some years from now. Will this speech help you enlarge your vocabulary, improve your grammatical skills, increase your knowledge of the world in general?

2. *Listen for the major arguments of the speech, and try to relate the details or supporting materials to them.* A speech will usually follow one or more of the organizational patterns discussed in Chapter 4. Is the organization problem-solution, cause and effect, chronological, or one of the other patterns? Whatever the pattern, there will usually be just two or three major points or claims. Try to isolate these points, and then listen for the speaker's supporting materials. Which of the main points does a particular example, statistic, or piece of testimony support?

   It has been estimated that college students remember no more than 25 percent of a communication when tested immediately afterward. This seems a small portion, but how much you remember is not as significant as what you remembered. A person who remembers only scattered bits of poorly related material (and this is what often happens) has done a poor job of listening. But people who remember the key ideas of the talk and are able to relate several pieces of significant supporting material to those ideas have done a good job of listening, even if they can recall only 25 percent of the total material. Try taking notes to improve your ability to separate and relate main points and supporting materials.

3. *Don't evaluate or criticize until you understand.* When a speaker states a point and begins developing it, some listeners have a strong tendency to assume that they know what the speaker is going to say. This is especially true of listeners who have had some continuing contact with the speaker or of listeners who know the speaker's attitudes and political position. Thinking that they know what will be said, such listeners no longer listen. Instead, they busy themselves with evaluating the speaker's supposed position. It is better to hear the speaker out before evaluating. You may be correct in assuming that you know the position he or she will take, but you could be wrong. Being a good listener means being sure you understand clearly what it is that you are criticizing.

4. *Don't let the speaker's reputation, appearance, or delivery cause you to listen poorly.* Listen to the President of the United States just as critically as you would to one of your classmates. Follow the same rule for other high-status figures, such as college presidents, corporation executives, and entertainment personalities. Sometimes people are led to accept uncritically the messages of such highly respected sources, although those messages would not stand up under proper logical scrutiny. On the other hand, don't downgrade the ideas of someone of unknown reputation or of someone whose reputation is not completely positive. Remember that a good listener evaluates ideas, not personalities.

Like reputation, physical appearance and delivery often disrupt listening. Just because a person wears shabby clothes and delivers speech awkwardly and hesitantly, you should not assume that that person has nothing worthwhile to say or that his or her proposals are necessarily faulty. Likewise, a well-dressed person who delivers a speech with magnetic force should not automatically be believed. Substance and appearance are two different things. You should judge a speaker on the former, not the latter.

5. *Don't get an emotional block because of the speaker's subject.* You may have strong preformed ideas on some subjects, such as abortion, taxes, student government, and grading practices. These attitudes may cause you to hear only what you want to hear. Some experimenters have suggested the existence of a process called "selective exposure." This process is defined as the human tendency to listen and attend to messages that support personal beliefs and attitudes and to avoid messages that are neutral or hostile. Various experimenters have found that people exposed to taboo words take longer to recognize them than people take to recognize neutral words. From this finding, it seems likely that, unless you guard against it, you may respond to offensive and nonsupportive messages by blocking out large sections through inattention or distortion of meaning; thus, you may attend to and correctly hear only those sections that are consistent with your present attitudes and beliefs.

To summarize what has been said up to this point: You can improve your listening by avoiding certain tendencies that cause you to concentrate poorly, that keep you from understanding a message because of inattention or inability to recognize its meaning and internal structure, or that cause emotional blockages against the speaker's subject. Avoiding all of these tendencies will make it possible for you to listen more accurately, understand more fully, and evaluate more soundly.

LISTENING DEFENSIVELY IN PERSUASIVE SITUATIONS

Some persuasive speakers may try to manipulate or victimize you. Such persons tend to operate from pure self-interest, with little regard for your welfare. A salesperson may try to persuade you to buy a used car that costs more than you should pay, costs more to operate than you can afford, and has hidden defects that will plague you for months. In political and social affairs, many schemes are proposed to the public that will surely enrich the proposers but will be too costly and defective to serve society in general. This does not mean that you should be eternally suspicious or resistant to persuasion. In fact, experimental studies have shown that intelligent, educated people are more open to persuasion and change than others. You should, however, exercise healthy skepticism and caution. You should be able to listen defensively. Here are a number of suggestions:

1. *Evaluate the communicator's motives.* Motives are sometimes difficult to determine. On some occasions they are fairly clear. A key question is: How will the speaker profit from what he or she is proposing? If the speaker will make money by persuading you, be cautious. A legitimate profit is O.K.; windfall profits suggest that you will be taken advantage of if you cooperate. Will the speaker profit by gaining power and prestige? Will the proposal violate the rights and liberties of others? If so, it should be turned down. Is the speaker justifying his or her behavior? If so, watch out. Newman and Newman point out the pitfall of relying too uncritically on the testimony of those who have something to gain—in this case, former communists who provide information about their fellow communists:

   On the face of it, when a communist has left the party and is no longer subject to discipline, he is "free" to tell the truth. But in place of the stringent demands of ideological conformity, a whole host of new pressures begins to operate. As Herbert Packer points out in his extensive study, *Ex-Communist Witnesses*, these people profited handsomely from ratting on their old associates; naturally they wanted what they had to say to be useful to their new sponsors, the FBI and the Department of Justice.[3]

   Basically, you should try to read motives to determine whether the communicator is operating from purely selfish motives that ignore the true interests of the audience or the cause of truth generally.

---

[3] Robert P. Newman and Dale R. Newman, *Evidence* (Boston: Houghton Mifflin, 1969), pp. 64–65.

2. *Evaluate the speaker's qualifications.*   Any person is entitled to express an opinion on any subject imaginable. An opinion is to be
taken for what it is, however. Do not confuse mere opinion with
knowledgeable or expert opinion. On topics requiring technical
or other special knowledge, ask yourself whether the speaker is
really qualified to speak with authority. Who, for instance, is
qualified to speak with authority on the environmental impact of
building a suburban mall on tidal marshlands near a coastal city?
If the developer tells you that there will be no destructive impact
on marine life, you may fairly ask: How does the developer
know? The testimony of a marine biologist would be more
appropriate.

3. *Watch out for extravagant promises.*   If someone paints an especially
optimistic picture of the benefits of adopting a new policy or of
buying a new product, be careful. As we have implied, people
tend to believe whatever is represented as being likely to satisfy
their needs, especially if the needs will be satisfied in abundance.
Con artists know this tendency and play to it by promising
unrealistic results. Think of some of the unrealistic claims offered
in advertising: a mouth wash, toothpaste, or deodorant that will
make you popular with members of the opposite sex; a public-
speaking course that will make you a company executive; an
extra-strength pain killer that will cure arthritis; and so on.
Characteristic of all these appeals is an extravagant promise that,
when examined logically, is often ridiculous.

4. *Be careful of highly emotional language.*   There is nothing wrong with
stirring up the emotions. Indeed, emotional reactions are often
inevitable, especially with topics that touch on cherished values.
But speech that is heavily laced with emotional terms, such as
crook, liar, traitor, un-American, un-Christian, oppressor, and *tyrant,*
should be carefully judged. The terms may be justified; if a case
is made, you may respond positively. Often, however, the use of
such terms represents mere name calling and is calculated to get
you to respond uncritically. Note the emotional language of the
following example. Do you believe the speaker, or would you like
a little more substantial proof?

. . . self-discipline is of little concern to the modern non-objective painter. All he needs is pigment and press agent. He can throw colors at a canvas and the art world will discover him. He can stick bits of glass, old rags and quids of used chewing tobacco on a board and he is a social critic. He can drive a car back and forth in pools of paint and Life magazine will write him up.

Talent is for squares. What you need is vast effrontery. If you undertake to paint a cow it must look something like a cow. That takes at least a sign-painter's ability. But you can claim to paint a picture of your psyche and no matter what the result who is to say what your psyche looks like? So our museums are filled with daubs being stared at by confused citizens who haven't the guts to admit they are confused.

But the Age-of-Fakery in art is a mild cross that American civilization bears. Much more serious is our collapse of moral standards and the blunting of our capacity for righteous indignation.[4]

5. *Don't be taken in by the claim that "everybody's doing it."* The Institute for Propaganda Analysis calls this kind of claim the bandwagon technique. The basic argument is that since so many people are doing something, that something must be all right. This is a common appeal in advertising: "Three million people smoke X brand of cigarettes; why don't you?" "X is the largest-selling aspirin in the world; it must be good." The bandwagon technique is also used often to establish or try to establish moral standards: "Everybody cheats, why shouldn't I?" "Every political party plays dirty tricks; why do people get so upset about Watergate?" What a lot of people believe or do may be right and good, or it may be the opposite. That they are doing it is not, by itself, a sufficient reason for you to do the same thing.

6. *If you have to act fast, consider waiting.* Back off if someone urges you to act immediately because an opportunity will be gone or because a situation is such an emergency that there is no room

[4] James Jenkins, "Who Is Tampering with the Soul of America?" *Vital Speeches of the Day,* 28 (1961-1962), 181. Reprinted by permission.

for delay. This tactic is a classic attempt to squeeze a decision out of you that you might not make if you had time to consider carefully. For example, the used-car salesperson may say, ''You'd better act fast, someone's going to snap this up right away.'' Likewise, the military establishment often urges the nation and Congress to endorse a new weapons system immediately on the grounds that the United States will remain perilously weak until it has that system. Of course, on some occasions the ''act fast'' argument may have merit, but it should be viewed with suspicion until convincing reasons are given to support it.

7. *Be sure to separate facts from guesses, rumors, and other suppositions.* Many times, people will report not facts, but their reaction to the facts. For instance, a witness to an automobile accident may assert that the driver was drunk because there was an odor of alcohol on the driver's breath and a beer can on the seat. The statement of this witness is an unproved assumption, not a fact. Newspapers sometimes report rumors as if they were facts. This happens especially under circumstances in which facts are difficult to come by, as during warfare or after an earthquake or some other natural calamity. On such occasions, newspapers will sometimes report that hundreds have been killed, only to reduce that figure later to about a hundred and, finally, to seventy-eight or some other specific figure. As a specific illustration, the May 7, 1965, issue of *Time* magazine reported on a revolt in Santo Domingo as follows:

No one had an accurate account of the casualties as frenzied knots of soldiers and civilians roamed the streets, shooting, looting, and herding people to their execution. . . . The rebels executed at least 110 opponents, hacked the head off a police officer and carried it about as a trophy.

One wonders how *Time*, after acknowledging that no one could get an accurate account of casualties, came up with the figure of 110. We can only believe that it was some reporter's guesswork.

When you read criticism of opera, symphony, literature, motion pictures, and theatrical productions, you should remember that the message will consist almost entirely of opinion. True, the opinion will be stated as if it were fact ("The acting was atrocious, the dialogue silly . . ."), but it will be opinion nevertheless. You should judge it accordingly.

LISTENING AS A KNOWLEDGEABLE CRITIC

In the classroom, you may be asked to listen to and evaluate the speeches of your classmates. In some cases, you may be asked to grade your classmates' efforts. During college and after you leave, you will listen to speeches by persons such as your minister, the mayor of your city, your congressional representative, or a corporate representative from your locality. You may not be called on for a formal evaluation of such speeches. Nevertheless, you will probably judge whether a speech was good or bad. How will you make such a judgment?

If you make a judgment solely on the basis of moral criteria, you will probably be unfair to the speaker. Obviously, moral judgments enter into the evaluation of a speech and should be considered, but some persons tend to allow moral judgments to blind them to other indications of effectiveness in speech. For instance, you might say that a person advocating abortion rights, the legalization of cocaine, or the right of our government to tap citizens' telephones is not speaking well because these positions seem unethical to you. In dismissing a speech as poor because it offends your moral sensitivities, you may overlook that the speech is well organized, uses good evidence and argument, shows superior style, and is delivered well.

Likewise, it is shortsighted to judge a speech solely by its results. Good speaking, you might argue, should be effective speaking; therefore, if a speech gets results, it is a good one. This standard might, at times, be valid. But think of the difficulties that result from such an assumption. Suppose I had made several speeches supporting the election of Ronald Reagan as president. Since Ronald Reagan was elected, I claim, the speeches I made were good speeches. It is obviously an unwarranted assumption to suppose that my speeches, by themselves, resulted in Reagan's election. One problem of judging a speech by its results is that it is hard to determine how much effect a speech has on the events that follow it. In many cases, the events a speaker supports would occur even if he or she had not spoken.

Similarly, is it correct to say that every speech that did not gain the effect desired by the speaker was a poor speech? By this logic, there could have been no good speeches on behalf of Jimmy Carter in 1980, because he was not elected to the presidency. A good speaker may fail to get results, not because the speech was poor, but because other powerful influences on human behavior conteracted the impact of the speech.

To sum up, then, if we judge a speech only on its ethical content or its probable effectiveness, we are overlooking other elements that deserve consideration. In fact, a speech should be measured by a set of critieria or principles developed from experimentation and practice. A novelist, to take a parallel case, should be judged not by whether the novel sold 10 million copies or by whether it took a morally agreeable position, but rather by how well the novelist applied the accepted principles of novel writing. The same goes for speakers. We should ask ourselves, after listening to a speech, not only whether it was morally agreeable or whether it was successful in getting results, but also whether the speaker applied sound principles of good communication practice.

In Chapter 1, we spoke of the factors a speaker must keep in mind when preparing a speech. We revealed, from the speaker's point of view, the nature of good communication practice. In the present chapter, we are interested in those same practices as viewed by the audience. What is it in the speaker's behavior that the audience should observe and evaluate in making a critical judgment of the quality of a speech? We will first discuss these principles in general terms and then offer some practical help in applying them to a given speech situation.

In judging a speech, you should ask first: What kind of communication did the occasion demand? Did it call for an informative speech, a ceremonial one, a persuasive one? You can judge, in answering the question, how well the speaker understood the speaking problem and how well the speaker applied accepted practices in meeting the demands of the situation. In later chapters, you will learn about particular demands put on speakers who are trying to speak informatively, ceremonially, and persuasively; the analysis here will give you a basis for judging how well a speaker meets these responsibilities.

Second, you should ask whether the speaker understood the needs of the audience and adapted his or her message intelligently to those needs. Since speaking is a mutual exchange between audience and speaker, speakers must understand their audiences. To do this, they must analyze factors such as those discussed in Chapter 2. Then they must adjust their communication to those factors. Moreover, the give-and-take of communication requires that the speaker recognize and respond to feedback from the audience. You should judge how well a speaker fulfills these obligations to the audience.

Third, you should judge the quality of the speaker's material. Does it seem to be the best available, made up of sound evidence from reliable sources? Are the conclusions drawn from the evidence logically defensible? And is the material organized and developed in such a way as to be readily understandable to the audience?

Fourth, you should judge the impression made by the speaker as a person. Does he or she come across as a person of character, one whose motives and abilities are to be trusted? This evaluation will be based on such questions as: Is the speaker fair with the audience, or is he or she trying in some way to take advantage of them? Does the speaker appear knowledgeable about the subject, well prepared, and intelligent in the judgments rendered? What kind of person is the speaker in general terms? Does the speaker show self-respect and respect for others? Does the speaker seem opinionated or judgmental in temperament? You have been briefly introduced to the concept of speaker credibility. A speaker's credibility is a part of the total judgment that you will make about the effectiveness of the communication. Credibility will be discussed later in more detail.

Finally, you should make a judgment about the speaker's use of language, body, and voice—the instruments by which the message is transmitted to the audience. The ability to command these instruments effectively is crucial to successful communication. You should use the information gained in the preceding chapters to judge the speaker's abilities in style and delivery.

These five general principles are the yardstick by which speeches are judged. Experienced critics apply these principles with ease (but with much thought as to final judgment) when they listen to a speaker. As an inexperienced critic, you may have some trouble remembering all these standards and deciding how a given speaker should be rated. To help with these problems, formal rating scales have been developed. Several such rating scales are shown in Figures 8.1–8.4. These scales have been used in communication classes at a large university and are adapted from a variety of sources. They probably do not improve the judgments of experienced critics, but they do help the critic to see all aspects of the judgmental process so that important factors are not overlooked. Also, they provide a numerical rating system that helps in pinpointing differences among speakers. The scales should be particularly useful to you in judging the speeches and other communication efforts of your classmates, as may be required by your instructor. The first is a sheet for rating an informative speech, the second is for a persuasive speech, and the third and fourth are for evaluating discussion participants and leaders. (Discussion is an activity that may or may not be included in your class; it is discussed in the final chapter of this book.) With practice, you should find that these scales will help you to become a knowledgeable critic.

Figure 8.1   INFORMATIVE SPEECH RATING SHEET

RATING	ITEM	COMMENTS
_____	Choice of subject:	
	____ Appropriate to speaker and listener	
	____ Appropriate to assignment and time limit	
_____	Development of introduction:	
	____ Gains attention	
	____ Establishes relationship with audience	
	____ Discloses purpose	
	____ Motivates learning	
_____	Organization:	
	____ Is clear and simple	
	____ Has an appropriate pattern	
_____	Development of the body:	
	____ Variety of supporting materials	
	____ Quality of supporting materials	
	____ Appropriate and effective use of audio-visual aids	
	____ Use of reinforcement techniques	
_____	Bodily control:	
	____ Use of facial expression, eye contact	
	____ Use of gestures	
	____ Posture and movement	

(Continued)

RATING	ITEM	COMMENTS
_____	Language:	
	____ Clarity	
	____ Vividness	
	____ Forcefulness	
	____ Oral style	
_____	Voice and pronunciation:	
	____ Quality	
	____ Flexibility	
	____ Emphasis	
_____	Conclusion:	
	____ Summary	
	____ Final appeal	
_____	Attitude toward listeners and speaking situation:	
	____ Urge to communicate	
_____	Overall effectiveness	
_____	Total rating	

Explanation of ratings (rate on a 1–10 scale)

10 Superior   Critic _____
 8 Excellent
 6 Good
 4 Fair
 2 Below average

Figure 8.2 PERSUASIVE SPEECH RATING SHEET

RATING	ITEM	COMMENTS
_____	Choice of subject:	
	____ Appropriate to speaker and listener	
	____ Appropriate to assignment and time limits	
_____	Introduction:	
	____ Gains attention	
	____ Builds prestige for speaker	
	____ Discloses or otherwise deals with purpose	

(Continued)

RATING	ITEM	COMMENTS

_____ Motivates audience

_____ Organization:

    _____ Explicit disclosure type

    _____ Inductive type

    _____ Appropriate clear pattern

_____ Supporting material:

    _____ Appeal to logic and consistency needs

    _____ Use of emotional proofs (fear, guilt, etc.)

    _____ Appeal to social conformity needs

    _____ General quality of motivation

    _____ Quality of proposals for need satisfaction

_____ Conclusion:

    _____ Summary

    _____ Final appeal

_____ Bodily control:

    _____ Use of facial expression, eye contact

    _____ Use of gestures

    _____ Posture and movement

_____ Voice and pronunciation:

    _____ Quality

    _____ Flexibility

    _____ Emphasis

_____ Language:

    _____ Clarity

    _____ Vividness

    _____ Forcefulness

    _____ Oral style

_____ Attitude toward audience and occasion—urge to communicate—credibility

_____ Overall effectiveness

_____ Total rating

(Continued)

RATING	ITEM	COMMENTS

Explanation of ratings (rate on a 1–10 scale)

10	Superior	Critic _____
8	Excellent	
6	Good	
4	Fair	
2	Below average	

Figure 8.3 DISCUSSION PARTICIPANT RATING SHEET

RATING	ITEM	COMMENTS

_____ Adequacy of participation

    ____ Helps manage conflict (harmonizes)

    ____ Acts as gatekeeper

    ____ Responsive to the question and to the group

_____ Cooperative, problem-solving attitude:

    ____ Ability and willingness to integrate own ideas

    ____ Doesn't try to monopolize

    ____ Not combative

_____ Analysis:

    ____ Powers of reasoning

    ____ Helps summarize thought processes

    ____ Calls for critical evaluation

_____ Evidence:

    ____ Quality of material contributed

    ____ Knowledge of subject

    ____ Asks for evidence when needed

_____ Speech processes:

    ____ General effectiveness of delivery

    ____ Use of voice

    ____ Use of nonverbal bodily communication

_____ Total rating

(Continued)

RATING   ITEM   COMMENTS

Explanation of ratings (rate on a 1–10 scale)

   10   Superior   Critic _____
    8   Excellent
    6   Good
    4   Fair
    2   Below average

Figure 8.4 DISCUSSION LEADERSHIP RATING SCALE

Instructions: Circle one number after each statement. The range is from 1, poor, to 7, superior.

TASK AREA

1. Leader's introductory remarks were informative, thought-provoking.

         1   2   3   4   5   6   7

2. Leader seemed familiar with the subject being discussed.

         1   2   3   4   5   6   7

3. Leader asked questions that encouraged critical thinking.

         1   2   3   4   5   6   7

4. Leader skillfully and tactfully kept irrelevant issues to a minimum.

         1   2   3   4   5   6   7

5. Leader made effective transitions and summarized at appropriate times.

         1   2   3   4   5   6   7

6. Leader presided easily and efficiently.

         1   2   3   4   5   6   7

7. Leader helped the group reach a defensible conclusion.

         1   2   3   4   5   6   7

INTERPERSONAL AREA

1. Leader established a relaxed, permissive climate.

         1   2   3   4   5   6   7

(Continued)

2. Leader encouraged all to participate.

     1   2   3   4   5   6   7

3. Leader made participants feel that the discussion was important and that they were needed.

     1   2   3   4   5   6   7

4. Leader listened with interest and without prejudice.

     1   2   3   4   5   6   7

5. Leader was pleasant, easy to talk to.

     1   2   3   4   5   6   7

6. Leader handled interpersonal conflicts tactfully but firmly and effectively.

     1   2   3   4   5   6   7

7. Leader proved to be skilled in human relations.

     1   2   3   4   5   6   7

SUMMARY

Listening is the average person's most common communication experience, accounting for 45 percent of one's communication activity. There are three basic types of listening: listening for pleasure, listening for understanding, and listening for persuasion. Listening to a message involves attending, understanding, assimilation, and reaction. Listening may be improved by paying careful attention to a message, focusing on major points and their supporting materials, withholding evaluation until you have understood the material, reacting objectively to the speaker's reputation and appearance, and avoiding emotional blocks caused by your preformed attitudes toward the subject. You can listen defensively to attempts to persuade by evaluating the speaker's motives and qualifications and by watching out for extravagant promises, highly emotional language, and claims that you must act immediately or that everybody's doing it. Finally, you must thoughtfully separate facts from guesses, rumors, and suppositions. If you wish to listen as a knowledgeable critic you must judge speeches by the general principles set forth in this book.

Exercises

1. You should act as listener-evaluator for all speeches delivered in class. Forms to help guide you are included in this chapter. These forms should provide the basis for class comments and discussions of speech performances. The instructor may require evaluation forms to be handed in occasionally, and sometimes, at least, each student should receive written evaluations from every member of the class.
2. Listen outside class to a campus speaker or to an address broadcast on television. Rate the talk and use your rating as the basis for a classroom discussion.
3. Listen to television commercials for a period of three or four days. Criticize these according to the principles in this chapter in the section titled "Listening Defensively in Persuasive Situations." Discuss your reactions in class.

Chapter Nine

INFORMATIVE SPEAKING

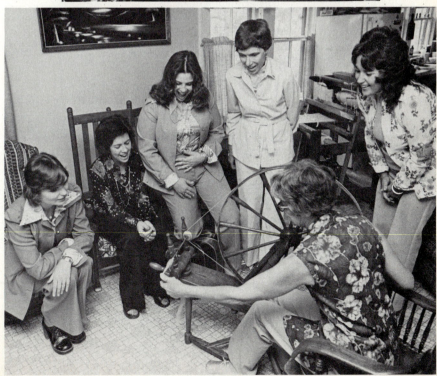

OVERVIEW

Major types of informative speaking

Motivating an audience to listen to information

General methods of preparation for informative speaking

Specific directions and sample outlines for the preparation of a
descriptive speech, a speech combining description and
narration, and a speech explaining a process

Informative speaking is characterized by accuracy, completeness, intelligibility, interest, and usefulness. If an audience hears an address on a subject such as how an electron microscope functions, they have a right to expect correct information that is complete enough to give at least a basic understanding of the instrument. They also expect the information to be presented in a way that is understandable and that keeps their attention. Finally, they expect the information to be useful. If an audience hearing a speech were a group of scientists who already knew the details of electron microscopy, the speaker would be violating the rule of usefulness in choosing that subject, unless talking about some new aspect of the technology.

Possible subjects for informative speeches are limitless, but they may be roughly classified into three types: (1) description; (2) narration and description; (3) explaining a process. These distinctions are not absolute. A single address, while perhaps falling mainly into one type, would certainly contain elements of each. A person uses *description* when dealing with happenings or events. History professors and news reporters rely heavily on this type of discourse—the history professor in describing an event like a battle, the reporter in relating an attempted assassination or the hijacking of an airplane. A person uses *narration and description* to reveal the causes, the meaning, or the operation of some thing or some concept. Simple narration may involve no more than telling why a volcano erupts. Narration may also be complex, however, as when someone tries to explain how DNA molecules function in transmitting hereditary characteristics. A speaker resorts to *directions* when explaining a process or procedure that can be accomplished in orderly steps. For example, a drill sergeant uses directions to tell a group of recruits how to disassemble, clean, and reassemble their rifles.

As we said, these three informative types overlap in any given speech. Nevertheless, you will probably be required in your classroom to give a speech that emphasizes one or another of these techniques. In light of this probability, some sample topics will now be offered.

Topics like the following would be useful for a speech that emphasizes description:

1. What really happened to Custer at Little Big Horn
2. The Gold Rush of 1849
3. The great San Francisco earthquake
4. How air controllers at a busy airport bring incoming planes to a safe landing.
5. How the New England town meeting functions
6. The tactics of civil-rights protesters in the 1960s
7. The characteristics of the Theater of the Absurd

The following topics could be used for a speech that emphasizes narration and description:

1. The frontier hypothesis of Frederick Jackson Turner
2. How a solar water heater works
3. The economic theories of John Maynard Keynes
4. What causes an earthquake
5. What causes inflation
6. How a space vehicle is launched and guided to its target
7. The mechanics of heredity
8. Principles and procedures underlying public-opinion polling

For a speech that emphasizes the giving of directions, the following topics might be used:

1. How to prepare a federal income-tax form
2. The making of a macramé pot hanger
3. How to instruct a computer
4. Reading a weather map
5. How to decorate and fire a ceramic ashtray
6. How to conduct a meeting according to Robert's Rules of Order
7. Building a ship model
8. How to make a linoleum block print

MOTIVATION AND LEARNING

An informative speaking situation is a learning experience for the audience. On one occasion they may simply accumulate facts; on other occasions they may learn to understand concepts or to follow directions. But whatever the material being communicated, they are asked to learn. An informative speech, therefore, should be constructed in line with good principles of learning. Basically, these principles are two: motivation and reinforcement. Five ways for motivating and reinforcing an audience follow.

Audiences are motivated and reinforced if you show how your message meets their needs. What use has the audience for the information you are about to disclose? Sometimes the use will be apparent. Such a speech may explain how to do something the audience would like to learn: diving from a high board, operating a snowmobile, making a macramé pot hanger, painting a chair, and so forth. But why should a person listen to you talk about various types of insurance, mental illness, social structure, or computer languages? In these cases, you must somehow show the audience the relevance of the material to their needs and desires. This means showing them how your information will help them understand themselves, improve their relations with other people, get a better job, enjoy more status, and the like. Here is an example of motivation by a prominent speaker who wanted his audience to learn about mental illness:

[My] first observation is that mental illness is something that may occur in the lives of any of us. It always develops rather unexpectedly. Nobody plans to get mentally ill, you know, and nobody expects to get mentally ill. We all expect we may get pneumonia or we may get a bad cold next winter. We expect physical illnesses of certain kinds. But no one expects a mental illness.

Nevertheless mental illness does come; it strikes down friends and acquaintances, the prominent and the lowly, rich victims and poor ones. It is no respecter of persons. It may come to any one of us.[1]

[1] Karl Menninger, "Healthier Than Healthy," in *A Psychiatrist's World* (New York: Viking Press, Inc., 1959), p. 635.

In this case, the speaker has provided audience members with a motive to learn more about mental illness by showing them how common it is and how likely it is that anyone might experience it.

Audiences are motivated and reinforced when their attention and interest are aroused. Audiences are interested in what is useful to them. Consequently, the best way to get them involved is to show how your material can serve them. But interest and attention may be aroused by the nature of the material apart from its usefulness. This topic was discussed in Chapter 4, but it is helpful here to re-emphasize two things.

New and startling information catches our interest even if not immediately tied to the satisfaction of one of our desires. It may not be very useful to audience members to learn that a person's head has 150,000 hairs on it, but the figure is certainly startling and may have some relevance if you choose to talk about wig making or hair dyeing. In the following example, the speaker is discussing how blind obedience to orders from authority figures can lead persons into criminal behavior. He uses the example of Lt. William Calley, the only army officer convicted of massacring Vietnamese villagers at My Lai. The startling information for most people is the result of a Harris Poll on how Americans would have behaved in Calley's shoes.

English writer C.P. Snow states: "More hideous crimes have been committed in the name of obedience than have ever been committed in the name of rebellion."

Calley claimed that Capt. Ernest L. Medina gave orders to kill all My Lai villagers. The jury never had to agree on that charge because they agreed that even if Calley had received such an order, he was duty-bound to disobey it because it would have been patently illegal. A Harris Poll following the trial revealed that 43 percent of Americans would have "followed orders" if they had been in Calley's shoes. Forty-one percent felt that if they were a soldier in Vietnam and were ordered by superior officers to shoot men, women, and children suspected of aiding the enemy—41 percent said they would be more right to refuse orders in an act of disobedience. The other 16 percent were not sure what they would do.[2]

---

[2] Marvin Sacks, "The Value of Disobedience," in *Contemporary American Speeches,* eds. Wil A. Linkugel, et al. (Dubuque, Iowa: Kendall/Hunt Publishing Co., 1982), p. 157.

Humor, also, helps to motivate and reinforce an audience. If you are making a serious point, you may use a humorous example or illustration to reinforce the idea. This is the tactic used by Neil Postman in a speech designed to illustrate how human beings tend to be irrationally impressed with the validity of numerical data. He illustrates with a reference to the Miss Universe beauty pageant.

Everyone must have a favorite and real example of the tyranny of numbers. I have several, the most recent having occurred a couple of months ago. I and several people of reputed intelligence were together in a hotel room, watching a television program called "The Miss Universe Beauty Pageant." Now, even in a non-technicalized culture, a beauty pageant would be, it seems to me, a degrading cultural event. In this one, pure lunacy was added to the degradation by the utilization of computers to measure the measurements, so to speak, of the women involved. Each of the twelve judges was able to assign a precise number to the charm of a woman's smile, the shapeliness of her bosom, the sensuality of her walk, and even to the extent of what was called her poise. But more than this, as each judge assigned a number, a mother-computer, with legendary speed, calculated the average, which was then flashed on the upper right-hand corner of the TV screen so that the audience could know, immediately, that Miss Holland, for example, was a 6.231 on how she looked in a bathing suit, whereas Miss Finland was only a 5.827. Now, as it happened, one of the people with whom I was watching believed, as he put it, that there is no way Miss Finland is a 5.827. He estimated that she is, at a minimum, a 6.3, and maybe as high as a 7.2. Another member of our group took exception to these figures, maintaining strongly that only in a world gone mad is Miss Finland a 5.827, and that she should count herself lucky that she did not get what she deserved, which, as he figured it, was no more than a 3.8.[3]

Audiences are motivated and reinforced when the speech is well organized. A good informative speech is organized in a way that aids learning. Experimental

---

[3] "The Technical Thesis," *Vital Speeches of the Day,* 46 (1978–79), 182. Reprinted by permission.

studies of speeches have reached certain conclusions about how organization is related to understanding. Several studies have shown that audiences can retain only two or three main points in a fifteen- to thirty-minute address. This finding supports the general assumptions that learning progresses step by step and that learners overloaded with learning tasks are less able to perform. Undue complexity or too many main points should therefore be avoided.

Other studies have shown that audiences retain more information from a well-organized speech than from a poorly organized one. In Chapter 4, we discussed patterns of organization—chronological, spatial or geographical, problem-solution, cause and effect, and so on. Strong organization results when the speaker follows the advice given in that chapter. Weak organization is represented by errors like the following: (1) Material is presented in incorrect chronological or spatial order, or material is randomly organized when it should be presented in either chronological or spatial order. (2) Material used in problem-solution order is mistakenly presented in the solution stage when it should be in the problem stage and vice versa. (3) Cause-and-effect relationships are confused. (4) Material that is complex and involved is presented without any clear organizational pattern.

Characteristics of organization that experimental research has demonstrated to be effective are as follows:

1. An explicit statement of the purpose in the introduction aids understanding of the main point of a speech. Some studies have shown that when the main idea of the speech is not stated explicitly, hearers are often unable to recognize it from the supporting evidence given.

2. Setting forth the structure of a speech in the introduction tends to improve understanding, as does repeating that structure by transitions in the body of the speech. Some studies do not support this generalization, and others do. It is very difficult in such studies to control the content of the speech so that only the organizational pattern can be said to be responsible for the result. However, it has been discovered that people have less ability to learn lists of nonsense words than to learn logically related terms. It is probably safe to say that when a speaker emphasizes the structure of the speech, he or she aids in the learning of its content. Research has also shown that repeating an idea or piece of evidence

throughout a speech improves the learning of that idea, even
when the audience feels that the repetition is disruptive and
annoying.
3. One aspect of content that may also be considered an organizational factor is the speaker's use of verbal cues about the relative
importance of ideas or items of evidence. If a speaker introduces
material with statements such as "This is important and should
be remembered" or "Please get this," the audience is more
likely to remember the material so emphasized.

Audiences are motivated and reinforced when the speech uses audio-visual aids. To
the extent possible, an informative speech should employ audio-visual
aids. Research has shown that a multichannel presentation through use of
audio-visual aids helps an audience assimilate certain materials much
more than if such aids are not used. The reason is evident. Without charts
or pictures, it is almost impossible to describe an object that an audience
has never seen, such as the middle and inner ear of a human being.
Likewise, a speaker cannot show differences in styles of musical composition without audio-visual aids. Thus, a multichannel presentation results
in better audience understanding. Audio-visual aids should be used when
they will help to clarify concepts you are discussing and to sustain interest
and attention. You should return to Chapter 5 and carefully reread the
material there on the use of visual aids.

Audiences are motivated and reinforced when the speech is delivered well. An
informative speech should be delivered in ways that help the audience to
remember content. Studies that have dealt with specific aspects of delivery
have shed some light on those factors that seem related to understanding.
For instance, a speaker who uses gestures and other visible actions
generates better recall than one who uses little or no visible action. Poor
vocal quality does not seem to affect understanding adversely, nor does a
monotonous tone. However, a monotonous (frequently repeated) pitch
pattern does seem to reduce audience comprehension.

When a speaker emphasizes important points throughout delivery,
such as by pausing before a point, raising or lowering the voice while
uttering a point, or emphasizing a point with gestures like banging on the
table, he or she helps the audience understand better. Poor eye contact
tends to reduce understanding; good eye contact improves it. Neither the
manuscript nor the extemporaneous style of delivery seems superior

in affecting the audience's grasp of the message. What is important is the degree of skill shown by the speaker in whatever style of delivery employed.

GENERAL STEPS IN THE PREPARATION OF AN INFORMATIVE SPEECH

In preparing an informative speech, you may find the following outline of steps helpful:

I. Preliminary analysis:
 A. *Analyze your subject.* What do you want your audience to learn? Obviously, they cannot remember everything you say. You must therefore determine the essential pieces of information they need to learn in order to have a sufficient grasp of the subject.
 B. *Analyze your audience.* How much do they know about the subject? This information will help you determine where to begin and will tell you how detailed you need to be. Do they already have an interest in the topic, or will you need to generate it?
 C. *Analyze the speech environment.* Will there be distractions? How can you overcome them? Will the surroundings be pleasant and comfortable? What facilities are available for audio-visual or other aids?
II. Planning the speech:
 A. *The introduction.* You need material that will gain interest and motivate the audience to learn. The introduction should also clearly indicate what items the audience is expected to remember. Identifying the learning task for the audience helps them in the act of learning itself.
 B. *The body.* You must identify the central idea and the main and subordinate points that will support it.
    1. The central idea is what listeners are expected to be able to do with the information in the speech. If you are giving a narrative-descriptive speech on the battle at Gettysburg, how much of that battle can the audience be expected to remember? Probably they will remember only the broad

sweeps of strategy. Make this clear. If the speech describes a
process or gives directions, is the audience expected to be
able to perform some act? Or are they expected merely to
understand what is involved in a process?

2. You should phrase main and subordinate points so that
they reinforce the central purpose. You should also reinforce the main and subordinate points with materials that
vivify, clarify, and motivate because they relate to the
experiences and needs of the audience.

3. You should use techniques that help improve recall, such as
restatement, internal summaries, and repetition.

4. You should organize the speech in a pattern suited to the
content. Descriptive speeches will probably be organized in
the spatial and/or the chronological pattern. Process
speeches will probably be organized in the chronological or
perhaps the cause-and-effect pattern. Narrative speeches
may go from the simple to the complex or may be developed in a topical way.

C. *The conclusion.* You should restate the learning task and the
main and subordinate points that have supported it. Additional motivating material may be used in a final effort to
reinforce learning.

III. Planning the delivery:

A. The delivery should be varied and flexible. Your voice should
reflect interest in and enthusiasm for the subject. Conversational speaking is probably best.

B. You should use plenty of gestures and bodily movements.

C. You should include demonstrations and visual or audio aids
when appropriate and natural.

A DESCRIPTIVE SPEECH

Speeches that are solely descriptive are not common. Usually description and narration or description and explanation are combined. Sometimes, especially when you want to give new life and energy to something
old and familiar or when you want to satisfy curiosity about a fascinating
new object, speeches may be devoted entirely to description. You might,
for example, give a descriptive speech on the Statue of Liberty for the

purpose of revitalizing an old symbol. Then again, you might want to describe the space shuttle to capitalize on an exciting new technological innovation.

Description deals with such qualities in an object as size, shape, composition, internal and external structure, and other features. In the following example, note how these features are the focus of the speech.

OUTLINE: A DESCRIPTIVE SPEECH

Specific purpose: To describe the Statue of Liberty

Introduction

I. The Statue of Liberty was presented to this country by France in a Parisian ceremony in 1884. It was shipped to the United States in 214 huge crates in 1885.

II. In case you have never been to New York to see it, I would like to describe it for you today.

Body

I. *Location:* As the site for the statue, the authorities chose the center of old Fort Wood on Bedloe's Island, now known as Liberty Island.

II. *Physical characteristics:*
   A. The statue is 151 feet from the sandals to the top of the torch.
   B. From the base of the huge pedestal to the torch is a distance of 305 feet.
   C. An elevator runs through the pedestal 150 feet upward to the base of the statue.

III. *Construction:*
   A. The interior of the statue, designed by Alexandre Gustave Eiffel, is a framework of iron much like that of the Eiffel Tower. It weighs 450,000 pounds.
   B. The exterior is covered with more than 300 sheets of thin copper that weigh 91 metric tons.

IV. *Interior access:*
   A. There are two parallel spiral stairways that run from the base to the crown. Each has 168 steps and rest seats at every third turn of the spiral.
   B. The crown has a 25-window observation platform that can accommodate 30 viewers.

    C. The torch can be reached by a ladder inside the arm, but the
       public is not allowed to use it.
  V. *The designer:* Frederic Auguste Bartholdi, a French sculptor, de-
     signed the statue, which is one of the largest ever built.

Conclusion
   I. From the observation platform one can get a magnificent view of
     New York harbor and the city.
  II. In 1903, a poem by Emma Lazarus called ''The New Colossus''
     was inscribed on a tablet in the pedestal. Five famous lines are
     often quoted from it:

> Give me your tired, your poor,
>
> Your huddled masses yearning to breathe free,
>
> The wretched refuse of your teeming shore.
>
> Send these, the homeless, tempest-tost to me,
>
> I lift my lamp beside the golden door.

A NARRATIVE-DESCRIPTIVE SPEECH

While description sometimes provides the entire content of a speech, a
more usual pattern is for description to be interspersed with narration or
reporting. Narration is concerned with the unfolding and development of
events. The news reports that you get on nightly TV broadcasts are
filled with narration of airplane accidents, military actions, floods, and
tornadoes. In reporting these events, the reporter will be concerned
that the account be characterized by three things: interest, accuracy, and
significance.

As we have said often, people are interested in subjects that affect their
personal lives or that are unusual, extraordinary, even bizarre. Thus, TV
news reports tend to be selected on such criteria. Accuracy is extremely
important, also, as TV reports reach millions and affect their attitudes
and perceptions of events. To illustrate the importance of accuracy, when
an attempt was made on the life of President Reagan in 1981, most
networks reported that James Brady, the presidential press secretary, was
killed. Later, reporters had to retract that statement and disclose
that Brady, though seriously injured, had not died. They were obliged
to apologize to the public and especially to Brady's friends and
acquaintances.

Finally, reporters are at pains to deal with subjects of significance, that is, ones that relate to human welfare and human needs. They are careful to point out the potential impact on society of unfolding events.

OUTLINE: A NARRATIVE-DESCRIPTIVE SPEECH

Specific purpose: To describe the great flood that struck Florence, Italy, on November 4, 1966

Introduction
  I. The flood that inundated Florence, Italy, on November 4, 1966, was the most disastrous that ever struck the city. It deposited a ton of mud for every inhabitant.
  II. *Purpose sentence:* I want to acquaint you with the causes of the flood and the damage it did to this great artistic center.

Body
  I. *The causes of the flood:*
    A. The greatest rainstorm in its history hit Florence on November 3.
      1. In less than 24 hours, 7½ inches of rain fell on the city, a greater amount than ever before registered.
      2. Average annual rainfall in Florence is about 33 inches. This means that about a quarter of a year's rain fell in one day.
      3. Rain of equal or greater intensity fell throughout the region crisscrossed by the Arno river.
    B. Two unused dams, which formerly provided power for mills, still extend across the Arno in Florence. These barriers are 4 meters high and played a big part in forcing the river from its banks.
    C. The opening of the hydroelectric dam at Levane, above the city, came too late. When the gates were finally opened they released a terrifying quantity of water.
  II. *The damage done:*
    A. The damage done to the city's paintings, sculptures, and libraries was immense.
      1. In the Biblioteca Nazionale alone, there were 24,000 manuscripts, 705,000 letters and documents, 3,000,000 books, and 68,000 musical works. Of these, 1,300,000 were severely damaged or, in many cases, destroyed.

2. At the university half of the 100,000 books were damaged;
   60 percent of the ancient manuscripts were damaged; and
   at least 90 percent of the equipment used in medicine,
   chemistry, and the natural sciences was completely
   destroyed.
3. About 1400 paintings on wood, canvas, and the walls of
   buildings were damaged, as were 14 groups of sculpture
   and 122 individual sculptures.
B. Damage done to historic buildings was equally disastrous.
   1. Great churches like the Duomo (Santa Maria del Fiore),
      Santa Croce, and Santa Maria Novella were flooded to a
      level of 8 to 10 feet.
   2. The same high water struck buildings like the Museum of
      Science and the Archeological Museum.
   3. Oil floating on the surface of the water coated the walls and
      art works of these buildings as the water receded. Some of
      these stains can never be erased.

Conclusion
  I. Florence is a city whose art works are treasured by the entire
     world.
 II. With the help of a worldwide relief program that netted millions of
     dollars, Florence has repaired much of the damage.
III. However, the sad fact is that, although many years have elapsed
     since the flood, no real effort has been made to prevent or contain
     another such disaster.

EXPLAINING A PROCESS

You may want to explain to an audience how something is done. For
example, someone who is good at doing things around the home may
want to explain to others how easy it is to hang wallpaper or repair a
leaking faucet. In such cases, a simple form of organization suggests itself.
First, one needs to discuss assembling tools and materials. Second, the
process should be divided into clearly defined steps. With wallpapering,
for instance, the steps would be cutting and matching the paper, pasting
it, and applying it. Third, common mistakes and pitfalls should be noted.

To the extent possible, you should demonstrate the process about which you are speaking. If you were speaking about wallpapering, you would want to bring some of the tools and a roll of paper with you and actually show the audience how the job is done. If you can in some way get the audience to participate, they will learn more swiftly what they must actually do. Opportunities for audience participation are limited, however, and most of the time you will have to content yourself with demonstration.

OUTLINE: EXPLANATION OF A PROCESS

Specific purpose: To explain the process of making a stained-glass panel or window

Introduction
  I. In the 1890s homes were commonly built with stained-glass windows and door panels.
 II. In the early 1900s stained glass became a recognized art in the works of William Comfort Tiffany:
   A. Tiffany experimented with many remarkable patterns and with many colors and textures of glass.
   B. The Tiffany lamp shade is famous today, and an authentic Tiffany lamp is worth thousands of dollars.
III. *Purpose sentence:* I would like to explain how to make a simple stained-glass panel or window.

Body
  I. The tools you will need to work with leaded glass are:
   A. Glass cutters with which the pieces will be shaped.
   B. Pliers with a wide flat nose to break off pieces of glass too small to grasp.
   C. A hammer and small horseshoe nails or brads to hold the leaded pieces together till they can be soldered.
   D. A soldering iron and solder that is 60 percent tin and 40 percent lead.
 II. The basic materials are:
   A. Glass of several varieties.
     1. Ordinary colored, commercially rolled glass. This is the cheapest kind.

    2. Specially prepared glass, colored in the melting pot and poured out on a stone surface that gives the glass a pebbled texture of bubbles, ridges, and veins. Such glass can be quite expensive, costing as much as $25 per square foot.

    3. Glass that is streaked or marbled.

  B. Came, or lead strips, with grooves on either side into which the cut glass is inserted.

III. Glass is assembled on a pattern (the making of a pattern and choice of colors will not be discussed here):

  A. One copy of the pattern is fastened to the work bench and is used to assemble the glass. This pattern should have a strip of wood nailed across the bottom and left-hand side to hold the structure in place.

  B. Another copy of the pattern is cut into separate pieces to be used as guides for cutting the glass.

IV. How the glass is cut:

  A. Each piece of the pattern is placed upon the sheet glass and is used as a guide for the cutter, which is held in the hand much like a pencil.

    1. Straight edges are easy to cut. The glass is scored by the cutter using a ruler or other guide and then snapped apart with the hands.

    2. Curved pieces must be scored freehand, and the glass must be tapped with the rounded butt end of the cutter to begin the fracture. The pieces can then be snapped apart.

    3. Circular or highly curved pieces must be cut by scoring the glass bit by bit and breaking it away till the desired shape is obtained.

  B. Glass cutting requires practice, and you can expect to waste a good deal of material at first. Practice on cheap, colorless glass till you get the hang of it.

V. How the glass is joined:

  A. After the pieces are cut and assembled on the guiding pattern, strips of lead came are cut to hold them together. The came channel must often be opened by using a small wooden stick called a lathekin.

  B. Edges of the glass are smoothed with a file and inserted in the channels of the came starting in the lower left corner of the pattern. Each piece must be tapped snugly into place and held with horseshoe nails driven into the work surface till the next piece is ready to be assembled. In this way the entire pattern is gradually put together.

VI. How the came is soldered:

    A. After the pattern is completely assembled, each joint in the came is soldered. It is best to have your iron attached to a dimmer switch built into a box. In this way the correct temperature of the iron can be precisely controlled. This is important because, if the iron gets too hot, it will melt the came itself.

    B. Each joint is brushed with soldering acid and the tip of the iron is touched to the joint with a ribbon of solder melted on it from above. If done correctly the solder will flow swiftly and smoothly over the joint.

    C. When one side of the pattern is soldered, the whole panel must be carefully turned over and the joints on the other side soldered.

Conclusion

  I. This highly abbreviated account shows you the basics of creating a stained-glass panel or other design.

 II. With practice you can turn out beautiful pieces such as this (hold up a sample).

SUMMARY

Informative speeches are mostly of three kinds: description, narration and description, and explaining a process. The audience must be motivated to hear and learn the material in an informative speech. Suggestions for motivating and reinforcing learning are relating material to audience needs, arousing attention and interest, organizing the speech carefully, using audio-visual aids, and delivering the speech well. The general steps in planning an informative speech include the following: analyzing your subject, your audience, and the speech environment; planning the introduction, the body, and the conclusion; and planning the delivery.

Descriptive speeches, narrative-descriptive speeches, and process speeches follow similar but varied outlines. The structure of each should be studied carefully.

Exercises

1. Prepare and deliver a short informative speech on a topic that requires mainly narration and description. Refer to suggestions in this chapter for topics.

2. Prepare and deliver a short informative speech emphasizing the explanation of a process. Supplement your oral presentation with audio-visual aids or actual demonstration.

3. Bring to class and be prepared to analyze an informative speech or magazine article that you think illustrates the ideas discussed in this chapter. Evaluate the use of supporting materials. What did the author do to try to generate interest and attention? Is there an effort to show how learning the material will be useful to the audience? If so, how? How well is this done?

Chapter Ten

PERSUASIVE SPEAKING

OVERVIEW

Kinds of proof used in persuasive speaking
Ways of using emotional, logical and ethical proofs
Social conformity as a form of proof
Speeches to convince and to activate
Creating resistance to persuasion
Conflicts that are beyond persuasion

Persuasion, as we have defined it earlier, is an attempt by one person to change the beliefs, attitudes, or conduct of another person. A persuasive speaker communicates an essentially verbal message with its appropriate nonverbal components and then responds to the feedback received. Attempts at persuasion usually involve many messages distributed over a period of time, with each message being adapted to listener response. As we indicated in Chapter 1, persuasion is a social tool for resolving conflict or changing individual behavior. In the courts, conflicts between individuals and the law are resolved. Legislative assemblies reconcile clashes between conflicting interests (consumers versus merchandisers; hawks versus doves; haves versus have-nots; blacks versus whites). In all such situations, people argue persuasively before the institutionalized decision-making bodies of society. In a sense, then, persuasion serves as an instrument of social or personal change, guiding and channeling such change through the clash of idea against idea, selfish interest against selfish interest. It should be obvious, therefore, that to be an effective agent for change, a person must be able to persuade with some skill. This chapter is designed to teach you how to be an effective persuader.

Aristotle felt that a persuasive message should contain two basic kinds of proofs, which can be outined as follows:

I. *Logical proofs*: These are rational arguments based on evidence. They are subject to verification and rebuttal according to the accepted standards by which people define sound argument as opposed to unsound argument and by which they tell dependable evidence from undependable evidence. (See Chapter 5.)
II. *Psychological proofs*: These are proofs that are nonrational, although not irrational. They consist of reasons for behaving that do not follow the rules of logic or the standards of evidence. Aristotle identified two kinds of psychological proofs:

A. *Emotional proofs*: These are proofs that suggest an action because that action will be satisfying to the individual. The satisfaction (or emotional component) comes from the fact that a proposed course of action will meet a need. Thus, someone may be convinced to order a steak for dinner, simply because it will be emotionally satisfying to eat steak. The pleasant emotion comes from the power of the steak to satisfy hunger, not from any logic or evidence.

B. *Ethical proofs*: In ethical proof, an audience tends to accept a persuasive communication because of the respect and admiration they have for the person who is communicating. People who are intelligent, are of good character, and appear to be trustworthy and friendly toward us are highly credible sources. We tend to believe what they say quite apart from the logical and emotional proofs they provide. In modern times, as mentioned in Chapter 5, we do not usually speak of a person as having good ethical proof. Instead, we substitute the word *credibility*, saying that a person's credibility is good or bad. With respect to government, we may talk about a credibility gap, meaning that we do not consider the statements of government agents trustworthy.

Aristotle's analysis of persuasion touches on very basic concepts. Logical and psychological proofs are at the heart of successful attempts to influence others. His analysis, however, does need some expansion because of ideas and perspectives that have come to light since his day and because of the need to spell out the steps in a persuasive speech in greater detail. We will attempt in this chapter to describe a pattern for constructing successful persuasive messages and to show how that pattern can be used. We will describe a successful attempt at influence as follows:

I. Gaining the attention of the audience to ensure that the message is received.

II. Motivating the audience to take action or change their attitude.

A. *By use of emotional proof*: The speaker appeals to audience desires and vividly connects speech content to basic needs for food, clothing, shelter, jobs, love, esteem, and self-development. The speaker does not depend mainly on evidence and argument but on the importance and urgency of audience needs and on the satisfactions to be gained by following the speaker's advice.

   B. *By the use of logical proof*: The speaker uses evidence and inductive and deductive arguments to show how the material will
help the audience satisfy basic needs. Often the speaker will
compare advantages to show that his proposal will give greater
satisfaction to the audience than an existing policy or a competing new one.

   C. *By the use of ethical proof*: The speaker's character, charisma, and
general attractiveness become a reason for the audience to
follow his or her advice.

   D. *By the use of social-conformity proof*: Here the speaker appeals to
the values and beliefs held by the audience's peers or other
reference groups.

III. Showing the audience the proper action to take.

   A. By proposing a specific behavior that the audience can adopt
to gain the promised satisfactions.

   B. By showing the high probability that the satisfactions will be
forthcoming if the proposal is adopted.

IV. Making the audience resistant to counterpersuasion.

   A. By stating opposing arguments and refuting them.

   B. By encouraging audience commitment.

   C. By warning the audience that others will attempt to get them
to change their minds.

ATTENTION

A good deal of evidence shows that attention serves as a gatekeeper to
prevent the human mind from being overloaded. We can define attention
as the process by which a person selects a particular stimulus from the
many available at any given time and opens the sensory channels (eyes,
ears, and so on) so that the selected stimulus can pass into the central
nervous system with little interference. From this definition, it should be
clear that a selected, or attended to, stimulus has an advantage over one
that is unattended to. An attended to stimulus enters the mind sharply
and clearly, whereas an unattended to one is only dimly perceived or
entirely ignored. Thus, whatever controls attention tends to produce
action. Things not attended to are not responded to, whereas attended to
stimuli are at least within the listener's awareness, which is a response in
itself; being within awareness, these stimuli will receive some sort of
reaction, even if it is only rejection.

Clearly, then, a speaker must know what factors will cause a stimulus to catch and sustain the attention of an audience. You should review the principles of getting attention we have already discussed in Chapters 2 and 4. We will quickly restate these principles here.

What a person selects to attend to depends not on accident but on two kinds of factors: (1) People attend to stimuli that have inherent attention-getting characteristics. (2) People attend to stimuli that relate to their needs and goals.

Some stimuli, regardless of their meaning or relation to a person's needs, seem to demand attention whether or not the individual wants to pay attention. Into this class fall the following types of stimuli:

1. *Intense stimuli*   The stimulus that has the greatest sensory impact will be attended to over others. People will, for instance, attend to a shout over a whisper.
2. *Active stimuli*   Stimuli in both delivery and content that express activity will be attended to over passive ones.
3. *Varied stimuli*   Stimuli that change or that are out of the ordinary or novel hold attention.
4. *Patterned or organized stimuli*   Related stimuli are easier to attend to than jumbled, disorganized stimuli.

The second kind of attention-getting stimuli are those that relate to needs and goals of the audience. Much evidence supports the belief that bodily needs and social goals strongly influence a person's attention. The nervous system seems to monitor available stimuli and to favor the reception of (or attention to) those factors that are related to the individual's needs. For instance, Wispe and Drambarean found that when people had been without food and water for twenty-four hours, they recognized hunger- and thirst-related words more rapidly than other words.[1] We will now discuss at some length the ways by which a communicator can make material appeal to the needs of the audience.

EMOTIONAL PROOF

Emotional proof requires arousing the feelings beyond the usual every-day level. A person who is emotionally aroused feels extraordinarily

---

[1] L. G. Wispe and W. C. Drambarean, "Physiological Need, Word Frequency and Visual Duration Thresholds," *Journal of Experimental Psychology,* 46 (1953), 25–31.

stirred up both mentally and physically. He or she feels the physical side of emotion in the form of increased heart beat and respiration, muscular tension that creates jitters, internal feelings that result from changes in the workings of the digestive system, often called butterflies in the stomach, and an overall sense of agitation. The mental experience of emotion arises from the circumstances in which it is felt. If we see an automobile bearing down on us, we label our feeling as fear or fright. If someone insults us, we call our feeling anger. If we do something that violates our sense of justice or good behavior, we call our feeling shame. Love, anger, hate, disgust, fear, joy, happiness, grief—these are the names we give to our emotions.

A speaker who wants to arouse such emotions in an audience can do so in many ways. The speaker can cite examples of persons whose needs or values are being thwarted in especially moving ways. Or the speaker can vividly show how the needs of audience members themselves are being threatened or denied by some action. In the former case, our emotions are stirred out of sympathy for the victim. We feel the kind of emotion we would ourselves feel if we were in that person's place. Note the following example by a student speaker, Lisa Golub:

Neglect of our elderly is a serious problem in American society.

The first sign of neglect is isolation. Consider family isolation. There is a woman at a nursing home I visit frequently who is a case in point. Gloria is 95 years old. She has been a resident of the Madison Convalescent Home for 13 years. Though she is confined to a wheelchair and cannot speak well due to a stroke, she is a bright and interesting woman. Each day she can be found fully dressed, make-up, and jewelry, her chair near the lobby door—waiting for a friend . . . who never comes. Where is her family? Though she has outlived most, her remaining family lives in Florida. *Florida!* Tell me why have they left a 95 year old woman alone to die, over a thousand miles away from them? "Forgotten." Do you know that there is actually a service in California that you can call if you are near death and for $7.00 an hour they will have someone sit beside you while you die?! If you have no one. If they have forgotten.[2]

---

[2] "The Crown of Life," in *Contemporary American Speeches,* eds. Wil A. Linkugel, et al. (Dubuque, Iowa: Kendall/Hunt, 1982), p. 229.

In this case, emotion is aroused by what is happening to someone else, by our sympathetic response to the frustration of one of that person's basic needs.

Another way of stirring the emotions is to tell the audience what is happening or is about to happen to them personally. Often, a speaker informs the audience of a threat or danger to their welfare. The danger may be the loss of ability to satisfy an important need or the violation of a cherished right, such as freedom of speech. Note, in the following example, how Walter Cronkite makes fear the overriding emotional tone of his speech:

I want to direct my remarks tonight to what I consider a fundamental and dangerous threat to the institution of the free press in America. It is *fundamental,* because it attacks the free flow of information, literally at its source. And it is especially *dangerous* because it comes from the one group most responsible for guarding First Amendment rights—the judiciary, led by the Supreme Court of the United States.

A number of court decisions in recent years, culminating most recently in rulings by the *highest* court, have had the effect of telling the press that it has no special rights, no constitutionally protected function to inform the public—and, by extension, of telling the public that it may not have any particular right to know.

I don't want to exaggerate the danger. I don't think anyone is going to shut down the newspapers or shut off the television networks in the *foreseeable future* . . . but I don't intend to minimize the threat, either. The right of journalists to *publish* the news is not being challenged, but our ability to *get* the news to publish is being undermined in a variety of ways and challenged at the highest levels.

There is no serious effort underway (that I know of) to *junk* the First Amendment. But there is a growing effort in progress to *gut* it; to make it about as meaningful as—an appendix—or a campaign promise.[3]

---

[3] "Is the Free Press in America Under Attack?" in *Vital Speeches of the Day,* 45 (1978–79), 331. Reprinted by permission.

Still another way by which a speaker may set off an emotional reaction is through the use of emotionally charged words. Some terms such as *shameful, cowardly, foolish, liar,* and the like, are calculated to arouse anger. Thus, a speaker who wants members of an audience to reject certain persons or ideas will describe them in such terms. In contrast, some terms are ones of approval, and by using them when speaking about persons or ideas, the speaker stirs positive feeling. Back in 1854, the famous black abolitionist Frederick Douglass aroused shame by describing how little the Fourth of July, a holiday celebrating freedom, meant to American slaves:

What, to the American slave, is your Fourth of July? I answer: a day that reveals to him, more than all other days in the year, the gross injustice and cruelty of which he is the constant victim. To him, your celebration is a sham; your boasted liberty, an unholy license; your national greatness, swelling vanity. Your sounds of rejoicing are empty and heartless; your denunciation of tyrants, brass-fronted impudence; your shouts of liberty and equality, hollow mockery; your prayers and hymns, your sermons and thanksgivings, with all your religious parade and solemnity, are, to him, mere bombast, fraud, deception, impiety, and hypocrisy—a thin veil to cover up crimes which would disgrace a nation of savages. There is not a nation on the earth guilty of practices more shocking and bloody than are the people of the United States, at this very hour.[4]

Finally, a speaker may arouse emotion by showing emotion in delivery. Emotion is contagious. When we see another person in tears, we are made sad ourselves. So we tend to share the feelings that persons around us show. Showing emotion in delivery is especially effective when coupled with another of the means of arousing the emotions we have described. How could Douglass, for example, express those words about slavery without an appropriate emotional involvement himself? A speaker is not an actor, and he will not pretend the visible signs of emotion just to arouse an audience. But if the speaker is committed to the task and believes strongly in the message, then his or her emotion will reveal itself to the audience.

[4] "The Fourth of July," in *Rhetoric of Black Revolution,* ed. Arthur L. Smith (Boston: Allyn and Bacon, 1969), pp. 138–39.

A common type of emotional proof is called *fear appeal*. When using fear appeal, a speaker emphasizes a danger to the audience in the form of a threat to their welfare. The following are some examples of fear appeals: trying to get people to use seat belts by describing the bloody results of an automobile accident; trying to get people to stop smoking by documenting the increased probability of their getting lung cancer; urging people to have regular eye examinations for glaucoma by discussing the prospect of blindness; or even urging people to use mouth wash for fear of offending others. Because of the frequent use of fear appeals, scholars have studied their effectiveness in a variety of experimental situations. Most studies have shown that a proposal accompanied by fear appeals is more effective in changing audience attitudes than a proposal not tied to fear appeals. However, arousing high levels of fear sometimes results in less audience support of the speaker's proposal than does arousing moderate or low levels of fear. Some helpful guidelines in the use of fear appeals follow:

1. A highly credible source (one admired and thought trustworthy by an audience) gets a good response from a strong fear appeal. A less credible source does poorly with a strong fear appeal but does well with a moderate or low level of threat.
2. If a strong fear appeal threatens the welfare of a loved one (spouse, child, relative), it tends to be more effective than if it threatens the members of the audience themselves.
3. A strong fear appeal is more effective if the speaker gives the audience a clear means of coping with the fear and reassures them that their coping will avert the threat.
4. The effectiveness of a strong fear appeal may be related to the audience's personality characteristics. For example, fear appeals influence people with high self-esteem more than people of low self-esteem. (Some recent research, however, suggests that people of moderate self-esteem are the most influenced.) Another variable is coping style: People who cope well react more favorably to a strong fear appeal than do people who cope poorly.
5. Arousing fear in an audience seems to depend on the speaker's ability to convince the audience of the *probability* that the threat is real and of the *magnitude* of the consequences.

We can illustrate the application of these guidelines with the following examples. Suppose that you were trying to convince an audience to go to a health center and get flu inoculations. Clearly this proposal would have to be supported by a fear appeal, that is, by describing for the audience the probable misery they would suffer if, by failing to get an inoculation, they were to get the disease. Before addressing your audience, you would have to decide whether to use a high-, moderate-, or low-level fear appeal. You would base your decision on your judgment of your credibility with the audience and on any information that might shed light on their personality characteristics. Assume that you decided that your level of credibility was high and that the audience, because it was composed of successful professional men and women, had moderate to high levels of self-esteem and good coping habits. You would probably elect to use a high-level fear appeal. Your first job would be to convince the audience of the probability of the threat: If they don't get an inoculation, they may get flu, and if they get flu, they will experience extreme discomfort and serious and possibly permanent damage to health. To increase the impact of the message, you might dwell on the unfortunate impact on loved ones (spouse, children) if flu were to strike the listener.

Not much evidence is available concerning the use of emotional appeals other than fear. Some studies have been done on the emotion of guilt, and many of them suggest that guilt appeals follow the same principles as fear appeals. Lacking definite evidence, a speaker must use his or her own judgment on whether high or low levels of arousal are best. But in all cases, an attempt to arouse emotion is successful to the degree that the speaker convinces the audience that the threatening event will probably take place and that the impact of this event on the audience will be serious.

LOGICAL PROOF

In Chapter 5, we explained and illustrated various types of logical proof. Logical proof depends on the use of evidence in the form of facts, statistics, and the opinions of experts. From this evidence, justified conclusions are drawn. The aim, as with emotional proof, is to establish a link between the speaker's proposals and the needs of the audience.

In the example given below, the speaker, Robert W. Scherer, president of Georgia Power Company, builds a logical case for the construction of nuclear generating plants. He compares advantages to argue that nuclear power is more economical than coal.

There are highly personal, as well as theoretical, reasons why more nuclear power makes sense for all of us. How, for instance, does it affect those in this room? Well, each of you is a consumer of electricity. You have families who'll be needing electricity and other energy in the future years. You're probably questioning, if not complaining about, the rise in your electric bills.

You also drive cars—probably more than one—and have equally serious concerns about the availability of gasoline and what it is going to cost.

Well, let's just see what nuclear power can do for electric rates and the gasoline supply.

Last year, nuclear energy supplied just under eight percent of all the electricity generated in the United States. It saved electric utilities and their customers some 810 million dollars in fuel costs. It generated the power equivalent of some 185 million barrels of oil or 45 million tons of coal. The savings in terms of both dollars and fuel oil will be even more substantial in 1975.

Thus, in a sense, you could say that your cars are running on nuclear fuel to the extent that more fuel oil is available for conversion to gasoline. And the pennies you save on your electric bill will at least help to pay for the higher prices you're seeing at the gasoline pump.

The cost of fuel for the nation's nuclear plants last year was less than one-fifth as much per kilowatt of generation as that of coal or fuel oil. This is not too surprising when we consider that a thimbleful of nuclear fuel produces as much energy as 1100 gallons of fuel oil or seven tons of coal.

Nuclear power generation in 1974—including the higher costs of building nuclear plants—was forty percent below the cost of coal or oil generation. So this is clearly one way to cut down on future electric bills for everyone.

Far greater fuel savings are attainable with the plants now planned or licensed for construction. These plants would increase our nuclear power output more than sixfold above present levels. They would do the work of almost three billion barrels of oil per year, worth some thirty-six billion dollars at current prices.[5]

[5] Robert W. Scherer, "Industry's Prospectus for the Future of Nuclear Power," *Vital Speeches of the Day,* 42 (1975-1976), 28. Reprinted by permission.

A clash between logical proofs and emotional ones is nowhere better illustrated than in the attack made on the nuclear-power industry by its opponents since the time of Scherer's speech in 1975. Anti–nuclear power speakers have emphasized three highly threatening fear appeals and have succeeded in creating a vocal and active body of public opposition. The arguments run as follows:

1. A nuclear power plant is very likely to have a serious accident in which deadly radiation will be released, threatening the life and health of the surrounding population.
2. Water used to cool reactors is discharged into rivers and streams and along ocean shores, where it threatens the animal and plant life necessary for a balanced environment and productive fisheries.
3. Spent fuel remains radioactive for generations and cannot safely be disposed of. It will leak into the environment at great hazard to human life and health.

These emotional arguments have resulted in the slowing down, almost halting, of nuclear-power-plant construction in America. They are reasonable because there is a factual basis for the threats that are said to exist in nuclear-power generation. An emotional argument, therefore, is trustworthy to the degree that it can be supported by evidence and argument.

Evidence and argument, the two essential ingredients of logical proof, were discussed at some length in Chapter 5. You should review that material carefully. In addition, a short discussion of consistency theories, which have a logical base, should prove helpful here.

Consistency theories assume that people try to avoid contradictory or inconsistent beliefs, attitudes, and actions. For instance, people do not normally declare themselves to be staunch Democrats and then vote for a Republican candidate. Neither do they declare themselves to be in favor of abortion on demand and then support a Constitutional amendment to make abortions illegal. The earliest consistency theory, advanced by Heider, was called *balance* theory. It argued simply that a person preserves a balanced state among thoughts by disbelieving or explaining away thoughts that are inconsistent with his or her attitude toward a given concept.[6]

---

[6] Robert B. Zajonc, "The Concepts of Balance, Congruity and Dissonance," *Public Opinion Quarterly*, 24 (1960), 280–296.

Osgood and Tannenbaum extended balance theory with *congruity* theory.[7] This three-element consistency theory tried to predict the direction and extent of change to be expected when contradiction, or incongruity, existed. Balance or consistency theory may be illustrated as follows: A person, P, is seen as having either positive (+) or negative (–) attitudes toward an object, O, and a source, S. P receives information from the source that is either positive (+) or negative (–) toward the object. No imbalance or incongruity exists if the information given by the source is consistent with the person's attitude both toward the object and toward the source, as follows:

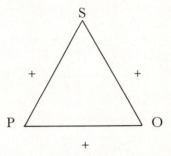

However, incongruity does exist if there is inconsistency among these three elements, as follows:

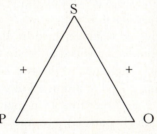

In the latter case, the person has a positive attitude toward the source and a negative one toward the concept. But the source speaks positively of the concept. In such a case, the person would be motivated by the prevailing incongruity to restore consistency to the situation. If S were delivering a persuasive speech with respect to concept O, he or she would hope that P would restore congruity by changing the negative attitude toward O to a positive one.

[7] Charles Osgood and Percy Tannenbaum, "The Principles of Congruity in the Prediction of Attitude Change," *Psychological Review*, 62 (1955), 42–55.

A couple of specific applications of this theory will illustrate its meaning. Let P represent yourself. Assume that you have a positive attitude
toward the governor of your state. Assume also that you have a positive
attitude toward building a new university stadium. The governor, however, makes a statement strongly opposing the building of the stadium.
The situation is thus an imbalanced or incongruous one and would be
diagrammed as follows:

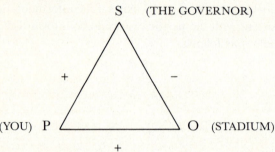

Since this situation is unbalanced, the theory predicts that P (you) would
restore balance by becoming less positive toward S (the governor), by
becoming less positive toward O (the stadium), or by somehow changing
your attitude toward both S and O. As Heider saw it, there was no clear
way to predict which of these alternatives you, P, would take.

Osgood and Tannenbaum felt that if you could measure the strength of
attitude, whether positive or negative, held by P toward S and O, you
would have a basis for predicting which direction the change would take.
They argued that the less ingrained of the two attitudes would be more
likely to change. By using a 7-point attitude scale, they could measure P's
attitude and assign a 1 to 3 positive or negative value to it. In our
example, if your attitude (P's attitude) toward the governor measured
$+2.5$ and your attitude toward the stadium measured $+1$, the diagram
would look like the following:

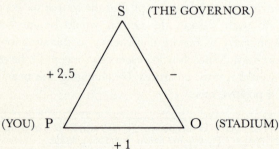

Given these measures of attitude strength, we could predict with some confidence that you (P) would restore balance to the situation by becoming much less positive toward the stadium, since that positive attitude was much weaker than the positive attitude toward the governor.

Osgood and Tannenbaum were remarkably successful in predicting the direction of attitude change in this kind of three-element situation, but their theory failed to cover situations involving more than three elements. Leon Festinger formulated a more broadly based consistency theory, which he called the theory of *cognitive dissonance*.[8] This theory builds on the theory of inner-need states. Festinger said that a person who responds to an inner-need state experiences conflict as he or she weighs alternative means of satisfying that need. This conflict is an uncomfortable feeling and motivates the person to make a choice or decision. While experiencing conflict, according to Festinger, a person is objective and unbiased in weighing the advantages and disadvantages of a particular decision. Once that person makes a decision, however, he or she tends to become biased in defense of it when presented with information that is inconsistent with it. When the person encounters information that conflicts with the decision, he or she experiences an uncomfortable inner state called *dissonance* and is motivated to take steps to reduce the dissonance. The extent of the dissonance is a measure of the person's motivation: the greater the dissonance, the greater the motivation to resolve it.

To apply this theory in persuasion, a speaker reminds the audience of decisions, attitudes, and actions they have embraced and then charges them with being inconsistent in some other aspect of their behavior. The speaker then recommends that the inconsistent behavior be brought into line with established attitudes. In the 1960s, it was common practice for black speakers to charge Americans with political and religious inconsistency in their treatment of blacks. They were echoing an argument of long standing, one that Frederick Douglass used so effectively when addressing a white audience on July 4, 1852:

Americans! your republican politics, not less than your republican union, are flagrantly inconsistent. You boast of your love of liberty, your superior civilization, and your pure Christianity while the

[8] Leon Festinger, *A Theory of Cognitive Dissonance* (New York: Row, Peterson, 1957), p. 291.

whole political power of the nation (as embodied in the two great political parties) is solemnly pledged to support and perpetuate the enslavement of three millions of your countrymen. You hurl your anathemas at the crowned headed tyrants of Russia and Austria and pride yourselves on your Democratic institutions, while you yourselves consent to be the mere tools and bodyguards of the tyrants of Virginia and Carolina. You invite to your shores fugitives of oppression from abroad, honor them with banquets, greet them with ovations, cheer them, toast them, salute them, protect them, and pour out your money to them like water; but the fugitives from your own land you advertise, hunt, arrest, shoot, and kill. You glory in your refinement and your universal education; yet you maintain a system as barbarous and dreadful as ever stained the character of a nation. . . .

You declare before the world, and are understood by the world to declare that you "hold these truths to be self-evident, that all men are created equal; and are endowed by their Creator with certain inalienable rights; and that among these are, life, liberty, and the pursuit of happiness;" and yet, you hold securely, in a bondage which, according to your own Thomas Jefferson, "is worse than ages of that which your father rose in rebellion to oppose," a seventh part of the inhabitants of your country.

Fellow citizens, I will not enlarge further on your national inconsistencies.[9]

Pointing out inconsistencies often leads an audience to defensive rationalizations rather than to changed behavior. A speaker, thus, should not expect that merely expressing inconsistency will be sufficient. He or she must resort to other arguments and kinds of proof. A speaker may also have to accept that changing the behavior of people with deeply committed views may take years or decades.

ETHICAL PROOF

The consistency theory of Heider and the congruity theory of Osgood and Tannenbaum were based on the assumption that people would like to

---

[9] In Arthur L. Smith, pp. 148–149.

have the same attitude toward a concept as they have toward an admired source. Thus, if an admired source favored a concept, the receiver would like to favor it, too; if the source rejected a concept, the receiver would like to reject it. Given this situation, a highly credible source would be more effective in changing attitudes than a less credible source. To take advantage of the theory, then, speakers should try to increase their credibility with the audience before disclosing the attitude that they want the audience to adopt. If, for instance, you know that your level of credibility with the audience is low and you proceed without trying to increase your credibility, you will not enjoy the advantage of consistency tendencies in the audience. On the other hand, if you increase your credibility, the audience will be inclined to support your proposal because of consistency tendencies.

How do you go about building credibility? One method is to arrange for the disclosure of favorable information about yourself prior to the delivery of the speech. Usually, a moderator or presiding officer presents such information in a speech of introduction. Experimental studies have shown that favorable information given in a speech of introduction can change a speaker's credibility level from low to high, with a corresponding increase in the persuasiveness of the message. The speaker may provide the moderator with the kinds of information necessary for a good introduction, such as evidence of the speaker's expertness on the topic as a result of education and experience and indications of the speaker's good character and trustworthiness.

A speaker may also build credibility by citing his or her credentials at the beginning of the speech. This approach was used, for example, by John R. Howard, president of Lewis and Clark College, when he was speaking to an audience of Oregon industrial and labor leaders. Howard felt that his audience might think him an impractical dreamer because he was an educator. Note how he cites evidence to overcome that impression:

Because I am president of a private liberal arts college, you may well question my credentials for speaking on economic matters to a gathering of Oregon's industrial and labor leadership.

Let me tell you. In the first place, the institution I serve employs more than 450 persons—not an inconsiderable enterprise even by corporate standards.

Secondly, higher education generally is one of this—and every—state's largest enterprises and perhaps the single most important investment area, underpinning and explaining the extraordinary progress in the United States since World War II. Few of you will fault the contribution of the colleges and universities in supplying educated and mentally-agile men and women for key positions in your companies. Most of the research that finally translated into sellable commodities was at least begun in the campus laboratories.[10]

Howard thus gives the impression that he is just as much a businessperson and manager as are the people in his audience.

Another way in which the speaker may establish credibility is by stressing that his or her background and ideology are like the audience's. Doing this makes the audience feel that the speaker is one of them and, consequently, a person worthy of belief. In the following example, the speaker is Neil O'Connor, chairman of the board of an advertising agency. As he addresses an audience of news personnel in Syracuse, New York, he stresses common ground with his listeners:

Thanks for the warmth of your welcome, a welcome back to Syracuse. One does feel old when he comes back to a place where he's been young. And while my sporting life in college here was pretty much confined to a parked car in Thorndon Park, I have to realize that on the Syracuse campus, I even antedate Ben Schwartzwalder.

I owe a lot to Syracuse. My father and mother both graduated from the University. Two of my father's brothers made their careers in this city. One was even President of this very hotel. I met a certain Nancy Turner, class of 1950, here. She is now Mrs. O'Connor. One of our oldest and most valued clients, The Carrier Corporation, has made this its headquarters city. I have many good friends here whom I see all too seldom.

I have a great respect for Syracuse, for the city and its people. It is an important and prosperous market for our clients' goods and services. We use it often to try out our clients' new products and ideas before we try them out on the rest of America. Local markets, and local marketing, have a lot of advocates in the advertising

---

[10] John R. Howard, "A College President Addresses Corporate Leaders," *Vital Speeches of the Day*, 42 (1975–1976), 50. Reprinted by permission.

business. Syracuse stands at the top of that list and I know the efforts of many of you here are going to keep it up there.

So it's nice to be back and I thank you for asking me and giving me this chance to talk with you.[11]

A clear delivery that is friendly and open tends to enhance credibility. The use of humor may also cause the audience to see the speaker as more trustworthy, but not necessarily as more competent.

We should note also that any change in attitude induced by a speaker's credibility tends to shrink over time. But, if a credible source uses credible evidence in a speech, the rate of decay can be slowed down. Finally, the credibility of a speaker may change from one speech situation to another. It may also change over time with repeated exposures to the same audience. (Take, for example, Richard Nixon's exposure to the American people.)

SOCIAL-CONFORMITY PROOF

Infants learn basic behavior patterns (how to eat, speak, walk, dress) from their parents. They also learn a vast array of values and attitudes. When they are old enough to move outside the home, they are influenced by the behavior of people at school, in the church, in neighborhood groups or gangs, and in a variety of other groups. They are influenced not only by the behavior but also by the opinions of others, which reach them directly or through the media. Thus, by the teen-age years, a child has become more a reflection of other people than a unique personality. This may be an overstatement, but consider the social forces that have shaped the child:

1. *Admired individuals* These may be parents, teachers, entertainers, politicians, friends, writers, or others. These admired persons provide role models for the child to imitate. The child tends to copy their lifestyle and behavior and to adopt their opinions and attitudes.

[11] Neil O'Connor, "The Freedom to Communicate," *Vital Speeches of the Day,* 43 (1976–1977), 179. Reprinted by permission.

2. *Peer groups*   People identify early with those of their own age who have common interests. In school, a student may identify with the student government, the debate squad, the drama club, or a variety of service or civic clubs. He or she may also identify with certain cliques or gangs and may mold thought and behavior out of a desire to be accepted and respected by these groups.
3. *Societal norms*   Standards of behavior are imposed by our social interactions with other people, even if we are not conscious of group affiliation with them. These norms are so widely accepted by society as a whole that they tend to become invisible rules for behavior. Our notion of what is masculine and feminine are examples. So, too, is our idea of correct social behavior in formal as opposed to informal situations. Even our definitions of *formal* and *informal* are taught to us by our society. Many of our prejudices against ethnic groups other than our own spring from unconscious imitation of the values of the society in which we move.

The persuasive speaking situation is open to several ways of bringing social pressure to bear. Some studies have shown that merely reminding an audience of group affiliation causes them to be aware of and influenced by the norms of that group. Thus, saying things like "Being Catholic, you know that . . ." or "You're aware of what the constitution of this organization says about . . ." is enough to set loose the persuasive force of group norms. Of course, a person's vulnerability to the persuasive power of such norms depends on the value he or she places on membership in the group.

Another way to use societal norms persuasively is to cite public-opinion polls and surveys. Data of this sort exist on almost every topic you can imagine, from the percentage of persons who endorsed the Equal Rights Amendment to the number opposing capital punishment. However, in the absence of survey information, a speaker may cite the respected leaders' opinions about the nature of group norms. The speaker may say, for instance, "George Meany assures us that the vast majority of laborers believe . . ." or something similar. In some circumstances, a speaker may use personal observations about the extent of opinion or the existence of compelling norms.

To illustrate the use of societal norms, here is a Harris poll used to underscore the seriousness of the problem the speaker is about to discuss. The speaker, Frank Lyon, Jr., senior vice president of Union Carbide, has used part of his introduction to outline the contributions that business has

made to society. He then contrasts the attitude one would expect from the
public with their actual attitude:

On the basis of these achievements, it would seem natural that
business, and particularly the economic system in which it operates,
would be held in the highest esteem.

But we all know that this is not the case. Far from it.

According to a public opinion poll conducted by Louis Harris last
May, only 19 percent of Americans voiced a great deal of confidence
in the executives of major corporations. Last year, the percentage
was 21 percent and ten years ago it was 55 percent. In another poll,
61 percent of the public stated that they believe there is a conspiracy
among the big corporations to set prices as high as possible. The
recent disclosures of corporate bribes and other corrupt activities
have given an even bigger push to the anti-business bandwagon. As
Supreme Court Justice Lewis F. Powell has written: "Business and
the free enterprise system are in deep trouble, and the hour is late."

Given the negative public opinion about business, it is not surprising to find considerable political support for legislative programs
whose basic thrust is to extend the scope of government intervention
into the private sector.[12]

Lyon's use of public opinion and of the opinion of a respected Supreme
Court justice gets the audience to listen to why government regulation of
business is undesirable and to Lyon's proposals for how the audience
should combat such regulation.

Speakers seldom rely on social norms as sufficient proof of their proposals. Other psychological and logical arguments are combined with
such proofs for maximum persuasive effect.

SPEECHES TO CONVINCE

In speeches to convince, the speaker aims to secure agreement to a
proposal by offering a series of sound reasons for support based on

---

[12] Frank Lyon, Jr., "Business and Government Controls," *Vital Speeches of the Day*, 42
(1975–1976), 83. Reprinted by permission.

evidence and argument. A speech to convince may also contain emotional, ethical, and social-conformity types of proof, but it depends mainly on careful cause-and-effect reasoning bolstered with statistics, factual evidence in the form of examples, and expert and lay testimony. A speech to convince is different from a speech to activate (which will be discussed in the next section) not only in the type of proof it uses, but also in that it does not call on the audience to take overt action. It simply asks the audience to share the speaker's belief. Thus, the specific-purpose statement may say, "The insanity defense in murder trials should be prohibited." The speaker wants only agreement with this proposal and does not ask the audience to take steps to see that it is put into practice. Again, you should go back to Chapter 5 to review the material there on cause-and-effect reasoning.

A sample outline for a speech to convince follows:

Introduction
  I. In October, 1967, two small Egyptian boats, miles away from their target, fired three Styx missiles at the Israeli destroyer, Elath. Unable to outmaneuver the missiles, the Elath was struck and sunk.
 II. The lesson of the Elath was simple. In an age of missiles, naval vessels are highly vulnerable.
III. *Purpose sentence*: Modern missiles are so effective at sea that large surface ships are no longer useful.

Body
  I. The large surface vessel is too large to go undetected at sea:
     A. United States nuclear-powered aircraft carriers are in the 90,000-ton class. The decks are as long as three football fields.
     B. Sophisticated radar, sonar, and spy satellites make it possible for the enemy to keep such ships under surveillance at all times.
     C. U.S. submarine commanders, in naval exercises, are repeatedly able to line up big carriers and cruisers in their periscope sights without being detected themselves.
 II. Once located, large surface ships like aircraft carriers, are sitting ducks for missiles that fly above the surface or swim beneath it:
     A. Examples of battleship kills in the Falkland Island war illustrate the surface ship's vulnerability.

1. The Argentine cruiser General Belgrano was sunk by two Tigerfish torpedoes fired by a British nuclear-powered sub.
2. The Sheffield, a British destroyer, was sunk by a single Exocet missile fired by an Argentine aircraft.
3. Shortly after these sinkings, the British frigates, Antelope and Ardent were destroyed, and later, other warships were struck and sunk or heavily damaged.

B. Reasons for the vulnerability of large ships are twofold.
1. The array of weapons that can be launched against them is awesome.
   a. "Smart" cruise missiles may be launched from as far away as 280 miles and home in on their target by computer calculation.
   b. The U.S. Tomahawk missile has a range of 1550 miles, slips through radar, and can carry conventional or nuclear warheads.
   c. The Soviet Backfire carries two AS-4 cruise missiles, which have a range of 500 miles, and travels two or three times faster than sound.
2. Big ships are floating gasoline stations and mobile ammunition dumps. Loaded with flammables and explosives, they can be destroyed, not by the original hit, but by their resulting internal explosions.

III. Such vulnerability limits the usefulness of a navy in wartime:
A. Experts think a U.S. carrier group would have little chance of surviving an all out Soviet attack. Therefore, admirals would be reluctant to engage the enemy for fear of destruction.
B. It would be better to have a navy composed of many small ships. Admirals could expect to lose a number of them in an engagement but would not have the entire force neutralized.
C. Small ships can now carry more arms and more destructive ones than big battleships used to carry.

Conclusion
I. In summary, large ships are so vulnerable to destruction by sophisticated weapons that they could not long survive in actual battle. Their usefulness in war is, therefore, extremely limited.
II. It would be wiser to build many small ships and expect to lose a number of them than to have fleets of huge vessels that admirals would be afraid to commit to battle.

SPEECHES TO ACTIVATE

In a speech to activate you will be calling on members of an audience not merely to believe in a proposition, but to do something about it. You may want them to do such things as spend money, volunteer services, or take action to promote a goal or solve a problem. Usually speeches to activate are constructed on the problem-solution pattern. The speaker first points out a problem that affects the audience and then offers a solution to it. But to actually get the audience to take action, the speaker must show convincingly that the benefits of the recommended solution outweigh the costs to the audience of acting on it. For example, if you want an audience to give money to a fund to be used to revive the Equal Rights Amendment, you would have to plan somewhat as follows:

I. Demonstrate that reviving and passing the ERA will be advantageous:
    A. The advantages will benefit members of the audience personally, their families and friends, and the community and the nation.
    B. The advantages stressed should be not only material ones such as better jobs, better pay, and the like, but also other satisfactions in the form of enhanced self-esteem, personal growth, and enforcement of such values as fairness and justice.
II. Disadvantages or costs should be honestly assessed:
    A. Disadvantages should be weighed against advantages.
    B. Advantages must be shown to be greater than disadvantages.

A good example of a speech to activate is "A Time for Peace," by Kenda Creasy. Creasy, an undergraduate student at Miami University, won first place in the Interstate Oratorical Association national contest in 1980. Note how she presents the problem of handling terminally ill patients, a problem that affects, or is likely to affect, audience members. She then shows by careful comparison the advantages of her proposal over the usual way of dealing with terminal illness.

A Time for Peace

"To all things there is a season; and a time to every purpose under heaven—a time to be born, and a time to die. . ."
Except today. Today modern medicine is better prepared to pro-

long life in all seasons. But for millions of Americans this year, it won't be enough. They will be diagnosed as terminally ill—and once labeled terminal, our medical know-how no longer applies. According to the Department of Health, Education and Welfare, you and I stand a one in four chance of suddenly assuming unexpected responsibilities because someone in *our* family has been diagnosed as terminally ill. But we could have help—with hospices.

A hospice is an alternative method of terminal care comprised of a team of doctors, psychologists, clergy, and volunteers who, basically, make housecalls. A hospice's aim is to help people die with as little discomfort and as much serenity as possible, involving family and friends along the way, and usually taking place in the person's home. Hospices do not cure; instead, they make medical, psychological, and spiritual help available to both the patient AND his family, before and after the funeral. As one health analyst put it, "A hospice is really more of an idea than a place." Unfortunately, even though the hospice movement is supported by the American Medical Association and HEW, hospices in the United States are too unknown to have the impact they could have. So what can we do? Well, first we must compare hospices with our present ailing approach to terminal illness, and then see what we can do to remedy the problem. At least then we can stop sacrificing a quality of life for a quantity of days.

The traditional American approach to terminal illness ignores three basic facts of life: the limits of curative medicine, the isolation of institutions, and the psychological impact death has on both the patient and his family. The first problem is the inherent limits of a medical system designed to cure. Hospitals *maintain* life: everything from visiting hours to progress reports are designed for the temporary stay. But the terminal patient's stay is *not* temporary; he will not get well. *Time* magazine pointed out in June, 1978, "Imbued as the medical establishment is with the idea of fighting at all costs to prolong life, it is naturally geared to the hope of success rather than to the fact of failure." But as *Changing Times* explained in April, 1979, "When care designed to cure and rehabilitate is applied to a person who knows he has a terminal illness, it creates a feeling of isolation and despair, especially if he senses the staff is just going through the motions."

Hospices make no such false promises. Dr. James Cimino explains, "For the hospice patient, it is too late for cures. The operations, radiation, and chemotherapy have been tried elsewhere.

They've been declared incurable and inoperable. The patient is entirely aware of his situation.'' Hospices provide two choices: either the person can go to the hospice or, more likely, the hospice will come to him, 24 hours a day, if necessary, with a team of doctors, psychologists, clergy, good neighbors, and volunteers. Treatment is palliative—that is, designed to ease pain and manage symptoms, such as nausea, but no heroic effort is made to cure the disease. The results? The person is comfortable, and his mind is clear.

Unfortunately, there is more to dying than just futile treatment of an illness. The second problem is institutionalization, which is more often easy than essential. Nearly 70% of terminally ill Americans spend their final year in a hospital or a nursing home—but at the moment, there is not much choice. For one thing, says John Abbott of Hospice, Inc., families doubt their own ability to care for a dying member, and find institutions more convenient. But in a hospice, he says, ''When families ask, 'Can we care for our loved one?' we say, 'Yes you can—and we'll help you.' '' The problem is, first you've got to find the hospice.

This summer, a family friend's grandmother spent the last six weeks of her life in the hospital begging to go home. The family was unable to find someone willing to provide round-the-clock painkillers to a ninety-three-year-old woman dying at home, and they called me to see if I knew of anyone. ''The physical pain,'' they said, ''doesn't hurt her half as much as not being home.'' Well, I didn't know of anyone—and two weeks later she died: in the hospital, by herself. To all things there is a season.

Had I known at that time that a hospice was located in Central Ohio, that expensive and futile hospitalization could have been avoided. And more importantly, a person who desperately wanted to be at home when she died could have been spared the trauma of an institution. Hospices in New Haven, Connecticut, allow 50% of terminally ill patients in that area to live at home—at a cost, incidentally, of about $25 a day, as opposed to $200 a day in a hospital. In those hospices which do provide residential facilities, rules are avoided, visiting hours are round-the-clock, and pets and personal effects are encouraged. Hospices allow that choice. Institutions do not.

But the third problem of terminal illness comes *after* the funeral, for in what psychologists call our ''death-denying culture,'' we ignore the family and deny them the catharsis of knowing they have done everything that they can. The Comptroller General's Report to Congress found that, as a result of a dying person's illness, family suicides jumped significantly. Three sociologists' study of widows found that 24% developed reactive depression, 12% became emotionally unstable, and 4% turned to alcohol within the first year of their husbands' deaths. Two separate studies show, that parents stand a 70% chance of divorce within two years of the death of a child.

Susan Silver, of the National Hospice Organization, explains: "When a family is intimately involved with a dying member, there is much less guilt afterward. They witness the natural dying process, they give of themselves, and their grief is not so prolonged." Hospice personnel do everything from drafting wills to feeding pets to providing family counseling—including a follow-up after the funeral. Volunteers either help out within the households or are trained by the hospice professionals. One woman, after a hospice team had helped her cope with her mother's death, said, "When she died it was a victory for all of us. None of us felt any guilt."

Today we appreciate life more—and go to greater lengths to preserve it—than any society in human history. But the fact is, for some of us, modern medical miracles will fail. Terminal illness is not discriminating: heart disease has no season, sickle cell anemia has no cure. There is a cancer death every 80 seconds—and one out of every four people you've met this weekend will eventually have cancer. What if, when you call home tonight, you find out it has hit there as well? It does happen.

The hospice movement in the United States needs our support, and with three simple steps we can provide it. First, encourage federal, state, and local government efforts to enhance the hospice movement. For example, as some states have already done, Medicare and Medicaid must be expanded to include hospice care for the aged and the poor.

Second, protect yourself. Buy insurance that covers hospices as well as hospitalization. Blue Cross and Blue Shield already do that; but with incentive, other companies would follow suit.

And most importantly, you and I have got to provide the personal concern that sets hospice care apart in the first place. Tell your parents about hospices: if they become ill tomorrow, wouldn't you want them to know? Or what if they did know, but there was no hospice that was near enough to help? Many hospices begin through local churches or community organizations, with grants available from HEW; consider them for yours. And above all, when someone *you* care for is diagnosed as terminally ill—and it *will* happen—don't simply say, "Well, if there's anything I can do. . ." Call him up, walk the dog, provide cassettes for last notes, help tie up school or business ends. The important thing to remember is that hospices are not places, they're people. But without the support of family and friends, hospice becomes just another empty room.

When Joseph Califano visited the New Haven hospice, he said: "I visited with the idea that hospice was about dying. I came away realizing it's about living." We can't give a dying person *more* time—for to all things there *is* a season. But with little effort and much compassion, we *can* give him back the time he has. . . A time to cry, and a time to laugh; a time for love, and a time for peace.[13]

The structure of Creasy's speech stands out if it is put into outline form. Also, the relationship of the outline to the finished form of the speech becomes clear. This outline was not prepared by Creasy but was made, after the fact, from the speech manuscript itself.

Introduction
  I. "To all things there is a season . . ." etc.
 II. American medical know-how has interfered with the time to die and has brought unexpected responsibilities to families of the terminally ill.
III. *Purpose sentence*: The hospice is a desirable alternative to our present way of dealing with terminal illness because it recognizes the limits of curative medicine, the isolation brought by institutionalization, and the psychological impact of death on the patient and the family.

Body
  I. Curative medicine is not equipped to cope with terminal illness:
    A. The patient cannot get well; the illness is not curable or temporary.

---

[13] *Winning Orations* (Mankato, Minn.: Interstate Oratorical Assoc., Mankato State Univ., 1980), pp. 81–83. Reprinted by permission.

B. A medical system designed to cure does not help a terminal patient; instead, it creates despair.

C. A hospice makes no false curative promises. Treatment is designed to ease pain, not to cure.

II. Under our present system, terminal patients are institutionalized—nearly 70% of them spend their final year in a hospital or nursing home:

A. Institutionalization may be convenient, but the isolation from home and family is bad for the patient.

   1. Example of a terminally ill patient—a friend's grandmother.

   2. Explanation of how this person could have been helped by a hospice.

B. A hospice allows 50% of its patients to live at home. The others are spared expense and futile hospitalization.

III. The third problem of terminal illness is the psychological impact on the patient's family:

A. We live in a death-denying culture that denies families the relief of knowing they have done all they can.

B. There is evidence of the tragic impact on families.

   1. Family suicides jump significantly after a dying person's illness.

   2. Twenty-four percent of widows develop reactive depression, 12% become unstable, and 4% turn to alcohol within a year.

   3. Parents run a 70% chance of divorce after the death of a child.

C. Susan Silver, of the National Hospice Organization, testifies as to how the hospice experience helps avoid these results.

IV. The hospice movement needs your support. You can help with three simple steps:

A. Encourage federal, state, and local efforts to expand the hospice movement.

B. Protect yourself by buying insurance that covers hospices as well as hospitals.

C. Use your influence to spread the hospice idea to your parents, your local churches, and community groups.

Conclusion

I. Quotation from Joseph Califano.

CREATING RESISTANCE TO COUNTERPERSUASION

A persuasive speaker may succeed in influencing an audience. But the influence may collapse under later attacks by advocates with contrary proposals. It becomes important, therefore, for a speaker to know how to make the audience resist counterpersuasion.

One of the primary methods is to present a two-sided or multisided case—one in which the speaker presents the arguments in favor of a proposal and then considers and refutes the opposing arguments. A two-sided presentation is usually more effective than a one-sided presentation. One-sided and two-sided presentations may be compared as follows:

1. A one-sided presentation seems best when an audience agrees from the start with the speaker's proposal and the aim is to strengthen agreement. A two-sided presentation is best with an audience that disagrees with the speaker's proposal.
2. Regardless of the audience's attitude, a two-sided presentation is best when they will later be exposed to counter-persuasion.
3. When the audience has a low level of involvement with the topic, or the position taken by the speaker is widely different from their views, a two-sided speech is most effective.
4. A two-sided speech seems to ensure that any change in attitude provoked by the speech will last longer than if the attitude change is secured by a one-sided speech.
5. A one-sided speech is more effective with subjects who are poorly educated, while a two-sided speech is more effective with well-educated people.

These comparisons show clearly that a two-sided presentation is generally best. It appears that a one-sided presentation is called for only when the audience already agrees with the speaker or is composed of poorly educated people.

Encouraging the audience to commit themselves to the position advocated by the speaker can also guard against counterpersuasion. A private commitment might involve having audience members write down on a card how fully they agree with the speaker. Those who indicate any degree of agreement will be less likely to change under counterpersuasion than if they had not made such an indication. However, a public commitment is a better way to increase resistance to future persuasive attack. In a public commitment, people might be asked to hold up their hands, stand up, sign a petition, or answer an attack on the speaker's position. Even such common signs of agreement as applause and shouts of "Yes, yes," "Give 'em hell," and so forth, are commitments that strengthen resistance. A public commitment becomes strongest when it involves behavior consistent with the belief. Thus, a person who answers an attack on the speaker's position makes a strong identification with it and becomes more resistant to change. Political candidates who induce people to make telephone calls for them, mail envelopes, solicit funds, and so on, have no fear that those people will drift to the other camp.

Another way to harden the audience against future attacks is to warn them against counterpersuasion. A number of experimental studies have shown that merely announcing to an audience that someone will try to persuade them will sometimes reduce the likelihood of their responding favorably to a persuasive attempt.

A warning that attacks the credibility of a future persuader has been shown to be effective in many cases. Thus, a speaker trying to get an audience to quit smoking may tell them that they may later hear other speakers deny a connection between smoking and lung cancer. The speaker would then point out to the audience that those speakers are representatives of the tobacco industry and are acting in their own self-interest.

The following paragraph is an example of an actual warning that was used in a debate concerning the effect of cola drinks on human health. Although it was used in an experimental setting, it represents a certain type of warning that speakers can actually give.

Dr. Dennis Alterman: Just a moment, I am very familiar with what Dr. Abelson is going to say on this issue. So, before he begins I would just like to say a few things. I do not think that carbonated cola soft drinks are harmful for the individual and any intelligent person will come to the same conclusion after considering the matter. Also, I do not accept and only the most uneducated individual will accept the arguments that he is going to present on cola soft drinks being associated with malnutrition, insomnia, heart disease, dental disease, and sclerosis of the liver.[14]

---

[14] Dominic A. Infante, "Forewarnings in Persuasion ...," *Western Speech,* 37 (1973), 190.

This warning includes nothing but the opinion of the speaker and a list of the types of argument that will be forthcoming in the counterpersuasive message. Other warnings might include evidence supporting the speaker's own position, evidence and arguments disproving conclusions to be drawn by the counterpersuader, and reminders of audience values and attitudes that would be inconsistent with acceptance of the counter-position.

In concluding this discussion of creating resistance to persuasion, we should repeat that the best method seems to be the two-sided presentation, in which the speaker predicts counterarguments, analyzes them for the audience, and refutes them. Common sense would call on the speaker to attempt a variety of ways of increasing resistance, not just one.

CONFLICTS BEYOND PERSUASION

By the process of persuasion described in this chapter, the people in American society are able to resolve most of their conflicts. In some cases, however, conflicts of interest are so incompatible that persuasion fails. For persuasion to succeed, both parties in a conflict must be willing to accept less than an ideal solution—to suffer some loss. When conflicting parties are unwilling to do this, when each insists on all or nothing, the process of persuasion tends to be supplemented by combative techniques that contain strong elements of coercion. These techniques include: (1)highly emotional, insulting, goading and even obscene verbal assaults on others; (2)symbolic behaviors, such as marching, demonstrating, draft-card burning, occupying buildings, and blocking traffic; (3)the use of threats of reprisal or the actual use of reprisals to ensure compliance; and (4)the use of symbolic acts of violence, such as smashing a window display, ransacking a draft-board office, or physically assaulting people. These tactics are labeled coercive because, for most people, they limit freedom of choice. A noncoercive communication is one that a listener feels allows for as much choice as possible; a coercive communication is seen as an attempt to limit the listener's choice to whatever is being advocated by the communicator. Thus, insulting or obscene language, symbolic behavior, reprisals, and acts of violence are seen by most people as attempts to restrict their freedom.

It may well be argued that all persuasive attempts have some elements of coercion in them. The purest kind of persuasion, however, provides

PURE PERSUASION	COERCIVE PERSUASION	PURE COERCION
Maximum Choice	Limited Choice	No Choice

Figure 10.1   A CONTINUUM OF PERSUASION TO COERCION.

listeners with the maximum amount of choice. This can be represented on a continuum, as shown in Figure 10.1. In the gray area, speeches that are not pure persuasion take place. This area contains reprisal threats that limit freedom of choice. The users of coercive persuasion often threaten, but either do not carry out their threats or make only minor reprisals. In the black area, however, words are backed up with symbolic deeds that result in forced compliance.

There is no question that coercive persuasion and pure coercion often work. Many people change their attitudes only after they have been forced to change their behavior. Attitudes toward school desegregation in America illustrate this point. But coercive persuasion has disadvantages also. It tends to get out of hand and to emphasize extreme behavior to the point that serious repressive measures are adopted against it. Second, it is generally not effective in persuading people unless they are vulnerable to such tactics and are unable to fight back. If they are not vulnerable (that is, if their property and goods cannot be damaged or stolen or their positions in the economic and social world threatened), they may be unmoved or provoked to hostility. Finally, such tactics may foster in society a feeling that any means is appropriate to bring about change. In some cases, this may be an acceptable position, but in the majority of cases, a society must insist on rational examination and reasonable justification of proposed change.

SUMMARY

The traditional proofs of persuasive speakers, according to Aristotle, are logical, ethical, and emotional. Another kind of proof is social-conformity proof, which rests on the desire of people to be like others. Proofs do not have much impact unless the audience attends to them; hence, a first requirement of persuasive speaking is to gain attention. The speaker gets attention by relating proposals to the needs of the audience and by using material that is characterized by intensity, activity, variety, and organization.

Emotional proofs spring from aroused feelings. Speakers can arouse feelings by citing examples in which needs and values of people or of the audience themselves are being thwarted. Speakers can also use emotionally charged words or show emotion in delivery. Logical proofs depend on the use of evidence and argument. Consistency theories, such as the balance, congruity, and cognitive dissonance theories, stress an audience's desire to maintain consistency among various beliefs and attitudes. Ethical proof results from the audience's perception of the speaker's intelligence, character, and goodwill. A speaker may project credibility by stressing identity of background and belief with the audience, by actually citing credentials, and by platform behavior that reveals friendliness, candor, respect for the audience, and humor. Social-conformity proofs appeal to an audience's desire to exhibit the same values and attitudes as peers and reference groups such as church, race, or nation.

Speeches to convince and speeches to activate are two common varieties of persuasive speech. The former stresses logical proof and seeks only to change beliefs or attitudes. The latter, while using logical proof, also makes use of psychological proofs and urges the audience to act to implement some proposal.

The speaker can guard against counterpersuasion by the selective use of one- or two-sided presentations, by getting the audience to commit themselves to the speaker's proposal, and by warning them that a persuasive attack on their belief is about to confront them.

Finally, some conflicts are beyond settlement by persuasion and may result in coercive techniques, such as marching, demonstrating, occupying buildings, threatening reprisals or actually harming people, and so on. These forms of coercion limit the receiver's freedom of choice and are, therefore, less desirable than persuasion that appeals to reason and seeks voluntary compliance.

Exercises

1. Prepare and deliver a speech in class in which you try to arouse a high degree of fear. Have members of the audience evaluate the degree of fear they felt on a scale of 1 to 7. What was the class median? Discuss the response you received in comparison with the results achieved by others making class speeches.
2. Prepare and deliver a speech emphasizing a single proposal that you support. Use logical arguments buttressed by social pressures. Try

to use survey reports, testimony of authority figures, and so on. Have class members evaluate your speech with written and oral comments.

3. Bring to class a persuasive article you have read in a magazine such as *Harper's, Atlantic Monthly,* or *Esquire.* Report on the means used by the author to influence belief and then evaluate them.

4. Select advertisements from newspapers, magazines, and television commercials and discuss the persuasive techniques used. Evaluate the probable success of these advertisements and give reasons for it. Could you improve them? How would you do it?

5. Listen carefully to one of your classmates delivering a persuasive speech. Do you agree with the main point wholly or in part? Why? What could the speaker have done to make the proposal more attractive to you? Did you think the speaker credible on this topic? What kinds of proofs were used? Did you respond favorably to these? Orally criticize the speech to the class on the basis of this analysis.

6. Prepare and deliver either a speech to convince or a speech to activate as described in this chapter. Prepare an outline for the speech using the models supplied in the discussion of these speeches.

Chapter Eleven

SPEAKING IN SPECIAL CIRCUMSTANCES

OVERVIEW

How to plan special-occasion speeches like the following:
    Speech of introduction
    Entertaining speech
    Speech of praise (eulogy)
    Welcoming speech
    Commencement address
    Critical book report
Speaking under parliamentary rules
Job-related speaking in situations like the following:
    Interviews
    Oral reports
    Public relations speeches

Sometimes speeches must be so closely adapted to the occasion that they cannot easily be categorized as informative or persuasive, although informative or persuasive elements may be evident in them. A speech of introduction, for example, may well be informative, but it may also be designed to enhance the credibility of the upcoming speaker. An after-dinner speech may give a speaker an opportunity for persuasion, but many times speakers regard it solely as an opportunity to entertain. The opportunity (or perhaps obligation) to deliver such speeches is so frequent and their structure so distinctive that we will discuss the more common special-occasion speeches separately in this chapter.

THE SPEECH OF INTRODUCTION

Although the speech of introduction is probably the most common type of special-occasion speech, it is often absurdly bad. Many introductory speeches are hastily prepared, contain information that is embarrassing to the person being introduced, and are too long.

The speech of introduction has several clear functions that the speaker should take care to fulfill. First, an introductory speech should get the attention of the audience, allow them the opportunity to settle down, and create interest in the speaker's topic. Second, it should try to build credibility for the speaker by acquainting the audience with his or her fitness to discuss the topic. Third, it should enhance that credibility by presenting the speaker as a genuine human being who shares the desires and values of the audience. These tasks may be done as follows:

I. *Get attention and build interest in the speaker's topic:*
   A. Use a humorous anecdote associated with the occasion.
   B. Use a variety of the supporting materials discussed in Chapter 5, especially those that are known to excite interest. Also, use the techniques described in Chapter 2 to hold the audience's attention.
   C. Announce the speaker's topic and illustrate its relevance to the needs of the audience. (Do this briefly, with only a reference or two.)
II. *Build credibility for the speaker:*
   A. Describe the speaker's professional achievements, education, degrees, and writings.
   B. Reveal the speaker's background of experience: jobs held, government appointments, organization memberships, offices held, awards won, and so forth.
III. *Humanize the speaker:* Reveal something about the speaker's family, hobbies, or personal philosophy of life. Use his or her own comments, gathered beforehand, to reveal character, sense of humor, or quirks. You may use quotations from the speaker's writings or the testimony of friends.

In making a speech of introduction, a number of cautions are in order:

1. Be sure that you are accurate in what you say. Don't make factual mistakes about where the speaker was educated, the titles of his or her works, and his or her job experience. Above all, get the name right.
2. Keep your introduction short. Three or four minutes is generally long enough.
3. Avoid flattery. Let your praise be genuine, but don't embarrass the speaker.
4. In referring to the topic, don't try to give the speaker's speech yourself. One example or reference to the relevance of the topic is enough.

5. Some speakers are so well known that they do not need the complete kind of introduction just outlined. Supply only what is necessary. Don't be afraid to say, "Ladies and gentlemen, the President of the United States."

Below is the text of an actual speech of introduction. Note that the introducer arouses interest in the speaker, Phyllis Schlafly, by noting her influence on the progress of the ERA. Next, she reveals her education and accomplishments, and finally something of her family life.

Speech of Introduction

Our guest tonight is Phyllis Schlafly. Many feminists believe that she is the person most responsible for bringing ratification of the Equal Rights Amendment to a dead halt just as it seemed sure to be adopted. Mrs. Schlafly is too modest to take so much credit for retarding adoption of the ERA, but she is outspoken in her criticism of it. "It is the worst constitutional amendment ever proposed," she says. "ERA will take away from women a long list of rights, benefits and exemptions that women do possess. These include exemption from the military draft and combat duty, the rights of a wife to be financially supported, provided with a home, and to have her minor children supported, and the right of factory women to have the benefit of protective labor legislation."

Mrs. Schlafly's emergence as one of America's best known women began when, as Phyllis Stewart, she attended Washington University, graduating Phi Beta Kappa. Her record at Washington won her a scholarship to do graduate work at Radcliffe in Cambridge, Massachusetts. There she got an MA in political science in 1945. Since then, she has run twice for Congress as a conservative Republican, but her greatest political recognition came in 1964 when she supported Senator Barry Goldwater for President of the United States. She wrote a political biography of Goldwater called *A Choice Not an Echo*, which was printed in paperback by a company she herself created in her home town of Alton. The book became a best seller. Over 3 million copies were distributed before election day.

Altogether she has written eight books. Best known of these today is *The Power of the Positive Woman*, first published in 1977. The theme of the book is that a positive woman understands the physical, psychological, and emotional differences between women and men and knows how to capitalize on those differences.

In addition to being a well known author, Phyllis Schlafly has earned a reputation as a radio and TV personality. In the mid-seventies she was a commentator on the CBS radio editorial series, *Spectrum,* and she was, for some years, commentator on a weekly radio broadcast sponsored by the Alton Chapter of the National Conference of Christians and Jews. Since then, she has appeared on numerous TV talk shows, and if you have recently tuned in to CNN, Cable News Network, you may have seen and heard her discussing contemporary issues in one of that network's opinion segments.

With so many accomplishments to her credit, has Phyllis Schlafly had time to be a "positive woman" herself? Her answer is "Yes." She married in 1949 and has raised six children. When asked how she managed a family amid all her other activities she replied, "As a nursing mother, I took all my children to political meetings across the state." She says she is just a housewife managing all her varied interests, including STOP ERA and the Eagle Forum, out of her six-bedroom Tudor house overlooking the Mississippi River in Alton.

Ladies and Gentlemen, it is my privilege to present to you a woman who has been called the Gloria Steinem of the Right. She will speak on the topic, "Right and Wrong: Crime in Our Schools."

THE ENTERTAINING SPEECH

Frequently a speech is called for in a situation where overt persuasion or serious informative content would not be appropriate. The light-heartedness of the audience and of their purpose in meeting calls for an amusing talk. The speaker's purpose then becomes that of giving the audience momentary pleasure and enjoyment without making heavy demands on their intellect. The speaker tries to arouse laughter or good feelings and to avoid such disturbing responses as anger, fear, and grief. Generally, the speaker will deal with simple, easy-to-grasp concepts and will depend heavily on humor. A speaker can arouse laughter by using a number of devices, some of which we will now explain briefly.

EXAGGERATION AND UNDERSTATEMENT

Exaggeration and understatement are related devices in that each achieves humor by describing some concept or thing in grossly inappropriate terms. Exaggeration overstates a circumstance until it becomes ridiculous. Note how, in the following example, the delays in early airline travel are exaggerated until they become funny, with a final climactic exaggeration. The story was taken from a speech by T. A. Wilson, chairman of the board of Boeing Company:

Speaking of personal affairs brings to mind a story during the early days of air travel when saving time wasn't always what the airlines provided. In the mid-1930s the British decided to link the empire with air transport. Their equipment consisted of large but slow airliners with limited range.

One of the first flights from London to Australia attracted a full passenger load. The plane took off and flew to northern France where it was delayed by a long spell of bad weather. It finally arrived in southern France where one of the engines failed and it was necessary to wait for another engine to be shipped by sea from England.

Other delays along the route occurred in Rome, Cairo, the Middle East and India. Finally the flight reached Singapore where more repairs were needed.

At this point a lady passenger asked the manager in Singapore if he thought the airplane would arrive in Australia in the next few weeks because she was expecting a baby shortly.

"My dear lady," sniffed the manager, "you should never have commenced your trip in that condition."

She replied, "I didn't."[1]

Understatement, the opposite of exaggeration, treats a subject in terms so ridiculously inadequate that they make it amusing.

---

[1] T. A. Wilson, "A Cloudy Future for Our Air Transportation Industry," *Vital Speeches of the Day*, 43, (1975–1976), 27. Reprinted by permission.

PUNS, SPOONERISMS, MALAPROPISMS

Puns, spoonerisms, and malapropisms are humorous twists of language. The pun relies on the double meaning of words: the literal meaning becomes secondary to a second, more out-of-place meaning. Examples are the cannibal chieftain who says to the captive newspaper editor, "Tomorrow you will be editor-in-chief," or the line penned by Jerome Beatty, Jr., in the *Saturday Review*: "If you're traveling in Scandinavia and you come to the last Lapp, you must be near the Finnish Line." The spoonerism mixes up the first syllables of two adjacent words; thus someone who means to say *crushing blow* actually says *blushing crow*. A malapropism occurs when a person tries to use a big word but uses an incorrect word that is comically close to the one he or she intended. An example is the case of the minister of a church who advised a visiting parson to speak loudly and clearly because the agnostics were terrible. The television character Archie Bunker is famous for his malapropisms.

SATIRE

Satire makes fun of social customs or of the manners and behavior of people. A speaker may satirize the loudness of rock bands; the hairiness and gymnastics of popular singers; the ridiculous claims of advertising for perfumes, soap powders, or other common products; the outrageous "dramatic" situations in soap operas; and so on. Satire relies heavily on carefully selecting details for emphasis and then exaggerating them.

Often, satire appears in the form of a short anecdote that ridicules a social trend or pokes fun at a recognized problem. The following story, for instance, is designed to satirize businesspeople's habit of cheating on their expense accounts:

"Let me have the check, I'll put it on my expense account," said one executive to his two dinner companions.

"No," protested the second, "let me have it; I'm in such a high bracket it will be practically painless."

Then the third spoke up. "I'll take the check," he declared with a masterful gesture. "My company is on a cost-plus basis. We'll make a 15 percent profit on the deal."

The most common form of satire, however, involves extended commentary on events of the day. Columnists like Art Buchwald and Ellen Goodman follow this kind of pattern in their newspaper columns. The example below is by Jeff Greenfield, writing in the *St. Petersburg Times*. Note how Greenfield locks in on a political trend and questions its sincerity by satirical commentary and a ludicrous parody.

If you live in Ohio, you've been seeing an eye-opening TV commercial in which Jerry Springer, candidate for governor and former mayor of Cincinnati, talks about a skeleton in his closet.

"Nine years ago I spent time with a woman I shouldn't have," Springer says. "And I paid her with a check. I wish I hadn't done that." Then, in a classic case of political judo—turning a rival's advantage into a liability—Springer explains how this incident might help him.

"Ohio is in a world of hurt," he says. "The next governor is going to have to take some heavy risks and face some hard truths. I'm prepared to do that. This commercial should be proof."

Springer's ad is the most remarkable example of a burgeoning trend in public life: the quick confession of error. In Arkansas, former Gov. Bill Clinton is running commercials in which he admits that in his first term, he wasn't listening to the people enough. In Massachusetts, former Gov. Michael Dukakis is basing his campaign on the same blend of contrition and a pledge of reformation.

This tactic has its modern roots in the 1969 mayoral re-election campaign of New York Mayor John Lindsay—a campaign in which I worked. One of Lindsay's problems was that he was seen as an aloof, superior, almost condescending official, insensitive to the needs of the blue-collar, middle-class New Yorker, so in what was dubbed the "Lindsay Eats Crow" commercial, the mayor looked into the camera and talked about mistakes in the context of his overall record.

"The things that go wrong are what make this the second-toughest job in America," Lindsay said, "but the things that go right are what make me still want it."

The tactic never really caught on, since politicians, most of whom are trained as lawyers, never like to acknowledge error, preferring instead to explain that "I was misquoted," "I was conducting my own undercover investigation of vice," "She was my cousin from out of town and I was administering mouth-to-mouth resuscitation" and other protestations of innocence.

Now, however, contrition—once described as "bull feathers" by former White House press secretary Ron Ziegler—may be an idea whose time has come. We will know that for certain when the following political commercial begins running on TV in your state:

"Hi, I'm Ralph Dithers, and I want to be your United States senator.

"I know what it means to suffer from economic hardships, because I took a thriving small business and ran it into the ground in six months.

"I know the heartache of personal dilemma, because I walked out on my wife and small children to indulge my kinkiest sexual tastes with a 19-year-old exotic dancer.

"I know the shortcomings of our criminal justice system, because I did 18 months in the state pen for embezzlement and forgery.

"I know the desperate need for tax reform, because I'm under indictment for 13 counts of income tax invasion.

"My opponent claims he is a model of morality and honesty. I ask you, ladies and gentleman: Do you want to gamble on a senator who has no place to go but down?

"If you elect me, you have absolute confidence that I cannot possibly be a disappointment to you—because you know what to expect going in. So vote for a senator you can feel superior to—vote for me."

"Paid for by Dithers for Senate Committee. Dithers: a humble man—with so much to be humble about."[2]

THE STORY OR ANECDOTE

The story or anecdote dramatizes an event, usually with scene setting, character descriptions, and dialogue. What often makes a story funny is its misleading development. As the story progresses, the audience is made

[2] *St. Petersburg Times,* May 26, 1982, p. 14A. Copyright, 1982, Universal Press Syndicate. Reprinted with permission. All rights reserved.

to believe that it will have a certain outcome, but at the last moment (usually in a tag line) an unexpected turn of events produces laughter. Abraham Lincoln once told the story of his experience with Thaddeus Stevens, who had made unflattering remarks about the honesty of Lincoln's secretary of war, Simeon Cameron. Lincoln asked whether Stevens thought that Cameron would steal. Stevens replied: "I don't think he would steal a red hot stove." Lincoln thought the comment was so good that he told it to Cameron, who became furious and demanded an apology. Stevens went to Cameron and said, "I believe I told Lincoln that you would not steal a red hot stove. I now take that back."

Stevens's final remark is unexpected and funny; its humor arises from its surprising logic. Another example in which the punch line is an unexpected logical twist is a story told of George Bernard Shaw who, while dining in a restaurant, was told by the waiter that the orchestra would respond to customer requests. "What would you like them to play?" "Dominoes," responded Shaw.

Some funny stories rely less on unexpected turns in the final line than they do on exaggeration and satire, particularly concerning the behavior of the characters or their responses to common situations. James Thurber used this type of humor in his stories.

The subject of a humorous speech can be almost anything. It is not the topic of the speech but the manner of treating it that makes it funny. With few exceptions, the same subject could be treated in an informative, persuasive, or entertaining fashion. In choosing to treat a subject entertainingly, a speaker may convey information and may indirectly be persuasive (especially by the use of satire, sarcasm, or parody), but the primary aim is to amuse the audience, not to inform or convince them.

An entertaining or humorous speech may be organized in several different ways. First, there is the *string-of-beads* type of organization, in which the speaker loosely links a series of humorous anecdotes about a central theme. John Watson, a highly successful commercial lecturer around the turn of the century, delivered a humorous speech again and again, to the delight of his audiences. The speech's title was "Scottish Traits." In the introduction, Watson pictured the character of the Scottish people as consisting of traits like slyness, wit, stubbornness, and thrift. He then illustrated each trait with one or more amusing anecdotes. He concluded with a sentimental tribute to the sturdiness of the Scottish people.

A second type of organization is essentially a chronological narrative, spiced with humorous episodes that are built around the speaker's personal experiences. Topics that lend themselves to this kind of organization might include "My Experience as a Babysitter," "How I Get Along with the Opposite Sex," and "My Life as a Soldier." Often in such a speech, the speaker will begin with a humorous anecdote and then emphasize common ground with the audience (something we've all experienced). This is followed by several stories with funny developments and outcomes. The conclusion is often a climactic joke or a semiserious appeal for mutual sympathy in shared frustrations.

A third type of entertaining speech has, like the string-of-beads type, a thematic structure and is peppered with numerous examples instead of stories. Its purpose is social commentary through satire. The speaker will usually begin with an example, story, or quotation that reveals the theme. The theme is analyzed into subtopics, each of which is illustrated with examples, cases, parodies, and so forth. Toward the conclusion, the relevance of the theme to contemporary life may be explained, either seriously or humorously. The final portion of the conclusion is made up of an appropriate quotation from literature, such as a poem, an epigram, a fable, or a maxim.

An entertaining speaker avoids excessive formality and firmness in delivery and uses instead a casual, spontaneous, friendly manner.

The following example of a humorous speech is organized on the string-of-beads pattern. The subject, teachers, provides a thread upon which the speaker hangs a series of loosely related funny anecdotes.

Bombing the Teachers

Some of you are preparing to be teachers and will, therefore, be concerned about the problems teachers have to face. Others of you are already familiar with the problems of teachers because, since kindergarten you have been contributing to them. Because kids are forced to go to school most of them don't have a very high regard for teachers. Near our school, when I was in the early grades, there was a sign that read "School—Drive Carefully—Don't Kill a Child." Beneath was a childish scrawl. "Wait for a teacher."

Not too long ago, I heard my little brother and a couple of his second grade friends playing war games—dropping bombs on imaginary cities. This exchange took place.

"Hey, that's great," said Jeffrey. "A direct hit. First grade too!"

"That's nothing," exulted his pal, Donnie. "I just got a direct hit on the high school, tenth grade."

This went on for some time till my mother couldn't take it any longer, and, pulling Jeffrey aside she said, "Even in real wars, Jeffrey, there are such things as rules. Fighting other soldiers is one thing, but bombing schools—soldiers wouldn't drop bombs on helpless, little children. Jeffrey looked shocked and incredulous at her words.

"We weren't bombing the children, mother. We were bombing the teachers."

I guess bombing the teachers is a favorite pastime. At any rate, thousands of jokes are told at their expense. Maybe we like to ridicule teachers because they are always putting us on the defensive and showing up our ignorance. How would you have felt if, like the little boy in third grade, you were asked, "Where was the Declaration of Independence signed?" and you responded without thinking, "At the bottom."?

Or how would you like to have been the student in the following situation. The professor of logic was illustrating how logic sharpens your thinking. "Suppose two men climbed out of a chimney," he said. "One is clean and the other is dirty. Which takes a bath?"

"The dirty one, naturally," replied the student.

"Remember," reminded the professor, "that the clean man sees the dirty one and notices how dirty he is."

"Now I get it," answered the student. "The clean one, seeing his dirty companion, concludes he is dirty, too—so he takes a bath. Am I right?"

"Right," said the professor, "but not for the reason you give. Logic asks, how could two men climb out of a chimney, one dirty and the other clean?"

You can really get yourself into trouble if you try to outsmart a teacher. This example is said to have happened at Boston College during a lecture by a young priest.

The professor, after long discourse, asked for questions. A student arose and demanded documentary proof of various statements made in the lecture. The professor admitted he had no proof with him, although it was easily obtainable. Unabashed, the show-off replied, "Well, sir, until you can produce documentary evidence, do you mind if for the time being I call you a liar?"

The stunned audience waited for the professor to find his voice. Then he quietly asked the student for his parents' marriage certificate. Unable to produce it, the student sat dumfounded as the professor said, "Well, sir, until you can produce the documentary evidence, would you mind if I called you an impertinent young bastard?"

Another thing about teachers is that you can never be sure of what they mean. Did you ever look at the comments a teacher writes on a student's report card? These require translating. For instance:

Michael doesn't socialize well. This means Mike is always beating some other kid's brains out.
John is progressing very well for him. Your Johnny is a dummy. If he keeps going at his present rate he'll get out of the third grade in 12 years.
Frank's personality shows poor social integration. This means Frank criticizes the teacher, smarts off to other kids, and generally behaves like a stinker.
Robert is a well-adjusted, wholesomely integrated individual. Robert knows how to butter up to the teacher, and does it without shame.

But sometimes kids get back at the teacher and puncture the pedagogical ego. Like the little boy who remained after class one day till the teacher said, "What do you want, Jimmy?"

"I'd like to know what we learned in school today."

The teacher responded, "Why in the world do you ask a question like that?"

"Well," said Jimmy, "My dad always wants to know what I learned in school today, and I don't know the answer."

Most of us remember a little bit of what we learned in school—enough to realize that, although we have a lot of fun at their expense teachers are remarkable people. Teachers must have the wisdom of Solomon, the courage of Daniel, the strength of Sampson, and the patience of Job. Few professions are so demanding. Mark Twain once said, ''Few things are harder to put up with than the annoyance of a good example.'' I am glad my teachers set me a good example, and, despite the annoyance, I am willing to put up with it.

SPEECHES REQUIRING COMMENDATION AND PRAISE

There are two basic types of speeches of praise. One is the formal eulogy, usually given at a person's death, and the other is a less formal speech of praise that is often associated with a person's retirement or with the presentation of an award.

The formal eulogy is sometimes organized in strictly chronological fashion, a practice that often results in a dull, anticlimactic presentation. A better style of development is the thematic-selective form, in which a central idea or theme about the achievement or character of the person is stated and illustrated with incidents from his or her life. Some of the themes that may be used are the following:

1. This is a person who achieved much with few resources.
2. This person's achievement was made in the face of extraordinary difficulties.
3. This person performed acts beyond normal or habitual human powers.
4. This person's achievement was beyond what is expected or beyond what duty requires.
5. This person's achievements have been of great benefit to humanity.

More than one of these themes may be stated and illustrated if appropriate. Here are some suggestions for composing a formal eulogy:

1. Begin with a striking, attention-getting incident in the person's life.
2. Show how this incident illustrates a basic trait of the person's character.
3. Select other events and incidents that illustrate the person's character.

4. Reveal the significance of the person's work to society. Tell how such work has benefited humanity.
5. Humanize the person with a tasteful reference to some of his or her frailties or quirks.
6. Focus your treatment of the person's life around one or more of the themes in the preceding list.
7. Conclude with a statement or written comment by the person or by recounting an action that exemplifies the person's best qualities.

The informal speech of praise given on the occasion of a retirement can follow the same pattern. Since the subject of the speech is present, praise must be stated gently so as not to embarrass him or her.

A good example of the formal eulogy is the speech given on January 15, 1978, by then Vice President Mondale following the death of Senator Hubert Humphrey. The eulogy was delivered at a Washington memorial service attended by the Senator's wife, Muriel, other members of the family, and guests. You will note that Mondale uses many of the techniques recommended in this section for the construction of a formal eulogy.

Dear Muriel, the Humphrey family and guests:

There is a natural impulse at a time like this to dwell on the many accomplishments of Hubert Humphrey's remarkable life, by listing a catalogue of past events as though there were some way to quantify what he was all about. But I don't want to do that because Hubert didn't want it and neither does Muriel. Even though this is one of the saddest moments of my life and I feel as great a loss as I have ever known, we must remind ourselves of Hubert's last great wish:

That this be a time to celebrate life and the future, not to mourn the past and his death. I hope you will forgive me if I don't entirely succeed in looking forward and not backward. Because I must for a moment. Two days ago as I flew back from the West over the land that Hubert loved to this city that he loved, I thought back over his life and its meaning and I tried to understand what it was about this unique person that made him such an uplifting symbol of hope and joy for all people. And I thought of the letter that he wrote to Muriel 40 years ago when he first visited Washington.

He said in that letter:

"Maybe I seem foolish to have such vain hopes and plans, but Bucky, I can see how some day, if you and I just apply ourselves and make up our minds to work for bigger things, how we can some day live here in Washington and probably be in government, politics or service. I intend to set my aim at Congress."

Hubert was wrong only in thinking that his hopes and plans might be in vain. They were not, as we all know. Not only did he succeed with his beloved wife at his side, he succeeded gloriously and beyond even his most optimistic dreams.

Hubert will be remembered by all of us who served with him as one of the greatest legislators in our history. He will be remembered as one of the most loved men of his times. And even though he failed to realize his greatest goal, he achieved something much more rare and valuable than the nation's highest office. He became his country's conscience.

Today the love that flows from everywhere enveloping Hubert flows also to you, Muriel, and the presence today here, where America bids farewell to her heroes, of President and Mrs. Carter, of former Presidents Ford and Nixon, and your special friend and former first lady, Mrs. Johnson, attest to the love and the respect that the nation holds for both of you. That letter to Bucky, his Muriel, also noted three principles by which Hubert defined his life: work, determination and high goals. They were a part of his life's pattern when I first met him 31 years ago. I was only 18, fresh out of high school, and he was the Mayor of Minneapolis. He had then all the other sparkling qualities he maintained throughout his life: boundless good humor, endless optimism and hope, infinite interests, intense concern for people and their problems, compassion without being patronizing, energy beyond belief, and a spirit so filled with love there was no room for hate or bitterness.

He was simply incredible. When he said that life was not meant to be endured but rather to be enjoyed, you knew what he meant. You could see it simply by watching him and listening to him.

When Hubert looked at the lives of black Americans in the '40s, he saw endurance and not enjoyment, and his heart insisted that it was time for Americans to walk forthrightly into the bright sunshine of human rights.

When Hubert looked at the young who could not get a good education, he saw endurance and not enjoyment. When Hubert saw old people in ill health, he saw endurance and not enjoyment. When Hubert saw middle-class people without jobs and decent homes, he saw endurance and not enjoyment.

Hubert was criticized for proclaiming the politics of joy. But he knew that joy is essential to us and is not frivolous. He loved to point out that ours is the only nation in the world to officially declare the pursuit of happiness as a national goal. But he was also a sentimental man and that was part of his life, too. He cried in public and without embarrassment. In his last major speech in his beloved Minnesota, he wiped tears from his eyes and said, ''A man without tears is a man without a heart.'' If he cried often, it was not for himself, but for others.

Above all, Hubert was a man with a good heart. And on this sad day, it would be good for us to recall Shakespeare's words: ''A good leg will fall. A straight back will stoop. A black beard will turn white. A curled pate will grow bald. A fair face will wither. A full eye will wax hollow. But a good heart is the sun and the moon. Or rather the sun and not the moon, for it shines bright and never changes, but keeps its course truly.'' Hubert's heart kept its course truly.

He taught us all how to hope and how to live, how to win and how to lose, he taught us how to live and, finally, he taught us how to die.[3]

In making an award or presentation, the general pattern of the eulogy may be modified as follows: The occasion and the purpose of the award should be described first. The significance of the award should be mentioned: the high standards held for it, the social value attached to it, and the number of able competitors for it. Then the person who is to receive the award should be named. (Don't try the worn out tactic of laboriously withholding the name until the last minute.) At this point, the procedures of the formal eulogy may be adapted to show why this person is receiving the award. The conclusion of an award speech is highlighted by the formal presentation of the award.

---

[3] Text of eulogy supplied by Walter Mondale. Reprinted by permission.

THE SPEECH OF WELCOME

Often a speaker will publicly acknowledge the arrival in the community of a distinguished guest or of a body of people, such as those coming to a convention, a seminar, or a memorial celebration. A speech of welcome should be short and sincere. The usual practice is to comment on the importance of the occasion for the visit and to illustrate the probable benefits for both visitor and sponsor. The speaker should note the expected contributions of the sponsors to the enjoyment and welfare of the visitors and should assure the visitors that the sponsors anticipate rewards from their presence. A simple declaration of welcome is enough to conclude the speech.

THE COMMENCEMENT ADDRESS

When a high school or college senior class graduates, a commencement address is almost always part of the ceremony. Commencement addresses are also called for at the graduation of specialized groups like those getting diplomas from law, medical, or nursing schools. Even the graduates of police academies, electronics schools, business colleges, barber colleges, and so forth, have graduating ceremonies that include an address. This type of speech is so common that you should know a little about its purpose and makeup.

A commencement represents a coming of age, a point at which a group of people have completed their preparations and are now ready to take part in business or professional life. A commencement ceremony calls for inspiration and advice, which form the substance of practically all commencement addresses. In Chapter 4, we quoted the introduction to a commencement address delivered by Mary Lou Thibeault. In it, she disclosed how most of the commencement addresses she had heard were structured. Her advice is useful enough to be repeated here: "Typically," she said, "they [commencement addresses] commend the graduates on what they have accomplished . . . warn them there are obstacles ahead, but . . . by applying what they have learned at college, and facing the future with strength, determination, faith and courage, they shall win professional and personal fulfillment."[4]

---

[4] Mary Lou Thibeault, "The Hazards of Equality," *Vital Speeches of the Day,* 41 (1974–1975), 588. Reprinted by permission.

Ms. Thibeault's formula is not far from standard commencement practice. Indeed, a rough outline of a commencement address might look like the following:

  I. *Introduction:*
    A. An attention-getting device or devices such as:
      1. A reference to the importance and meaning of the occasion.
      2. A humorous anecdote about your own school experiences (or the humorous experiences of others).
    B. A statement of purpose showing your intention to deal either with the general challenges facing society or with the specific prospects, demands, and opportunities of the profession or business for which these graduates have been trained.
  II. *Body:*
    A. A discussion of the conditions that have existed in the past in society generally or in the graduates' particular business or profession.
    B. A discussion of changes needed in the future as a result of new problems and the development of new knowledge and techniques.
    C. A discussion of how the education and training of the graduates will enable them to meet the challenge of change.
  III. *Conclusion:* An inspirational charge to the graduates consisting of one of the following:
    A. A moving quotation from poetry or literature.
    B. A quotation from an authoritative source.
    C. A personal prediction of things to come.

A commencement address should usually be short (twenty minutes or so) and should be tailored carefully to the situation. Although the basic pattern of the speech is often the same, it need not be littered with truisms and hackneyed clichés.

In the commencement address that follows, the speaker, John W. Hanley, chairman and chief executive officer of the Monsanto Company, was speaking to the graduating class of Webster College, St. Louis, Missouri. His introduction is a humorous reference to the occasion, and the body of the speech is made up of three lessons Hanley learned during his career that he feels could be of value to Webster graduates. The conclusion reinforces his message by citing the example of Moses in the movie *The Ten Commandments*.

I offer you my hearty congratulations on your graduation today. This ceremony, like the thousands of graduations held across the country, is a celebration—a celebration of formal education, of personal achievement, and of that process of learning that is so vital to our nation and its prosperity.

A few days ago, as I was working on some notes and ideas for this address, one of my associates at Monsanto stopped by with some advice about commencement speeches. "Never," he said, "tell the graduates that the future is theirs."

As I quickly covered up my notes, I asked, "Why not?"

"Because," he replied, "you would be saying that the future belonged to them, and they would be sitting in the audience knowing they didn't even own the caps and gowns they had on."

I can't even say that the present moment is mine—my cap and gown are borrowed as well!

In addition to our borrowed clothes, there are other, more significant ties between Monsanto and Webster College—ties with your Board of Directors, your faculty and your student body. In fact, the close relationship we've shared over the years has often made me feel like an alumnus myself!

I recall being in your place some 40 years ago. I sat in the middle of the graduation class feeling that I knew everything there was to know—at least, everything important.

Since then, I've been astonished at how much more I've had to learn, just to get along in business.

Three lessons were particularly important to me. Today I would like to tell you what those lessons were, why I believe they made a difference in my career, and why I believe that they can be helpful to you as well.

Lesson No. 1: Cultivate your curiosity.

What do I mean by curiosity? I mean that sense of wonderment which we find in a child. That desire to try something new, to learn how all the pieces fit together, to be taught how to do things, and how to do things better.

Your presence here today shows that you possess that vital sense of wonderment. I was interested to learn that 60 percent of your graduating class is at least 25 years old. Many of you have jobs now or have had jobs in the past. Given those commitments, I am encouraged to see how important you consider the process of learning, since learning, after all, is really organized curiosity.

When I arrived at Monsanto in 1972, one of the first things I told my top executives was that they had the responsibility for training John W. Hanley, that I made mistakes every day and that they would have to catch them.

They took me at my word, and decided to help satisfy my curiosity by signing me up for a crash course in petrochemical technology—a course which has since paid me back many times over.

I also asked them the question: What kind of company do we want Monsanto to be? A variant of that question also applies to each of us here: What kind of person do we want to be? You've given a partial answer with the degree you're receiving today in your chosen field.

But your degree is only one small step. To paraphrase Sir Winston Churchill, your degree is not the beginning of your education or the beginning of the end of your education. Rather, it is the end of the beginning. Now come the really tough courses of life itself.

To pass these courses, the only real life-preserver you have is your curiosity—your willingness to try something new.

Consider President Reagan's novel proposals to control inflation and get our economy moving again. Whether you agree with them or not, you have to admit that they embody the courage to try something new. Considering the howls of protest many people expected, these proposals represented either a supreme act of courage and faith or the ultimate political folly. The votes are not yet counted, but there has been surprisingly broad support for the new approaches.

Whatever the outcome, the proposals offer an example of what it means to cultivate your curiosity, the courage to try something new.

But let me emphasize that—like the degree you're receiving— curiosity does not guarantee success. It does not mean that you will ultimately be handed the job of your dreams. And like curiosity, your degree does not mean that you're *entitled* to anything.

In fact, your degree means only one thing, but one very important thing, that you had the interest and the courage to follow through a course of study and learning to completion.

This brings us to Lesson No. 2: Enlarge your enthusiasm.

Enthusiasm encompasses the ideas of joy and excitement, but to my mind, it means much more—the pursuit of excellence, and the perseverance to get the job done.

In the past two years, much has been said and written about the decline of productivity in the United States, about all the ills that are affecting our economy and society.

But I believe there is a new mood in America. Our society is now at a turning point, one that bodes well for all of us and especially for you. In effect, we are turning back to an old American virtue—the idea of accepting the risk that accompanies the pursuit of excellence.

Two years ago at Monsanto, we were looking at the sales goals for our *Roundup* herbicide. Since its introduction in the United States in 1977, it had averaged an annual sales growth of 42 percent, an enviable record for any product.

Looking at the projections for 1984, we asked the question, what if we doubled our sales force in the field and our marketing support? Could we achieve the 1984 goal even earlier?

We knew we would be running a risk, and in terms of dollars, a big risk. But we also knew that we had a winner in *Roundup*—it's the kind of product that sparks enthusiasm. So we did double our sales force and backup support, with the result that in 1980, we doubled our sales over 1979.

Enthusiasm, in addition to the pursuit of excellence, includes perseverance—carrying every project through to completion, even when you reach the point of total frustration. The successful men and women of history invariably reached that point, and their enthusiasm carried them on in spite of it.

In 1976, the city of St. Louis was trying to raise the funds needed to finish the Convention Center downtown. The problem was that inflation had increased construction costs beyond what was originally projected.

The then-Mayor John Poelker came to my office. He was determined that the center was going to be completed. He told me how the center would attract business, how it would be good for the metropolitan area, and why it would benefit all of the people and companies that call St. Louis home.

I was impressed with his presentation, but particularly with his enthusiasm. I talked to a few people at Monsanto, and we proposed a challenge grant of an additional half million dollars to help attract the needed funds. Looking back, I am proud of the role my company played, along with the other companies in St. Louis, in helping to see the Center through to completion. But without John Poelker's enthusiasm and perseverance, I'm convinced that there would have been no Convention Center for the city.

Enthusiasm, when combined with the curiosity I mentioned earlier, often yields an added result—serendipity, the accidental discovery of something important. The Procter & Gamble Company, where I worked for 25 years, witnessed a classic example of this.

A worker in a P & G soap factory went out to lunch one day without remembering to turn off his blending machine. When he came back, he saw that the resulting batch had tiny air bubbles beaten into it. He realized he had something, and so did his supervisors. When the soap reached the market, the public loved it. Since then, Procter & Gamble has sold more than 30 billion bars of Ivory Soap—the one that floats—because one worker saw something of promise in air bubbles.

At Monsanto, we routinely test every compound we develop, on the off-chance that it may have a use the developers didn't realize. In fact, we discovered an important herbicide while studying a rubber-processing chemical.

Curiosity and enthusiasm, and their hybrid serendipity, still require one additional element.

That's Lesson No. 3: Make the law of averages work for you.

By budgeting your time more carefully than most people do, you can make more time available. If you use this "bonus time" properly, you can take full advantage of the law of averages.

When I started my career as a soap salesman in Los Angeles, I noticed that most salesmen averaged a 50 percent sales-to-calls ratio—about six sales for every 12 calls during a normal day. I figured that if I gave up one hour of sleep in the morning, and shortened my lunch period, and used that time to call on four additional stores, I might be able to improve the average sales record. As a result, I averaged 16 sales calls a day, with 8 contracts.

What I did was make the law of averages work for me. This simply means I made hard work and the extra effort pay off.

Another example closer to home shows how institutions can make the law of averages work for them. Webster College is gaining a national reputation for bridging the worlds of work and education. It is one of the first institutions of higher learning that has realized the growing need to reach new kinds of students with programs designed to help them in their jobs and careers.

At the same time, Webster is solving a major problem faced by colleges and universities across the country. With the notable decline of the birth rate starting in the 1960s, it became obvious that the number of traditionally aged college students would also decline. The question Webster asked was: How do you preserve the college as a growing institution of learning in the face of declining enrollment trends?

The answer was deceptively simple—you stop thinking of students as being between 18 and 21 years old. But the implementation of that answer was the tough part. Through hard work and the extra effort, the administration and the faculty are making the law of averages work for Webster, and for Webster's graduates.

Does the combination of curiosity, enthusiasm and the law of averages guarantee success in life—or your money back?

Indeed, it does not!

Herbert Bayard Swope, the great St. Louis-born newspaper editor, was once asked for his prescription for success. "I can't give you a sure-fire formula for success," he said, "but I can give you a formula for failure: try to please everybody all the time."

Furthermore, success, in the final analysis, always involves the element of chance or luck. Louis Pasteur grasped this well when he said that chance favors the prepared mind. The three lessons I've learned since graduation did no more than prepare me to seize that moment of opportunity when it occurred.

First, cultivate your curiosity. Keep it sharp and always working. Consider curiosity your life-preserver, your willingness to try something new.

Second, enlarge your enthusiasm to include the pursuit of excellence, following every task through to completion.

Third, make the law of averages work for you, so that you win more than you lose.

I've always been something of a movie buff. One picture that made a lasting impression on me was Cecil B. DeMille's "The Ten Commandments," which was re-run in St. Louis on Easter Sunday.

In true DeMille style, we were treated to scene after scene of Moses warning the pharaoh, Moses talking to the Lord, Moses leading his people out of bondage. Charlton Heston, playing the lead role, gave new meaning to the definition of leadership.

The more I reflected on that movie, the more impressed I was with what it said about Moses.

First, he was curious, and extremely so, about the burning bush. Because he was willing to investigate something new, he was transformed from a humble shepherd into a great leader of his people. Curiosity was, in effect, his life-preserver.

Second, his leadership of people was animated by enthusiasm—the kind of enthusiasm that kept him going despite adversities. And 40 years in the wilderness is a long time to be enthusiastic about *any* responsibility.

Third, confronted with a stubborn pharaoh who refused to free the Israelites, Moses never wavered in his confidence in the eventual outcome. For one thing, he had the law of averages working for him.

While I do not presume to compare myself to the great lawgiver, I have been helped by those three lessons of his life— curiosity, enthusiasm and the law of averages.

I believe they can be important to you as well. I won't predict that the practice of these principles will bring you manna from heaven, for that required a little supernatural assistance.

But I do predict that these lessons will prepare you to recognize and grasp that moment of opportunity in your life, to enable you to part your own, personal Red Sea.[5]

---

[5] "Lessons I've Learned Since Graduation," *Vital Speeches of the Day,* 47 (1980–1981), pp. 598–600. Reprinted by permission.

THE CRITICAL BOOK REPORT

The critical book report is a common type of speech that has mixed purposes. It is primarily informative, but it almost always has elements of persuasion in it. Its specific purpose is to tell an audience of a classical or currently well-known fiction or nonfiction book, to interpret the contents for them, and to stimulate them to read the book. (Civic clubs, men's or women's clubs, and educational and service organizations often solicit this kind of presentation.) The speaker approaches the book from two points of view: first, its literary value and, second, its value as a comment on society's faults, problems, and prospects.

After reading the book carefully and looking at available reviews of it, the speaker may construct the report following an outline similar to the one that follows:

I. *Introduction:*
   A. Attention-getting materials about the author: his or her status, views on the world, personal habits and quirks, previous works, and so on.
   B. Some reference to the social questions with which the book is concerned and their importance.
II. *Body:*
   A. A brief selective summary of the action (if a novel) or of the topics dealt with (if a nonfictional work). To maintain interest, you may quote short, selected passages of the text.
   B. An interpretation and judgment of the book's quality.
      1. If a novel, you may comment on the plot and its development, the point of view, the characterization, the style of the work, and so forth.
      2. If a nonfiction book, you may comment on its coverage of the subject, its logic, the adequacy of its sources, its organization, and the like.
   C. An interpretation and judgment of the work as social criticism:
      1. Criticize how well the author recognizes the problem, his or her analysis of it, and the usefulness of the solution (if one is suggested).
      2. Relate the author's criticism to other works of literature and to other types of social criticism.

III. *Conclusion:* Try to summarize the book's meaning and its probable impact on the reader. Perhaps you can end with a well-selected quotation from the book and a recommendation that the audience read it themselves.

The following outline shows the structure of a critical book report on *The Jungle,* a classical work of muckraking fiction written in the early twentieth century. The speaker uses comments about the significance of the work and its social impact to arouse interest. Then he presents a summary of the action and shows how it revealed an important social problem. He then evaluates the writer's solution to the problem and, in the conclusion, assesses the contribution of the work as a social document.

Introduction
  I. The book I am about to review made a tremendous impact on American society when it was published in 1905:
    A. Jack London wrote of it: "Here it is at last. The book we have been waiting for these many years. The *Uncle Tom's Cabin* of wage slavery! Comrade Sinclair's book, *The Jungle!* And what *Uncle Tom's Cabin* did for black slaves, the *Jungle* has a large chance to do for white slaves today . . ."
    B. In fact, Upton Sinclair's book did change things in the meat-packing industry.
      1. President Roosevelt, who was much impressed with the book, appointed a commission to investigate the Chicago stockyards.
      2. Congress later passed a pure food and drug bill and a beef inspection act.
  II. The author, Upton Sinclair, wrote the book when he was twenty-six years old, after spending seven weeks observing life in the Chicago stockyards and meat-packing plants. He had found he could go anywhere in that huge complex simply by wearing old clothes and carrying a dinner pail.

Body
  I. Synopsis of the action:
    A. The novel is about a Lithuanian family that comes to the United States and whose members find employment in the

Chicago packing houses. Jurgis Rudkus and his wife, 16-year-old Ona Lukoszaite are the principal characters. Through the experiences of this couple and their friends, the story condemns the capitalist economic system.

1. Vote buying by industrialists.
2. Cheating workers through company housing projects.
3. Blacklisting of workers who try to organize unions.
4. Unsafe and degrading working conditions.
   a. Quote effect of chemicals on workers, p. 77.
   b. Lives lost in digging the telephone tunnel, p. 224.
5. Unsanitary packing practices.
   a. Quote methods of beef curing, p. 61.
   b. Quote illegal butchering of pregnant cows and use of "slunk" calves, p. 62.

b. The end of the book forecasts improvement of the worker's condition as Jurgis becomes active in the socialist party.

II. According to historians the book accurately pictures the life of workers in the packing plants:

A. All of Sinclair's charges except one (that human beings had fallen into lard vats and were rendered instead of being rescued) were confirmed by an investigating committee.

B. David Graham Phillips, one of the renowned muckrakers, wrote of it: "It is . . . simple, . . . true, . . . tragic and so human."

III. The book is well thought out, focuses on fully developed characters, and has an engaging plot. It is actually, however, a propaganda piece advocating socialism as a cure for the excesses of capitalism:

A. The book introduces the audience to actual socialist personalities and events. (Illustrate with references to the text.)

B. Sinclair's belief that socialism would come to the rescue of the American worker proved wrong.

Conclusion

I. What, then, was the contribution of *The Jungle?* The book was written in the muckraking period, a time when numerous writers such as Ida Tarbell, Ray Stannard Baker, and David Phillips were exposing the excesses of greedy capitalists.

II. As one historian put it, "The great role of the muckraker was to publicize the need for reform." Possibly no muckraking document succeeded better at this task than Upton Sinclair's book, *The Jungle.*

SPEAKING UNDER PARLIAMENTARY RULES

Any formally organized group with a regular schedule of meeting times can profit from the use of parliamentary rules. As the name indicates, parliamentary rules were created to serve governing bodies. Rules were adopted to ensure (1)that business was conducted in an orderly way, (2)that all members of the organization were treated fairly, that is, that all had equal opportunity to debate and thereby influence action, (3)that decisions could be made by majority vote, and (4)that the right of the minority would be respected. In the United States Congress, a complicated set of rules have grown up that cover every kind of situation the Congress could possibly confront—from the election of officers to the certification and expulsion of members, from the adoption of simple resolutions to the handling of complex, highly detailed matters like the national budget.

Most organizations need only a simple set of rules that can take the form of a two- or three-page pamphlet. Anything not covered in this rule book can be decided by majority vote at the time the need arises. Rules should establish an order of business and a chart of motions for handling debate. (Of course, a set of bylaws are also needed to indicate qualifications for membership, dues, how officers will be elected, and the like, but bylaws will not be discussed here.)

ORDER OF BUSINESS

There is no reason a group has to proceed in a certain order in handling its business. Although custom has established the following as a usual pattern, groups should feel free to vary from it if they wish.

1. The chairman or chairwoman calls the meeting to order.
2. The secretary reads the minutes of the last meeting for correction and approval. The minutes may be printed and circulated in advance if desired.
3. Officers and chairpersons of standing committees make their reports. Reports are received and acted on.

4. Unfinished business from previous meetings is taken up.
5. New business is proposed and acted on.
6. Announcements are made.
7. The meeting is adjourned.

The order of business can be changed at any time with the approval of the majority of the members. If some item of new business requires immediate action there is no reason why it cannot be put ahead of committee reports and old business. The purpose of parliamentary rule, after all, is to make action easier, not to hinder it.

MOTIONS

Action by a group using parliamentary rules begins with a formal proposal known as a *main motion.* Such a motion usually originates with either a standing or specially appointed committee that has been studying a particular problem and has prepared a solution to it. Motions may also come from the members at large, however, when members are knowledgeable about an issue and have taken the trouble to write a carefully worded proposal. On page 277 is a chart summarizing the motions discussed in this section. A main motion asks the organization to take some action, such as preparing for a coming workshop, appropriating money, or simply, through a resolution, going on record for or against some current issue. The form of a main motion is something like the following: "I move that the Sierra Club donate $450 to the fund being raised by John Daniels to bring suit against X Chemical Company."

Once a main motion is on the floor, it must be taken care of before the organization can turn to other matters. The usual way of dealing with a main motion is to debate its merits and then vote on it, either accepting or rejecting it. Sometimes, however, members may not want to take a vote on the motion as is, but will take care of it in some other way. For this purpose a number of *subsidiary motions* exist.

Several motions may be used to delay action. A member may move to *postpone to a definite time.* Usually, this means postponing to the next or a later meeting. An alternative is a motion to *postpone indefinitely.* This motion is not often used; when it is, it is usually an attempt to kill a motion without a vote. Both motions may be debated, and the time in a motion to postpone to a definite time can be amended. A third motion, called a motion *to lay on the table,* is technically a lot like the motion to postpone indefinitely. It appears to mean that the motion can be taken up again later by a motion to remove from the table. In fact, however, it is generally used to prevent action and to do away with the motion without a vote. Authorities on parliamentary procedure say it may not be debated. Logically, though, it should be open to debate because it is used to perform the same task as the motion to postpone indefinitely.

A motion *to refer to a committee* may also delay action. This motion is used when there is wide disagreement on the details of a motion but wide support for it in principle. Referring to a committee allows the committee to resolve disputed details so that an amended motion may be brought to the floor for vote at a future date.

The motion *to amend* is probably the most frequently used subsidiary motion. Amendments may consist of striking out portions of a main motion, or adding to it, or changing its wording. Consider, for instance, the motion, ''I move that this organization go on record as supporting the Equal Rights Amendment and that a copy of our motion to support the ERA be sent to the governor and members of the legislature.'' Such a motion could be amended in a number of ways. Someone could move to amend by striking out ''And that a copy of our motion'' and all following words. Or someone could move to insert after the word ''governor'' the words ''and members of the cabinet.'' Or someone could move to substitute the word ''endorse'' for ''go on record as supporting.'' What members may not do in an amendment, however, is offer changes that substantially alter the meaning of the motion. For instance, you could not propose to substitute the word ''condemns'' for the words ''go on record as supporting.''

Proposed amendments can also be amended. But to attempt more than one amendment to an amendment is to risk snarling the motion in so many threads of change that it becomes impossible to untangle.

A final subsidiary motion is called *moving the previous question.* The purpose of this motion would be much clearer if it were phrased, ''I move we end debate and vote immediately,'' rather than, ''I move the previous question.'' At any rate, the motion is used to end debate and bring the motion to a vote. It is not open to debate and requires a two-thirds vote.

Incidental motions are ones that deal with procedure. The most important of these is the motion *to limit debate.* A limit on debate may become necessary because time is restricted and a number of persons want to speak on an issue. A member may then propose, ''I move that debate on this issue (or motion) be limited to five minutes per person.'' The motion to limit debate may not be debated, but the time limit may be amended.

Another incidental motion is the *point-of-order motion*. If a member thinks the rules are being violated, as say, in the election of officers, he or she may rise and say, "Point of order." The chair must respond to this motion before further debate takes place and must acknowledge the mistake and correct it or explain how, in fact, the correct procedure is being observed. This may lead to a motion *to appeal the decision of the chair.* In any circumstance in which the chair makes a ruling about procedure, the correctness of the ruling may be voted on by the members. If they reject the chair's ruling, they must then vote a proper one.

At times, in voice votes, the chair will rule that a motion was approved or defeated, although a member might think that the voice vote was not clear-cut. The member may then use a motion called *division of the house,* which requires the chair to take a vote by having the members raise their hands or stand.

If an organization wishes to change the voting procedure, or the method of appointing a certain committee, or any other established rule, it may do so after approval of a motion *to suspend the rules.* Such a motion is

Motion	Second?	Debate?	Amended?	Vote
Main	Yes	Yes	Yes	Majority
Postpone (definite time)	Yes	Yes	Yes	Majority
Postpone (indefinite)	Yes	Yes	No	Majority
Lay on table	Yes	No	No	Majority
Refer to committee	Yes	Yes	Yes	Majority
Previous question	Yes	No	No	Two-thirds
Limit debate	Yes	No	Yes	Two-thirds
Appeal the chair's decision	Yes	Yes	No	Chair decides
Division of house	No	No	No	Chair acts
Point of order	No	No	No	Chair decides
Suspend rules	Yes	No	No	Two-thirds
Reconsider	Yes	Yes	No	Majority

not open to debate and requires a two-thirds vote. Often, the chair may handle inconsequential changes in the rules informally. The usual practice is for the chair to say, ''If there is no objection, we will permit an officer to serve on this committee for the coming year only.'' If such an announcement were challenged, then a formal motion to suspend the rules would have to be voted.

Finally, a member may make a motion *to reconsider* after action on a main motion has been taken. This can be moved at the same meeting in which the original motion was adopted. But a member should only make such a motion if information important to the debate was neglected or if a number of members, for some legitimate reason, were unable to take part in the original debate. The motion may be debated and requires only a majority vote. The only person who can make such a motion, however, is one who voted with the majority on the original motion.

JOB-RELATED SPEAKING

Once they have graduated, most students will find that the majority of their communication opportunities are associated with their jobs. At the outset, when applying for a job, they will be interviewed (a challenging communication situation) and, once hired, they will have to communicate daily with peers and supervisors in interpersonal and formally structured situations. As they advance in an organization, they will be called on to communicate in ever more demanding circumstances. They may have to speak at business conferences and conventions; or they may have to represent the organization to the general public. Everything that has been covered in this book should help a person perform job-related speech tasks. But there are some job-related speaking situations that need specific treatment.

THE JOB INTERVIEW

An employer conducts a job interview to size you up as a potential worker. During the interview, you will make a crucial impression. If the impression is good, you may well get the job; if the impression is poor, you will most certainly be scratched from the list. It is important, then, to know what to expect and how best to conduct yourself in the job interview. Here, in outline form, is a brief sketch of the information that the employer will want about you:

I. *Indications of the kind of character you have:*
   A. Your honesty and general moral character; personal habits that might be job related.
   B. Your trustworthiness and reliability.
II. *Indications of your intelligence, education, and skills:*
   A. Your general educational background.
   B. Specific job-related skills.
III. *Indications of your ability to work well with others:*
   A. Effectiveness of your interpersonal relations; how well you would get along with coworkers.
   B. Your ability and willingness to take directions and criticism from supervisors.
   C. Any leadership skills that might be useful on the job.
IV. *Your goals and ambitions:*
   A. What you want your life to be like generally.
   B. How you see your future development with this company.

To get this information, the interviewer will ask you a battery of questions. You should prepare in advance to answer them. There are two basic types of questions commonly asked in interviews. Some are simple *information-seeking* questions, such as "What high school and college did you attend?" Others are *judgment-seeking* questions by which the interviewer hopes to assess your general intelligence, adaptability, value systems, and so on. Often these judgmental questions will give you an opportunity for an extended reply. A sample question might be: "What do you think are the most important qualifications for this job?"

In answering all types of questions, be honest and don't try to oversell yourself. On the other hand, it is wise to find out before the interview what this particular company specializes in, what its attitude is toward employees, what it expects from them generally, and, if possible, what it seeks as qualifications for the specific job you want. Knowing these things, you will be able to avoid responses that will hurt your chances. Here is a list of questions of the type you may expect in a job interview. Before you enter an interview situation, you ought to have formulated appropriate responses:

1. Why are you interested in this job?
2. Why would you like to work for this company?
3. Why are you dissatisfied with your present job?

4. How did you become interested in this particular line of work?
5. What education and experience have you had that you think qualifies you for this job?
6. How much money do you expect?
7. Can you work well with other people?
8. What do you think you can offer this company?
9. What do you want your life to be like when you reach the age of forty?
10. Are you a good team worker?
11. If you had a serious conflict with a coworker, how would you resolve it?
12. What things would make you satisfied with a job?

In answering these questions, try to understand the interviewer's purpose and respond accordingly. For instance, in responding to question 11, you might say, "I don't expect to have serious conflicts with coworkers. I'm the type of person who works well with colleagues. In case there were a disagreement, however, I think I could solve it by talking it over frankly with the person and not have to involve the boss."

The job interview does not consist of a one-sided information flow; the interviewer will expect you to be seeking information also. The kinds of things you will want to know can be brought out by questions like the following:

1. What are the responsibilities of the job? Is there a written job description?
2. Does the job have a salary range? Does it have a minimum starting salary? Is salary adjusted to experience and training?
3. When will I earn a vacation? How much vacation will I get?
4. What are the fringe benefits, such as health insurance, retirement, pension or employee discounts?
5. Will I be expected to work overtime, on weekends, or on holidays?
6. Can I expect to be promoted rapidly? Can I move from this job to other positions of greater responsibility? Are there management-trainee opportunities for which I might later qualify?
7. When will I know whether or not I have been hired?

Usually the interviewer will indicate when the interview is over by saying something like: "Well, Ms. Jones, I believe I have gotten all the information I need. Is there anything else you would like to know?'' At this point, it is unwise to prolong the interview. You might ask another brief question and then conclude by asking question 7.

GROUP AND CONFERENCE SPEAKING

Chapter 13 covers communication in small groups. This kind of speaking is especially important for people who reach policy-making positions in business and industry. Small-group communication in a business context will focus mainly on how the company can achieve its mission. Settling conflicts will be important in this process.

ORAL REPORTS

Oral reports are of two basic kinds: the committee report and the convention or conference report. In modern business organizations, fact finding and policy proposals are frequently assigned to committees. Fact-finding committees are usually asked to investigate new procedures (such as different accounting systems) or to pinpoint what's happening within the company (for example, the nature of an employee training program and what it costs). Often, the report of a fact-finding committee will underscore the need for policy change. To examine possible policy changes and to recommend an appropriate policy, another committee may be appointed. In making committee reports, whether on facts or policy matters, a speaker need not worry about attention-getting and interest-holding materials. Interest is there already. What is wanted is a concise, clearly stated, easily understood presentation of the topic. Either a fact-finding or a policy committee report should follow a format similar to the one shown here:

I. *Introduction:*
   A. Give the background of the committee's task, and clearly explain it.
   B. Indicate the importance of the committee's findings to the operation of the organization.
II. *Body:*
   A. Explain the committee's procedures.
      1. Where and how did it gather its data?
      2. How did it analyze and interpret its data?
   B. What do the data mean?
      1. How do the data affect the quality of the product or service?

    2. How do the data affect productivity and profit?

  C. If the report is from a fact-finding committee, how do the data mesh with policy?

  D. If the report is that of a policy committee, what are the policy options?

    1. How are those policy options to be evaluated?

    2. Which policy should be adopted?

    3. What problems and outcomes will implementation yield?

III. *Conclusion:*

  A. Summarize the findings.

  B. Recommend appropriate action.

The convention or conference report is called for when you are asked to attend such a meeting as your company's representative. On your return, you will be expected to report any information from the conference or convention that might be useful to your company. Such a report will be similar in organization to the one just outlined, except the introduction will stress the nature of the conference or convention and how the information presented there applies to the operations of the home company. The body will deal with factual and policy matters that seem relevant and will handle them in much the same manner as already described.

PUBLIC-RELATIONS SPEECHES

When people have reached a position of responsibility in an organization, they are frequently called on to address civic clubs such as the Rotary, Kiwanis, and the Chamber of Commerce. They may also be asked to address special-interest clubs like the Economic Club, the PTA, and the Sierra Club. On such occasions the speakers may want to make a public-relations type of speech known as the goodwill speech. This kind of speech is especially desirable if a speaker's organization has received public criticism and poor publicity. Thus, an oil-company officer may wish to defend the company's production and pricing policies. A hospital administrator may wish to speak about the rising cost of medical care. Goodwill speeches under such circumstances are frankly persuasive in that the speaker tries to interpret company policies in a way that will reduce resentment and build understanding and goodwill. Such speeches do not usually take the form of argument, however. For the most part, they are informative: they present facts about the company's policies and procedures so as to win support for the organization. In other words, the speaker presents inductive evidence that will lead the audience to conclude that the speaker's firm is of great social worth, that it has honorable and kind intentions, and that it is run by individuals of character.

Such a speech follows the principles of good persuasive speaking given in Chapter 10, with some adaptations. A suggested outline follows:

I. *Introduction:*
   A. Begin with a novel statement about your work experience, or present one or two interesting facts about your company that will stir curiosity or interest and the desire to hear more.
   B. Indicate that your purpose is to present facts about your company that will help the audience understand it better.
II. *Body:*
   A. Show how your company is vitally concerned with the solution of some social need through its product or through a worthwhile service it offers.
      1. Support this claim by telling of interesting events in the company's history that demonstrate its social awareness and its importance to the community.
      2. Further support your claim by explaining the organization and operation of your company. Be selective. Pick those things that are interesting and that illustrate the fundamental values of your company. Be sure to point out the worthwhile things your company has achieved.
   B. Either directly or indirectly, mention the ill feelings toward your company that exist.
      1. Counter these criticisms by interpreting them in light of your company's constructive social role.
      2. Counter by showing that your organization is presently safeguarding the public interest and plans to do so in the future.
      3. Show that, when rightly understood, the conduct of your company is just and fair.
III. *Conclusion:* Have a strong summary that identifies your organization as being in the forefront in the search for a better, more stable social order.

Business and professional people, as this discussion has shown, need superior communication skills. The specific speech requirements mentioned here are only a few of the challenging occasions for communication that may arise. The best preparation for successful job-related speaking is mastery of the principles taught in this book.

SUMMARY

Special-occasion speeches must be adapted to the demands of the circumstance in which they are given. A speech of introduction, for instance, must fit the person being introduced and the audience that will receive the message. The same is true for entertaining speeches, speeches of praise, welcoming speeches, commencement addresses, and critical book reports. Outlines and sample speeches in this chapter illustrate the special requirements of these occasions and should be used as guides in preparing these speeches.

Parliamentary rules are used in groups that have formal, periodic meetings. The primary vehicle for doing business under parliamentary rules is the main motion. Main motions may be passed or rejected as presented, or they may be amended to make them acceptable. Consideration of a main motion may be delayed by motions to postpone, to refer to a committee, or to lay on the table. Certain procedural motions, such as to limit debate, to suspend the rules, or to appeal a decision of the chair, may be used to make business easier and maintain fair and orderly debate.

Job-related speaking involves employment interviews and on-the-job speaking like the presentation of oral reports of committee work or convention activity. Public relations speeches are delivered to project a favorable image of a business or industry to the public. Outlines for such job-related speeches are included in this chapter.

Exercises

1. Select a classmate and introduce him or her to the class. Follow the suggestions given in this chapter for the composition of the speech of introduction.
2. Plan and deliver a five-minute entertaining speech to the class. Use humorous devices like the ones mentioned in the text. Structure the speech in one of the three ways given in the section of this chapter on entertaining speaking.

3. Write a eulogy for a person you greatly admire. Hand this in to the instructor for evaluation and rewrite it according to his or her suggestions.

4. Make a speech nominating a person for a political office. To construct this speech, adapt the suggestions given in the sections of this chapter dealing with the speech of introduction and the eulogy.

5. Divide the class into teams. One person is to be designated as the employer who writes an advertisement for a job and conducts the employment interview. The other person answers the advertisement and plays the role of the applicant in the interview. Interviews should be conducted before the class and evaluated by class members.

6. Prepare a public relations speech. Select as the focus of this speech a profession or business you are interested in and might like to pursue after you graduate.

7. Organize the class as a parliamentary assembly. Divide the class evenly into four "committees." Let each committee formulate a motion on some issue of current interest. Then, let the class as a whole hear, debate, and handle these motions according to parliamentary rules.

Chapter Twelve

RADIO AND TELEVISION SPEAKING

OVERVIEW

How to adjust to radio and TV studio requirements
Some peculiarities of the radio and TV audience
How to plan, write, and deliver a manuscript speech
How to prepare for a discussion-debate program
How to answer questions and objections

Seventy-eight million American homes have at least one TV set and roughly half have two or more. Thus, there are probably 120 to 130 million TV sets in this country. The number of radios is probably twice that. (Just think of the number of radios in automobiles alone.) This mass of communication receivers is serviced by 750 commercial TV stations, 260 public TV stations, and 7000 radio stations. Most of these facilities transmit programs twenty-four hours a day, or very near that. This programming includes a high proportion of "talk" shows of several types: structured public speaking and debates and less·structured interviews, discussions, and public opinion forums. In recent years, thousands of Americans have found themselves communicating through such programs to audiences that number in the millions. And because of pressure on broadcasters to provide more public service programs, the number of talk shows is likely to increase.

Many of these shows offer ordinary people the chance to communicate through the mass media. Take the kind of radio program in which listeners call in, by telephone, to express their views on various issues. On an issue like abortion or drug abuse, callers swamp station switchboards. Typical callers may get two or three minutes to express their views. TV programs are common in which a local TV station has a camera crew go to a shopping mall or other public place to seek interviews. The crew asks individuals to express their opinions on topics of immediate interest, like school boards or property taxes. Cable television networks often have an entire channel reserved for local or regional programming. Much of such programming involves citizen editorials and public forum shows. Thus, the chances grow that you, an ordinary citizen, will have an opportunity to speak over radio or TV. If you should ever run for office, even such a modest one as school board member or city commissioner, you will almost certainly have to use radio and TV appearances in your campaign. Obviously, then, you should know how to communicate effectively over these electronic channels.

SPECIAL PROBLEMS WITH THE RADIO-TV CHANNEL

Who is the audience in a radio or TV show? Often, a speaker using a radio or TV channel will face an actual formal audience. When this happens, the electronic equipment tries to capture the occasion, as well as the speech itself. The TV camera, for instance, will focus not only on the speaker, but also on other platform guests and members of the audience. In such circumstances, speakers must decide how they will adapt their material—to the audience they face, which might number a few dozen or a few hundred, or to the unseen audience that may number hundreds of thousands or even millions. Of course, to some extent a speaker will try to serve or influence both audiences. The immediate audience, though, may be highly specific—composed, for example, of mostly mature adults who are labor union members. On the other hand, the larger audience is, in a sense, universal—consisting of old and young, union and nonunion, educated and uneducated. What may be especially right for one of these audiences may not be particularly effective with the other.

Another thing to remember is that a radio or TV audience is different in a number of ways from a live audience. Audience members are not, for example, captive in the sense that an audience in an auditorium is. They can turn to another station at any time if they don't like a speaker. If they do choose to hear a speaker out, they are still the target of many distractions. The phone may ring, the baby may cry, or a companion in the room may comment or ask a question. All such interruptions will disrupt understanding of a speaker's material. In addition, people are accustomed to radio and TV messages that are short, relatively simple, easily grasped, and presented in an entertaining way. Overall, the radio-TV audience usually has a mind-set requiring that a message be packaged in an attractive, compelling way.

Usually, therefore, radio-TV speakers try to make their material as universally appealing and attention-getting as possible. This means that they choose examples and arguments that will interest, appeal to, and be understood by almost everyone. Also, they try to use simple, clear, and concrete language, uncomplicated organization, and as much entertaining material as possible.

When you speak on TV, the audience will not see you in the same way they see a speaker in an auditorium. Instead, they see an image limited by a small screen. To make up for this compressed image, the TV director will use mainly close-up shots of the speaker showing the head and face.

Under these circumstances, the audience can't see hand gestures, but they have a better view than normal of facial expressions and eye contact. Be sure to look directly at the camera in formal speeches. (A red light on the front of the camera will glow when the image from that camera is being broadcast.) In interview and discussion formats look at the interviewer or the moderator, not at the camera.

In formal radio and TV speaking, careful timing is essential. Programs usually begin on the hour or the half hour and must end precisely at the close of the allotted time segment. Time must be preserved for an introduction and concluding remarks by the announcer. This means that a thirty-minute period may allow the speaker only about twenty-eight minutes. To work within such tight limits speakers usually write out and read the formal radio or TV speech from manuscript. Radio speakers usually hold the manuscript in hand and read directly from it, but TV speakers will be able to read from some kind of a teleprompter, which displays the text of the speech in large type just behind the camera lens. You should practice reading from a teleprompter till you get the hang of it.

Your adjustment to the microphone will not be difficult if you remember a few simple things. Most modern radio and TV studios are equipped with individual microphones that hang around the speaker's neck or attach inconspicuously to clothing. This relieves the speaker of worry about facing the microphone, but he or she must still attend to loudness. When the microphone is attached, the sound engineer will ask you to speak in a normal voice and will set the sound equipment accordingly. Although you may vary somewhat from this established level, you should avoid extreme changes because they will produce unwanted distortion. Also, remember that the microphone will exaggerate sloppy articulation. While you should avoid stilted pronunciation, you should be crisp and clear. Coughing, heavy breathing, and clearing your throat are all magnified by your microphone and can become serious distractions.

When you are on the air, the program director will need to communicate with you by silent hand signals. You should learn the director's signals before your program begins. Usually, they are simple. To let you know that you should begin speaking, the director will point a finger directly at you in a "from the shoulder" gesture. To get you to speed up, he or she will raise a hand above the head, forefinger extended, and rotate it in a swift circular motion. To get you to slow down, the director will raise both hands close together and then separate them in a "stretching" motion. If you aren't talking loudly enough, the director will hold out an arm, palm up, and give it a pushing-upward motion. If you are too loud he or she will reverse the action.

When you are in front of the TV camera, you need to think about dress and makeup. The studio will usually take care of the latter, but it is important to cooperate without self-consciousness. If you do not wear enough makeup, you may look very pale on camera, perhaps with dark shadows under your eyes or, if you are male, with a bluish cast to your chin from beard stubble. Both men and women need powder to prevent shiny noses or, in the case of bald men, to prevent glittering heads. Television audiences often respond unfavorably to an unsightly face. Richard Nixon once complained that he ''lost'' a debate with John Kennedy because his makeup failed to soften his jaw line and the dark shadows of his shaven skin.

Like badly done makeup, poorly chosen clothing may make a person unsightly on color TV. Some colors, certain greens for instance, may be reflected in your skin. Multicolored checks and stripes may blur together and can even appear to vibrate. Solid colors, of a muted shade, are probably best. Also, avoid bright jewelry, pins, rings, badges, or other items that may catch the light and glitter. If you are uncertain about dress, get advice from studio personnel.

PREPARING AND DELIVERING THE MANUSCRIPT SPEECH

The manuscript speech should not be read like an article or essay. It is written to be heard. Consequently you should write it in an oral style. We described the characteristics of oral as opposed to written style in Chapter 7. You should reread that section and try to word your manuscript according to the suggestions there. In particular, you should avoid long, involved sentences because they tax the attention span and will quickly cause listeners to tune you out.

The introduction to your speech should get the audience's attention and interest. One good way to do this is to tie your remarks to some striking news event that has just captured public interest. For example, in January of 1982 an Air Florida plane crashed into the 14th Street bridge just outside the National Airport in Washington D.C. A speaker discussing air-traffic safety could easily use the news accounts of this event as a springboard into his or her speech. Most people either travel by air or have relatives and friends who do so. Obviously, therefore, a plane crash and a discussion of air safety ties in closely with their vital interests.

Not only should the introduction get attention. It should also clearly state the speech's scope and purpose and offer an advance look at its main points. Two or three main points are all you can reasonably expect to cover in a short speech. They should be repeated at least once and should be summarized in the conclusion.

You should develop the speech by stating each main point and giving the evidence that supports it in as interesting and varied a way as possible. Using the air-traffic–safety topic, the speaker might outline one main point as follows:

I. Air-traffic safety suffers when out-of-date airports, built close to city centers, are forced to accommodate modern jet traffic:
   A. Runways of old airports are far too short and cannot be extended. Washington National's runways are only two-thirds as long as Dulles's runways.
      1. Short runways require sharp landing descents that are dangerous.
      2. Short runways prevent pulling out of takeoffs if trouble develops.
   B. Airports near city centers bring planes in at low altitudes over populated areas.
      1. The Air Florida crash killed six persons sitting in cars on the 14th Street bridge.
      2. San Diego airport causes planes to fly over the heart of the city, sometimes at less than 500 feet.

The conclusion of the speech should restate the purpose and the main points of the outline. This restatement should be followed with another vividly narrated example, illustration, or case history. End with some dramatic sentences, say, a striking prediction or question about the future of events—"Will we have another Air Florida crash? Must another plane fall into a congested city area and kill scores of people before we take action to make our airports safer? Let us hope we will act before another such tragic event occurs!"

THE INFORMAL DEBATE PROGRAM

Perhaps the most common type of radio or TV talk show pits speakers against each other in face-to-face confrontation. In some cases, you will speak in one-to-one opposition against a chosen member of another camp. You will usually have an opportunity to briefly present your side of the issue, as will your opponent. Then, in the remaining time, the two of you will respond to questions from each other or from the studio audience. On other occasions, you will be the only speaker. You will probably be allowed to speak briefly about the issue at hand, but during the majority of the program you will respond to questions from members of a selected panel (as on the programs "Meet the Press" and "Face the Nation") or from a studio audience. In either format, you will want to follow, roughly, a problem-solution pattern. You will need to know (1) how to present your position briefly and logically, (2) how to expose the shortcomings of a competing position, and (3) how to answer questions effectively. The material on logical argument in Chapter 5 will guide you in stating your position well.

PRESENTING YOUR CASE PRECISELY AND LOGICALLY

If you are recommending a change in some established practice or policy you must, to be logical, make certain claims and support them with evidence. The claims you must make are (1) that present practice or policy falls short or is undesirable for stated reasons, (2) that a new policy or practice will correct the shortcomings, and (3) that the new policy can be put into practice without serious problems. The following outline illustrates such a logical presentation (with evidence left out):

I. The quarter system in a university makes for serious problems:
     A. Short courses (usually ten weeks) make student learning difficult.
         1. Courses like novel reading, dramatic literature, and chemistry, cover more material than the student can learn in such a short time.
         2. Most quarter courses sacrifice full treatment of the subject because of time limits.
         3. Most quarter courses move so rapidly that students must give up discussion and mature consideration of the topics covered.
     B. Short courses put undue pressure on students.
         1. The number of examinations increases stress and fatigue.

    2. Preparation of term papers and class projects suffers because of lack of time.

  II. Changing to a semester plan would relieve the problems:

    A. Having enough time for the presentation of material would allow full treatment of the subject and thorough consideration, through discussion, of important topics.

    B. Examinations would be cut by one-third with a consequent reduction of student stress.

    C. The time for preparation of class papers and projects would be much more realistic.

III. The semester plan can be implemented with little trouble:

    A. The conversion will cost little.

    B. Quarter courses can be modified to fit semester presentation without much difficulty.

    C. The semester plan is better than any alternative, such as a trimester plan.

Not all controversial topics involve changes in policy or practice. Many times we are concerned about the value of certain aspects of our culture. These concerns commonly lead to what are called *propositions of value*. A sample proposition of value might be "Violence on TV programs is socially undesirable." Here the judgmental term is "socially undesirable." Consequently, the first step in establishing this proposition would be the definition of that term and of the criteria by which it may be shown that TV violence leads to "socially undesirable" consequences. An outline for a speech trying to prove this proposition might look like the following:

  I. A TV program is socially undesirable if it causes people to behave in ways that may harm themselves or society.

  II. A TV program causes people to harm themselves and society if watchers suffer the following conditions as a result of viewing the program:

    A. They are encouraged to harm themselves by seeing

      1. The use of dangerous weapons or explosives or the performance of unsafe feats of driving or other dangerous actions.

      2. The excessive use or condoning of drugs or alcohol.

B. They are encouraged to perform acts that harm others or society in general by
   1. Seeing aggressive behavior (beating, murder, arson, and so forth) shown as a model for manliness, or as a way to gain respect from peers.
   2. Being conditioned to view violent behavior as commonplace and acceptable.
   3. Losing their sensitivity to the human suffering caused by violent acts.
   4. Losing their respect for law and civility in society.

EXPOSING THE SHORTCOMINGS OF A COMPETING POSITION

To establish or prove a proposition a person must do two things: present evidence supporting the proposition and draw valid or logical conclusions from that evidence. To attack a competing position, therefore, you would attempt to discredit the opposition's evidence and to explose flaws in the reasoning by which conclusions were drawn from it.

In general, evidence may be discredited by claiming one or more of the following:

1. The evidence is insufficient to warrant the conclusion.
2. The evidence is out of date.
3. The evidence is contradicted by other evidence.
4. The evidence comes from poor and unreliable sources.

Examples will help clarify how these strategies work in actual practice.

Suppose a person proposes that there are widespread abuses in college football and basketball programs. That person must cite enough actual abuses on particular college campuses to make the charge credible. One or two abuses, however prominent and extreme, are not enough evidence to justify a claim about athletic programs at some 1200 colleges and universities.

Out-of-date evidence is common, and in exposing it a speaker can often offer contradictory evidence. Recently a student speaker quoted figures showing that only 9 percent of the doctors in this country were women. His data, however, came from a news article published in 1974. On the face of it, 1974 evidence can hardly be said to be true in 1982. An opponent's attack on the evidence was made convincing by more recent data—in 1978, 20 percent of the entry classes in U.S. medical schools were women, and women made up 16 percent of the total med-school population. Such figures strengthened the claim that 1974 ratios of men to women were no longer valid in 1982.

You can seriously weaken the impact of evidence if you can link it to poor and unreliable sources. Bias of a source is the most common reason to suspect its reliability. If it appears that a source will profit from the implications of the evidence it presents, we have reason to believe the evidence may not be all that reliable. For instance, the American Tobacco Institute has conducted ''scientific'' experiments that show no link between cigarette smoke and cancer in laboratory rats. People often scoff at this evidence because they suspect the source of bias springing from self-interest. If, historically, a source can be shown to have made mistakes or told lies, the source's credibility can be challenged. Richard Nixon's credibility, for instance, has suffered seriously because he made countless false statements about the Watergate cover-up. Many persons now hesitate to credit his testimony about any other issue in government either.

You can use several strategies to expose flaws in an opponent's reasoning. First, you can attack an inductive conclusion because it is based on insufficient or atypical examples. In the foregoing discussion of evidence, we saw that citing one or two highly visible cases of abuse in athletic programs would not be enough evidence to indict a large number of schools. But even if many cases are cited, they can be challenged if they can be shown not to be typical of the whole group. To return to the example, you could cast doubt on the representativeness of cited abuses if you could show that they are not well distributed geographically, that they apply primarily to very large schools or schools in a particular conference, that they occurred mainly in schools with very large athletic budgets, and so forth. These challenges will not disprove the charge that abuses occur, but they will put the charge in proper perspective and may help in remedying the problem.

Another way to test an opponent's reasoning is to look carefully at suggested cause-and-effect relationships. Often, speakers give little or no evidence to support a cause-effect connection. Ronald Reagan's administration, for instance, justified tax cuts on the ground that the money people saved in taxes would be put into savings, thus providing industry with cheaper and more-available capital. Cheap, readily available funds would presumably stimulate the economy, leading to greater prosperity all around. In challenging such a cause-effect prediction, an opponent could point out that the administration presents no evidence at all to show that people would actually save the money gained from tax relief. In fact, it is just as likely that they would spend such money as it is that they would save it. If they spend it, then industry has gained no new sources of funds for expansion, and the expected upturn in the economy would not happen. One might further strengthen the attack on this cause-effect chain by predicting that a different effect than the one predicted will result from the cause; that is, in this case, that millions of persons spending money they saved in taxes, would create a consumer demand that would fuel inflation.

Another way to question an opponent's reasoning is to show flaws in comparisons and analogies. For instance, a lawyer once argued that a corporation could not make an oral contract because it had no mouth. His opponent quickly pointed out that, if the analogy were true, a corporation could not make a written contract either, because it had no hand. Most analogies are more literal than that, however, and are based on the assumption that what has happened in one set of circumstances will happen again in similar circumstances. Thus, one may argue that we should not send military advisors to El Salvador because when we sent military advisors to Viet Nam we were led into a disastrous war. To counter such an argument, a speaker would have to show that the situation in El Salvador is different enough from the situation in Viet Nam so that what happened in Viet Nam will not occur in El Salvador.

Sometimes a speaker can accept another person's reasoning but may reduce or nullify its impact by reinterpreting it. One objection to the now-defeated Equal Rights Amendment, for instance, was that the Amendment would require men as well as women to be drafted. Many supporters of the ERA accepted this objection but tried to weaken it by arguing that women should be proud to shoulder equal responsibility with men. They also pointed out that, as with men, draft boards could exempt women with children, women with health problems, or women with hardships. Moreover, the armed forces would not have to assign women to combat duty.

ANSWERING QUESTIONS EFFECTIVELY

Most TV and radio talk shows consist almost entirely of questions and answers. A person who appears on such a program is usually asked an initial leading question or two, such as "Can you state your position on abortion (capital punishment, the proposed sales tax increase, or whatever) in a few sentences?" This allows the person to advance a few carefully organized, prepared remarks. From that point on, however, questions will come from all directions and with a variety of motives. The speaker must be able to respond to them effectively. In making the recommendations for answering questions that follow, we assume that you will be advancing a position that competes with others.

In preparing for a question-and-answer show, you should try to predict as many questions and objections as possible. If you are dealing with a matter of policy you should expect questions about whether there really is a problem that requires a change in present policy, what the nature and extent of the problem are, what the probable causes of it are, and why your way of dealing with it is desirable. On these points, you should have additional evidence and argument ready beyond what you will be able to present in your opening statement. The extra material can be used to explain and reinforce your position as you respond to questions.

You may expect questions from persons who have one of three kinds of motives. Some persons will support you and will ask questions that allow you to expand on strong points, to introduce new arguments, or to bolster evidence. Other persons will be merely curious: eager to learn more about the topic and to gain a clearer idea of where you stand. A third kind of questioner will be hostile and will, in the disguise of questions, raise objections and offer contrary evidence and argument that tend to undermine your position.

Answer a questioner who supports you or is simply curious in the following way:

1. Point out that the question relates to a particular aspect of your case, such as the nature and extent of the problem, the causes of it, or the workability of your proposed remedy.
2. Present new evidence or argument and show how it supports that aspect of your case.
3. Restate the validity of your overall position in view of the new evidence and argument you have presented.

Answer a questioner who raises an objection or who offers contrary evidence and argument as follows:

1. Relate the question to a particular aspect of your case.
2. Weaken the objection by showing the following: (a) it is based on a misunderstanding of your position; (b) it assumes cause-and-effect connections that will not operate; (c) experts in the field do

not agree that the objection is valid; or (d) although the objection
may be valid, the disadvantage that it points out is outweighed
by the benefits of your policy.

3. Counter any new evidence with new evidence of your own or
with questions about whether your opponent's evidence is sufficient, up to date, and reliable.

4. Attack a new line of argument by exposing logical weaknesses in
it.

5. Finally, state the validity of your overall position.

The following are some special considerations to think about in answering questions:

1. If a question seems silly, you may turn it aside with humor.
(Avoid heavy sarcasm at the questioner's expense, though.) Then
you can offer additional comments supporting your position on
an issue suggested by the question.

2. If your answer to an objection is weak, move swiftly into a
restatement and reinforcement of one of your strong points.

3. If a question asks for information you do not have, admit your
ignorance (don't try to bluff). Suggest where such information
might be found and what it is likely to show. Downplay the
importance of the evidence, if appropriate, by showing that it
relates to a minor point or that, even if it doesn't support your
position, the evidence you have already presented outweighs it.

A couple of questions and answers follow. The first is a question asked
out of support or curiosity. The question is intended to draw out the
speaker's position.

Question: Don't you think the presidential debates are a poor way for
people to measure the fitness of presidential candidates?
Answer: Yes, I do. The skills on display in the debates are quick spur-
of-the-moment adjustments to questions and objections desgned to
entrap and confuse. The debates might show how well the president
could handle a press conference, and that's about all. They give no
clue how the president will do when discussing policy with the
cabinet or legislation with leading members of Congress, or when
making a formal address to the nation. Occasions like those require

much more thought. They demand formal proposals. And they give much more opportunity for careful examination and consideration than the debates do. In other words, I am saying that the speaking skills required by the debates have little relationship to the kind of communication skills the president needs in office.

Note that, in the answer, the speaker relates the question to his or her total criticism of the presidential-debate format. The answer then proceeds to strengthen the speaker's position by presenting an argument that was evidently well thought out in advance.

In the next example, the question is really an objection and the questioner is trying to refute some of the speaker's material.

Question: How can you claim that grocery chains are earning big profits when stores like A&P earn only 1 percent on sales?
Answer: In a high turnover business like grocery chains, a 1 percent annual profit looks small, but the real indicator is: How much do they earn in relation to investment? Grocery chains have traditionally earned at least 10 to 15 percent annually. And this is after setting aside large sums as reserves that are not counted as profit. These facts underscore what I have been saying all along, that labor costs are not the only cause of high prices. Sometimes high profits increase prices, too.

This answer successfully points out a fallacy in the objection, corrects it with a proper view of the situation, and then shows how the response has strengthened the speaker's case.

SUMMARY

Radio and television are communication channels that reach millions of Americans. These millions make up an audience that, in the mass, is accustomed to entertainment and to relatively simple, easily understood messages. Two common types of radio-TV speech formats are the formal manuscript presentation and the informal debate or discussion program. The speaker must write manuscript speeches in oral style and must pay particular attention to making them interesting and easily understood. Discussion and debate speaking need to follow a logical sequence that is

basically a problem-solution pattern. You must know how to test the
evidence and argument that underlie your proposal and be able to spot
and expose weaknesses in the evidence and argument of opponents.
Responding to questions is important in a talk-show format. Questions
may be asked for information or to raise objections to your proposals.
Responding well to questions is an important part of successfully using
electronic media.

Exercises

1. The class should listen to a talk show like "Face the Nation" and
   observe the question and answer techniques used. Class members
   should discuss questions like the following ones:

   Were the motives of the questioners evident? Were they hostile or
   friendly?

   Did the answers seem to follow the suggestions given in this
   chapter? How did they depart from these suggestions? Were the
   departures good or bad in your opinion?

2. Have the class divide into teams of three questioners and one
   advocate. Let these teams perform in front of the class. Criticize
   questions and answers.

3. Use a tape recorder and a video-tape recorder to record students
   giving formal and informal presentations. Play these back for comment and criticism.

4. Have class members evaluate a formal TV presentation by the
   President of the United States or some other prominent figure.

Chapter Thirteen

GROUP DISCUSSION

OVERVIEW

Group discussion distinguished from public speaking
Discussion tasks and how to word a discussion question
Characteristics of questions of fact, value, and policy
Leadership responsibilities in a discussion
Participant responsibilities in a discussion
Influence of a group discussion situation on participants

The speaking situations that we have emphasized in this book are often called *one-to-many.* In the one-to-many context, a speaker directs a continuous flow of speech to an audience of people who mostly pay attention to the speaker and disregard each other. Any interplay of communication generally comes from questions and comments exchanged by the speaker and individual members of the audience and, of course, from the continuous nonverbal feedback that accompanies a speech.

This communication pattern is common, but it is not always appropriate. Many situations call for group discussion, a more informal pattern of speech. Instead of hearing long formal statements, participants exchange short contributions and pay attention not to a particular speaker but to all members of the group. Group discussion, then, can be defined as that form of communication in which a small group of people, usually ranging from three to a maximum of six or eight, interact by speaking with one another to achieve some common goal or purpose.

Group discussion may sometimes be public; that is, the group works before an audience that listens in. Some public service television programs have this format. For instance, the question, "What can we do to reduce the rate of inflation?" may be posed to a group of three or four experts (a banker, an economist, and a budget expert from Congress). Guided by a moderator, these people talk with one another, exploring the causes of and possible remedies for inflation. Their purpose is mainly to inform the listening audience about the problem of inflation and its complexities. Most group discussions, however, are not public in the sense just described; rather, they are private, in that they are not observed by people other than the participants. Such discussions take place to meet the needs of the group members themselves, rather than the needs of a listening audience. Private group discussions tend to be task oriented; that is, they are designed to yield some outcome expected by the group members.

DISCUSSION TASKS

Discussion groups arise from the participants' needs. For instance, the vice president for marketing of a corporation may call together a group of sales managers to discuss the question "What are the reasons for the declining sales of product X?" A minister may invite the deacons and selected members of the congregation to join in a discussion of the question: "What is a Christian attitude toward homosexuality?" Or a prison warden may assemble the prison's administrative staff to discuss the question "How shall we deal with the problem of racial strife among our prisoners?" Each of these topics was selected to meet a somewhat different type of need. The first topic illustrates a fact-finding or information-sharing situation, the second a value-assessment concern, and the third a policy or problem-solution need. We will discuss each type of question at some length, but first we should say a few words about the makeup of a discussion question.

WORDING A TASK-ORIENTED DISCUSSION QUESTION

When a task-oriented discussion group assembles, it does so in response to a problem. Members of the group should be aware that the success of the discussion hinges in part on the clarity with which the problem is stated. The statement of a good discussion question is governed by the following characteristics:

1. The topic should always be worded as a question that states the problem and specifies the goal of the discussion. If someone says, "This discussion is to be about the energy shortage" the participants will have very little information to guide them. Are all aspects of the energy shortage to be considered? Is the purpose of the discussion to inform the group about the causes of the energy shortage or about how long the known reserves of oil and coal will last? Is the purpose of the discussion to search for alternatives to existing energy sources or for ways of conserving present resources? None of these points is made clear unless you phrase the topic as a question. Suppose you ask, "How can we best conserve present reserves of oil?" The participants will know that the discussion will focus on ways to extend available oil supplies, either by restricting use or by discovering alternative sources of energy.

2. The question should be worded in an unbiased way. A biased question assumes judgments about the topic that may or may not be confirmed by the discussion itself. In this way, a biased question discourages investigation of a portion of the topic that needs exploration. Suppose someone asks, "How can the present wasteful and inefficient consumption of oil be reduced?" Worded in this way, the question assumes that waste and inefficiency are characteristic of oil consumption in this country. It also suggests that reducing waste and inefficiency will sufficiently reduce oil consumption. Both of these assumptions may or may not be true, and their presence in the wording of the question itself tends to limit and channel the thinking of the participants.

3. The question should be clearly phrased. If a group tried to discuss a question like "What is the present situation in international relations?" its members would have to spend a great deal of time determining what the terms *present situation* and *international relations* means. The latter term, for instance, might refer to disarmament talks, activities of the United Nations, tariff and trade agreements, or regulation of fishing rights. If the question is clearly stated, confusing terms will be defined and the intended area of discussion will be clear.

4. The question should be worded so as to avoid a mere yes or no judgment. For instance, the question "Should this school adopt the quarter system?" limits the discussion to the pros and cons of the quarter calendar only. A better discussion question would be "What academic calendar should this institution adopt?" The discussion would thus be open to analysis of semester, modified-semester, trimester, quarter, or any other type of academic calendar.

We have said that discussion questions generally arise out of the needs of the participants. In the classroom situation, students should select questions for discussion that have meaning for them as students or as young people trying to establish themselves in an adult world. In selecting a question, they should also consider the availability of material and the amount of time allotted for discussion. If the school library has little information on a proposed question, and if there are few resource people to turn to in the community, participants may want to select another topic. Likewise, if the topic is broad and there is a lot of material on it, but there is only an hour in which to hold the discussion, participants may want to select a more limited topic.

The nature of the discussion task influences the structure of a discussion. As we indicated earlier, some discussions are aimed at fact finding or information sharing, some are value oriented, and others are problem-solution efforts. Each type proceeds in a somewhat different way.

DISCUSSING QUESTIONS OF FACT

The aim of a fact-finding or information-sharing discussion is to determine the facts in, or exchange information about, a given situation. The discussion question usually begins with the words *What is* or *What are*. For instance, the discussion might turn on the question "What methods do college instructors use to assign student grades?" Analysis of the question would probably lead to a discussion outline somewhat like the following:

I. What has been the traditional theory used by professors in assigning grades?
    A. How does the norm-based system work?
        1. What are the assumptions underlying it?
        2. What effect does it have on students?
    B. How well do norm-based grades reflect actual student achievement?
II. What is the criterion-based method of awarding grades?
    A. What are the assumptions underlying it?
    B. What effect does it have on students?
    C. How well do criterion-based grades reflect actual student achievement?
III. What is the contract system of grading, and how does it compare with the norm-based and the criterion-based methods?
IV. What is the S-U pattern of grading, and how does it compare with other patterns?

The participants in this discussion would certainly evaluate the various systems discussed, and they might end up favoring a particular one. But the discussion would not be conducted to determine the relative merits of the various systems. A judgment might result later; but the discussion's first purpose would be simply to inform the participants.

DISCUSSING QUESTIONS OF VALUE

Value-assessment discussions usually fall into one of two categories: they are concerned either with utilitarian values or with ethical values. Sometimes both types of questions arise in the same discussion. A discussion centered on utilitarian values would probably be guided by an outline something like the following:

   I. What is the purpose of present scientific research designed to alter the genes of such bacteria as *Escherichia coli*? [In place of this topic, any other may be substituted.]
  II. Can this purpose actually be achieved? If so, how soon?
 III. If new forms of bacteria can be created by gene manipulation, what will be the results?
    A. Will these results benefit human beings?
    B. Will the results harm human beings?
 IV. To what extent is this kind of genetic research acceptable to society? To what extent is it unacceptable? Why?

A discussion centered on moral values often proceeds somewhat according to the following plan:

   I. Why is civil disobedience [or whatever the behavior in question] considered by some people to be morally wrong?
    A. What are the assumptions of those who condemn civil disobedience?
      1. The law must be obeyed if we are to have an orderly society.
      2. There are appropriate, legal ways of changing unjust laws. [etc.].
    B. What are the assumptions of those who approve civil disobedience?
      1. Laws that do not conform to principles of justice higher than human principles (laws that do not follow God's law, laws that erode the dignity and welfare of people, and the like) should not be obeyed.
      2. Laws decreed without the participation of the governed may be disobeyed [etc.].
  II. What are the undesirable social consequences of civil disobedience?
 III. What are the desirable social consequences of civil disobedience?

IV. Is civil disobedience morally justifiable, not justifiable, or somewhere in between? Always? Under certain circumstances?

It should be noted that value questions tend to involve questions about
social usefulness. This fact suggests that many of our moral values are
rooted in beliefs about the desirable or undesirable social consequences of
given behavior.

DISCUSSING QUESTIONS OF POLICY

Most discussions probably are stimulated by policy questions, which
invariably begin with the words *What shall we do about* or *What kind of action
should we take with respect to.* Policy discussions generally begin with a
description of the problem and proceed with an examination of solutions
to that problem. For instance, the management staff of a big retail
corporation might call for a discussion of the question "What kind of
action(s) should this company take with respect to theft by employees?"
An agenda for this question would undoubtedly include the following
items:

I. What is the size and scope of employee theft?
   A. How many employees are involved?
   B. How much do they steal?
   C. What products do they steal, and how do they do it?
II. What are the causes of employee theft?
   A. Is the problem the result of inadequate security?
   B. To what extent are employee morale and employee pay scales
      related to the problem?
   C. Are there other causes?
III. What criteria should be used in arriving at a solution to this
problem?
   A. Is it ethical to use devices that threaten employees' rights to
      privacy and to the presumption of innocence until proven
      guilty?
   B. How costly will proposed solutions be? And how effective?
   C. Will solutions cause employee resentment or affect how cus-
      tomers view the company [etc.]?
IV. What are some possible solutions to the problem?
   A. Increase security and employee surveillance by means of TV
      cameras, and the like.
   B. Use periodic lie-detector tests.

C. Launch a propaganda campaign to increase employee awareness of the theft problem.
D. Provide employee incentives for detection of theft [etc.].
V. What solution or combination of solutions will best solve the
   problem in terms of the criteria set for a good solution?

A discussion that follows this suggested pattern will probably lead to a
solution that is carefully weighed against alternatives. Such a solution
should attract the cooperation of those managers whose job it is to give the
proposal a fair trial.

LEADERSHIP RESPONSIBILITIES IN A DISCUSSION

Discussion leaders have different styles. Some leaders are *authoritarian,*
keeping tight control over who speaks and when. In addition, authoritarian leaders tend to force the participants in the direction of a solution they
prefer by criticizing participants with whom they disagree. They may
threaten participants with reprisals if they fail to cooperate with the
"boss." Such leaders inhibit the freedom of the group to explore ideas and
test solutions.

At the opposite extreme are *laissez-faire* leaders. Their concept of leadership is to do almost nothing to control or direct the discussion. They are
willing to give participants great freedom to express their ideas and to
wander from the discussion agenda. The laissez-faire style of leadership is
generally preferable to the authoritarian style, but laissez-faire leaders
tend to waste time and fail to focus the energy of the group toward clear
goals.

Democratic leaders practice laissez-faire to some extent. They certainly
allow freedom of ideas and criticism. But they also exert controls and offer
guidelines and procedures that further the work of the group. Democratic
leaders also tend to be objective in their criticisms and directions to the
group.

An early experimental study of leadership was done in 1939 by Lewin,
Lippitt, and White. During a six-week period, they compared the behavior of young male discussion participants under each of the three types of
leadership: authoritarian (autocratic), democratic, and laissez-faire. They
found that their experiment justified the following conclusions:

1. The participants in the laissez-faire groups did less work and
   poorer quality work than those in the democratic groups.

2. The autocratic groups did somewhat more work than the democratic groups, but democratic-group members showed more interest, motivation, and originality.
3. There was more hostility in the autocratic groups, and this hostility led to aggressive behavior against other members and more dropping out of members.
4. The autocratic-group members were more submissive and less individualistic.
5. The democratic group members were friendlier with one another and more group minded. They praised one another's efforts more and tended to work more frequently in spontaneous subgroups.[1]

Other investigators have studied the behavior of discussion leaders in a number of situations and have described characteristic leadership functions in terms of the way leadership behavior furthers group action. Bales, for instance, saw two basic categories of leadership behavior: the *socioemotional function* and the *task function*. Leaders who were good at the socioemotional function tended to be well liked by the groups. These leaders spent much time encouraging members to participate, commending them, and in general creating a friendly atmosphere. Task-oriented leaders had good ideas about the topic and made many contributions designed to help solve the problem being addressed by the groups.[2]

Discussion-group leaders should try to create an atmosphere of cooperation and goodwill among the participants. They should assure participants that the group needs to know their ideas and evaluations. They should stress that disagreement and conflict are inevitable and desirable, for it is through such clashes that a group tests and evaluates ideas. Leaders should be especially careful to avoid an atmosphere that is known as "groupthink." Groupthink occurs when the climate of discussion indicates that it is not good policy to disagree with a prestigious person, like the chairperson of the board or the president of the business. This attitude leads participants to seek favor by being agreeable, even to the extent of trying to determine what the boss wants and then deliberately speaking to satisfy him or her. Such a climate severely limits the

[1] K. Lewin, R. Lippitt, and R. K. White, "Patterns of Aggressive Behavior in Experimentally Created Social Climates," *Journal of Social Psychology,* 10 (1939), 271–299.

[2] R. F. Bales, "A Set of Categories for the Analysis of Small Group Interaction," *American Sociological Review,* 15 (1950), 257–263.

scope of a discussion and inhibits honest disagreement. As a result, the quality of decisions made by the group may suffer.

In addition to setting the climate, the leader does a number of things that fall under the heading of *task facilitation*. These are things that help the discussion members to understand and reach their goals. For instance, the leader generally suggests an *agenda,* which is an outline of the subissues to be discussed. (The outlines for fact, value, and policy questions given in the preceding sections are examples of typical agendas.) Once the agenda is agreed on, the leader tries to keep the group moving without too much wandering. He or she does this by summarizing what the group has accomplished, by indicating what still needs to be done, and by providing transitions between one step and another.

The leader can often do all of these things at once. It is common for a discussion leader to say something like "I think we all seem to agree that there are some occasions when civil disobedience is not only necessary, but ethical and proper. The question is when? Suppose we turn our attention now to defining the situational factors that make civil disobedience morally acceptable." The leader may also point out cases where additional evidence is needed and may stimulate critical thinking by evaluating arguments or asking that members make such evaluations themselves.

Another important aspect of leadership is the *constructive management of conflict.* Conflict tends to occur (1) because members compete to try to influence the outcome of the discussion and (2) because members compete for favorable attention within the group. A leader can handle the latter problem by making sure that no one participant talks too much and that all have an opportunity to express themselves. For instance, he or she may say, "I think we have heard from almost everyone in the group on this point except George. George, how do you feel about the use of polygraph tests to prevent theft among employees?" The leader may also encourage objective rather than belittling or emotional evaluation of ideas expressed by participants. Comments such as the following will generally help establish this point: "I don't think we should ridicule Henry's idea. A lot of people share his view. Let's look at the argument for what it's worth." By encouraging cooperation and evenhanded treatment of all participants and ideas, the leader tends to discourage egotistical remarks and power plays attempted through coalitions or bullying.

The conflict that arises from attempts to influence the outcome of the discussion should be encouraged, however, not surpressed. The quality of the final decision arrived at by the group rests on the extent to which

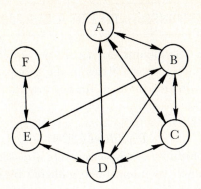

Figure 13.1
This pattern represents poor discussion interaction. While members A, B, C, and D communicate well with one another, E communicates only with B and D. F is almost completely isolated.

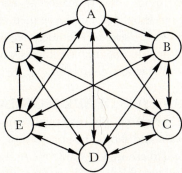

Figure 13.2
In this pattern, there is much greater interaction among the group as a whole. This kind of pattern facilitates task performance much better than does the pattern in Figure 13.1.

competing views have been presented and discussed. Thus, the leader should encourage all participants to express themselves fully and openly. He or she should emphasize the value of having conflicting views presented and objectively evaluated. The leader may use such comments as, "A moment ago Anne expressed a tentative view that we all seemed to frown on. I wish she would express it more fully for us now. It may have some good ideas in it that we ought to consider." Even if some group members react to challenging ideas with emotionally defensive behavior, the leader should still try to encourage the clash of views. The conflict of ideas is the best insurance the discussion participants have against groupthink. It also tends to improve the quality of the discussion. Figures 13.1 and 13.2 are diagrams illustrating good and poor participation patterns.

PARTICIPANT RESPONSIBILITIES IN A DISCUSSION

Good discussion participants do not sit and offer a few off-the-cuff comments. They have responsibilities to the group and to themselves. Unless those responsibilities are met, they cannot expect the discussion to be fruitful.

PREPARATION

A primary responsibility of all participants is *conscientious preparation*. A discussion group pools the information gathered by its members into a fund of knowledge that should be larger than what any individual member could amass. If members are not prepared, however, the group simply pools its ignorance, and the product is no better than what a member could have uncovered alone. If the leader or another member asks, "What evidence exists to show that employee theft is a serious cost in the operation of this business?" several members should have evidence to share on the point. If they do not, no one knows whether the problem is really serious enough to warrant discussion.

ANALYSIS OF THE PROBLEM

In addition to being prepared, discussion participants should *analyze the issues inherent in the problem* and should be able to raise questions about how well the group confronts these issues. Someone may say, for instance, "I don't think we have fully established the causal relationships here. I think we are just assuming a connection. Does anyone have any evidence that ties those two things together in a causal way?" Or someone may point out, "We haven't really considered the disadvantages of this alternative fully. What about its general acceptability to the public?" The purpose of such comments and questions is to probe the logic of what the group is doing and to further its task of fully considering the problem.

HARMONIZING

Discussion participants may assist the leader in the constructive management of conflict. We have already pointed out that conflict is desirable but must be managed to prevent stubbornness and communication breakdown. Thus, a participant may adopt the role of *harmonizer*. The harmonizer does not try to prevent conflict, but only to keep it from disrupting the discussion. The harmonizer may use such comments as the following: "Jane's point is certainly provocative, but I don't think we should attack her personally for it. Let's test the idea itself." "John may be right in getting upset about this statement. Let's hear what he has to say and try to judge his position on its merits." The harmonizer's aim is to divert emotional response away from people personally and to encourage the group to examine and test the ideas themselves. Sometimes this approach will not be enough, making it necessary to express disapproval: "I don't think we should resort to name calling or to condemning ideas we disagree with. I think we ought to give every person and every idea a fair hearing." Peer pressure that asks for open, if not friendly, behavior will usually help to manage personal conflict.

GATEKEEPING

Sometimes participants may add to the efficiency of the discussion by acting as *gatekeepers*. Gatekeepers try to secure a high level of involvement from all participants. They open the gate, so to speak, for people who are a little bit timid about talking. Gatekeepers often make encouraging remarks, such as "Joan, you look as if you have something to say on this point," or, "Bill, tell us how that remark strikes you." At the same time, they try to tactfully shut the gate on overeager participants who want to talk too much: "You've made a good point, Dave, but before you elaborate on it, I think we should get the reactions of others. Lenore, how do you feel about it?" If two participants are arguing and ignoring the others, a gatekeeper may say, "You two have opened up one of the issues in this matter, but there are other points that need consideration. Sarah, what other points do you feel need to be looked at?" Thus, the gatekeeper blocks the two from further argument and opens the door to a different person.

This discussion of participant responsibilities has focused on desirable behaviors. Obviously, certain other behaviors are undesirable and should be avoided. We will mention them briefly.

WITHDRAWAL

A participant who does not talk is of no value to the group. Some people hesitate to speak because they feel they have nothing important to contribute. If a participant has read and thought about the discussion topic, he or she cannot help having valuable evidence and ideas to share. A discussion gains much from the clash of ideas and from the discussion of evidence and its meaning. If all participants withdrew, the discussion would obviously fail. A discussion tends to lose effectiveness if a number of participants fail to contribute.

MONOPOLIZING

Monopolizing is the opposite of withdrawal. It is the urge to talk too much and thereby keep others from participating. In a sense, the monopolizer forces other participants to keep silent when they want to contribute. A discussion dominated by one or two monopolizers is, in effect, the same as a discussion from which the majority of members have withdrawn.

AGGRESSION

Aggressors tend to be overtly combative. They see the discussion as a contest to decide who can talk the most, refute opposing arguments most vigorously, and generally score the most points. They tend to ignore the feelings of others and to be pushy, if not rude, in their comments. They intimidate others with their behavior and thus hamper the free flow of ideas that is so necessary for successful discussion.

HOW GROUPS INFLUENCE INDIVIDUAL PARTICIPANTS

Earlier, we mentioned a tendency for discussion participants to engage in groupthink—to tailor their evidence and arguments to the expectations of high-status members they do not wish to offend. This phenomenon raises the following question: How does the behavior of individuals in a group differ from their behavior when they are acting alone? A number of studies have provided some clues to these differences. Dickens and Heffernan, after surveying the results of twenty-eight studies, felt the following conclusions were justified:

1. After discussion, extreme judgments tend to draw in toward a middle ground.
2. After discussion, judgments tend to improve in accuracy or correctness.
3. Knowledge of how the majority stands greatly affects an individual's judgment.
4. Right answers tend to be held more tenaciously than wrong ones.
5. Group superiority is greater in dealing with problems that permit a range of response.[3]

---

[3] Milton Dickens and Marguerite Heffernan, "Experimental Research in Group Discussion," *Quarterly Journal of Speech,* 35 (1949), 23–29.

These conclusions suggest that group performance is superior to that of individuals working alone. This judgment needs tempering, however. When a task has few steps, needs only a few facts for successful solution, and has a solution that is easy to verify (as in math or deductive-reasoning), a group will probably produce results no better than the individual members would have produced. Moreover, it will take a group longer to produce those results. If a problem has multiple parts, requires a lot of information for successful solution, and has a solution that is difficult to verify (as when one tries to project the consequences of adopting some course of action, like increasing gasoline taxes), a group is likely to produce results that are superior to those produced by an individual member acting alone.[4]

Before concluding this discussion of group influence, we should note two other consequences of group activity. The first is the tendency of groups to take greater risks in making decisions. This is called the *risky-shift phenomenon*. Risk, in this context, means the willingness to adopt a belief or course of action with less information and evidence than most people would normally want. Thus, groups tend to make decisions that the individual members of the group would probably not accept if acting by themselves. A number of explanations have been offered for this phenomenon, including the idea that Americans place a high value on risk taking. The most likely explanation, however, is that group participation spreads out responsibility for action and thus makes it easier for members to excuse themselves if the decision turns out to be wrong. It should be pointed out that, in spite of risk taking, group decisions still tend to be better than individual decisions under the conditions described in the preceding paragraph.

A second consequence of group influence has to do with member satisfaction. Generally, the members of a group experience various degrees of satisfaction with decisions that are reached. If conflict has been successfully managed, if an atmosphere of trust has been established, and if the individual has participated extensively in the discussion, he or she tends to be satisfied with the result. This fact is important to businesses and other organizations where the implementation of general policies is crucial. If employees participate in the formation of policies, they tend to

---

[4] For a good discussion of the effect of group influence, see Lawrence B. Rosenfeld, *Human Interaction in the Small Group Setting* (Columbus: Charles E. Merrill, 1973), pp. 65–96.

be more enthusiastic about putting those policies into practice. If, however, management tries to impose new procedures from above, workers
generally respond with resistance in the form of lower morale, greater
absenteeism, or reduced productivity.[5]

SUMMARY

Group discussion differs from public speaking in that participants do
not give long one-to-many speeches to a relatively passive audience.
Instead, they exchange short, informal comments with one another in
groups of three to eight persons. In a discussion, participants talk about
questions of fact, value, and policy. A good discussion question deals with
a single problem and specifies the group's goal in discussing it; it is
worded in an unbiased way; it is clearly phrased; and it is worded to avoid
a yes or no answer.

Fact-finding or information-sharing discussions try to verify what the
facts are in a given case. Value-assessment discussions try to assess the
utilitarian and moral values of an event or proposal. Policy discussion
explores a problem and tries to come up with a solution to it.

The discussion leader tries to further the group's progress by suggesting
an agenda and helping the group to follow it and by trying to manage
conflict among participants. Discussion participants must prepare by
informing themselves on the topic, analyzing the issues the topic raises,
and trying to further the work of the group by keeping members' minds
on the task and helping them settle conflicts. Participation in groups
affects individuals by making their judgments less extreme, more accurate, more sensitive to majority opinion, and more strongly held.

Exercises

1. The class should divide into groups of eight. Each group should
    select and word a discussion question on policy. After preparation,
    these groups should engage in a discussion before the class.
2. Students should evaluate all classroom discussions using a simple
    check list (like the ones shown in Chapter 8) of the points raised in
    this chapter. These evaluations should be shared with the discussion
    participants.

---

[5] L. Coch and J. R. French, Jr., "Overcoming Resistance to Change," *Human Relations,*
11 (1948), 512–532.

INDEX

PHOTO CREDITS